THE WAY WE WERE

The Way We Were

1900–1914

James McMillan

Based on the files of the Daily Express

WILLIAM KIMBER · LONDON

First published in 1978 by
WILLIAM KIMBER & CO. LIMITED
Godolphin House, 22a Queen Anne's Gate,
London, SW1H 9AE

© James McMillan and Express Newspapers Ltd., 1978

ISBN 0 7183 0186 2

Typeset by Watford Typesetters
and printed and bound in Great Britain by
The Garden City Press Limited,
Letchworth, Hertfordshire, SG6 1JS

Contents

List of Illustrations

List of Illustrations Appearing in the Text

Acknowledgements

My thanks are due to Mr John King and his staff of the *Daily Express* library; to Mr Ronald Frost of the micro-film unit and to Miss Lily Stewart for her invaluable typing.

Note

Conversion of pounds, shillings and pence into decimal coinage is as follows:—

One guinea	equals	£1.05
Six pence		2½p
One shilling		5p
Half a crown		12½p
Ten shillings		50p

As a rough guide cash figures should be multiplied by twelve to give their present day value though not in all cases: for instance in 1912 a pneumatic tyre cost £12. It does not cost twelve times that amount today.

The average income tax for the period was 1s 2d (6p) in the pound.

Introduction

Nowhere is the flavour and atmosphere of the past captured more truly than in the columns of the daily newspaper of the time. Historians may mull over what statesmen did and deduce cause from effect. Sociologists may draw conclusions about a society from reports of Royal Commissions. But only the newspaper – reporting things as they happened, sharing and shaping the prejudices of its readers, catching the human predicament – can bring the past to life.

So great have been the changes this century that those born since the last war would be totally bewildered if they were to find themselves transported back to Grandma's and Grandpa's day. The scale of transformation has been unique, taking place, as it has, within two generations.

This book is a window on yesterday. The window is the *Daily Express,* a newspaper exactly the age of the century : founded by Arthur Pearson in 1900, its first issue appeared on 24 April, price one-halfpenny. The eight-page paper, packed with fine print, contained about 96,000 words – the equivalent of a large-size novel. There were no photographs.

Its first classified advertising content conveyed the announcement by Messrs H. W. Thompson Bros that, to celebrate the opening of new premises in Oxford Street, six free shirts would be given away with every 27s 6d three-piece suit bought.

The news columns recorded this exchange in a coroner's court :

Coroner : 'As a chemist, you know you should not take anything for granted.'

Mr Cook, the chemist : 'Well I was looking at it as a gentlemen.'

Coroner : 'But chemists are not supposed to be gentlemen.'

These were the days of a class distinction so clear and unequivocal that it barely roused comment at home or abroad.

The aristocracy ran the (unpaid) House of Commons and naturally the House of Lords.

On the death of the Duke of Argyll, society dances were cancelled for three weeks as a gesture of proper deference to nobility: one hundred and sixty columns of news were devoted to the death, lying-in-state and funeral of King Edward VII – and $1\frac{1}{2}$ columns to the death of 136 miners in a pit disaster at Whitehaven at the same time.

In Germany Princess Sophie of Saxe Weimar was forbidden to marry Baron Hans von Bleichröder, a rich Jewish banker. In despair she committed suicide and her distraught father issued a statement that, despite his grief, 'all the money in the world would never have sufficed to bridge the gulf between a Princess of Saxe-Weimar and Baron von Bleichröder.'

In Vienna, no one without sixteen quarterings – aristocracy on both sides for four generations – was permitted to attend Court : officers at the Grand Military Ball who lacked such qualifications were barred from the principal ball room. In St Petersburg, an officer on guard duty at the Winter Palace committed suicide when a peasant desecrated his uniform by spitting on it.

Advertisements for 'lady' maids (as distinct from ladies' maids) offered post for girls of superior upbringing who were in need of extra money to supplement diminished family fortunes. They were paid £20-£25 a year, some £3-£10 more than their less well-endowed sisters. But it was pointed out that they were worth the extra 'because they are more trustworthy and sensible than ordinary domestics'. Even the poorest domestic was, however, better off than certificated pupil teachers in Lincolnshire, who were paid £12 a year.

On the other hand, if you wanted to leave the country, there were trans-Atlantic passages on offer at £2 (provide your own food) and 160-acre farms – for free – in Canada.

Although emigration was high, so was immigration : three and a half thousand Swiss and Germans a month were coming to England to serve the country's growing catering needs (though Germany, even then, was so prosperous that she had 1,500,000 guest workers). Immigrants were extremely unpopular, especially those from East Europe, but then in this hey-day of national pride and self-confidence so were all foreigners.

A report in January 1904 on the attempted kidnapping of Miss Gertrude Williams of Chelsea (believed to be a plot to have her transported as a white slave to South America) concluded : 'The one gratifying feature of this distressing and sensational story is that Miss Williams was abducted by a foreigner.'

Miss Williams was one of many girls in jeopardy on the streets of

London and other major cities. Scotland Yard revealed that 30,000 young women went missing every year and three excited correspondents wrote to the *Express,* apparently with more emotion than accuracy (for proof was never forthcoming) that beautiful Belgian girls were auctioned in houses near Regent Street.

If they were, it would have been in keeping with an age when women were – in many respects legally – regarded as no more than chattels and yet were also treated with a quite startling degree of chivalry. When Dr Marshall from America addressed an audience at the Exeter Hall in London on purity, women were excluded, partly because the gently-reared would be horrified by disclosures of impurity and partly because the lower type of women were the cause of impurity.

It was very much a man's world where good women were to be treated with the greatest courtesy. (An unfortunate labourer, Thomas Barrell, was sentenced to 21 days' jail by Woodbridge, Suffolk, magistrates for 'profaning and assaulting' Miss Bessie Alexander – by kissing her.)

Chivalry, however, did not extend to beauty contests. A report on a local competition in Hull on 25 October, 1906, observed that 'Mrs Foster won the consolation prize for receiving the least number of votes'. Mrs Foster's comment was not recorded.

The one woman who enjoyed universal approbation was the one who, in 1900, occupied the first position in the land.

CHAPTER ONE

Royal Occasions

When the White races ruled the world they had one great Queen – Victoria. Alone of rulers since Imperial Rome Victoria's name came to signify an age. She reigned for nigh on sixty-four years and her statues and portraits were to be found in every corner of the British Empire and in many other lands besides; her marriage to Prince Albert – who died forty years before her – was considered so perfect that it aroused a correspondent to write dismissively of a prospective Continental royal marriage :

> Duke Henry of Mecklenburg-Schwerin will not get much consolation when he contemplates his future as Queen Wilhelmina's consort.
> There is only one notable instance of a perfect union in this direction, and that was our own Queen Victoria's marriage with Prince Albert the Good. For the rest – unhappiness seems common for the position has almost always been found to be too difficult even for men of great tact and diplomacy as well as sagacity and soundness of judgement.

On her passing recollections of her life, little vignettes poured into the newspapers. The *Daily Express* alone ran a 26,000 word tribute which included touching reminiscences of the demure young woman who courted the slim, handsome German princeling Albert of Saxe-Coburg-Gotha.

As Queen she was obliged, by etiquette, to propose to Albert. This she did, implicitly, by shyly offering him flowers from her bouquet at a ball in Windsor Castle. The only drawback to this romantic gesture was that Albert was wearing a tight green military uniform. Nothing daunted and displaying that acumen which twelve years later was to triumphantly launch the Great Exhibition, Albert borrowed a knife

17

and cut the tight-fitting cloth above the heart to accommodate the posy.

Aspects of the glitter and pomp of the world's greatest reign were duly recorded : at her wedding Victoria wore a dress of pure white satin costing £1,000, but the homely side of the Queen's life was stressed at great length.

It was recalled how she and her young husband would ride for seven hours in the countryside around Balmoral, frequently staying overnight at humble inns where they insisted on remaining incognito. Secrecy was once maintained by one of the Queen's entourage telling the landlord that the Royal couple were newly-weds who yearned for privacy. When a well-loved old servant died the Queen broke down and wept repeatedly.

Yet the golden thread running through the recollections was Queen Victoria's total identification with the people : with their virtues, their strengths, their foibles and prejudices too.

Once an African chief had asked her, 'What is the secret of England's greatness?' She replied, 'The Bible.' And all in her family – at her death she had seventy direct descendants: six children, thirty-one grandchildren and thirty-three great grandchildren – were instructed to drink deeply from the spiritual well.

Faith. Duty. Service. These were Victoria's watchwords and she passed them on to one of her grandsons, the future George V, in a birthday letter accompanying the present of a watch.

> Hoping that it will serve to remind you to be very punctual in everything and v. exact in all your duties. I hope you will be a good, obedient, truthful boy, kind to all, humble, dutiful and always trying to be of use to others. Above all, God-fearing and striving always to do His Will. It is in your *power* to do immense good by setting an example and keeping your dear Grandpapa's name [Albert] before you.

As will be seen, these admonitions had considerable effect on young George who came to stand high in the old Queen's affections : 'a dear boy, so anxious to do right and to improve himself.'

It was these attributes of family devotion, extending the family to embrace the people of the British Empire, that called forth the most affectionate comments. Thus the *Express* editorial of 23 January, 1901 :

> In the history that shall tell future generations the story of the nineteenth century Victoria will stand out from the commonplace

list of English Sovereigns as one of those who were great.

Victoria gave with her heart as well as with her hands. When we heard of this or that good deed done by the Queen we did not think of it as something official, passed through the office of a Lord Chamberlain, but as the spontaneous benevolence of a dear old lady who loved children and dogs, and quiet chats with the old wives of Highland cottages, and all innocent and wholesome pleasures, who would weep readily for the suffering of her people, and join heartily in their enthusiasms and pleasures.

Gentle and kind as she was, Victoria was no mawkish humanitarian. The destinies of the British Empire had been entrusted to her, and if it were necessary in the interests of Empire, of Freedom, of Humanity, she would send her soldiers out to fight as readily as any War Lord of all the ages. She never paltered with the duties of her high destiny, and if the welfare of the many called for the sacrifice of the few she interposed no barrier of womanish scruples to the resolute policy of her Ministers. What it cost her to be thus faithful to her Royal trust, what tears the Woman shed in secret while the Queen was quietly firm in public, we can only guess.

And let it not be forgotten that the Queen gave her sons and grandsons to the nation with the same stern conviction of duty as when she called for the sons of other women – that Royal names have figured in the records of heroic service, in the lists of the wounded and the dead.

It is one of the duties of Royalty to be brave, and the Queen had the pluck of her martial ancestors, the spirit of a hero in the tender body of a woman. Time and again her life was attempted by assassins : she put the danger aside as lightly as if it were a common incident of the ceremonial of Courts, and never condescended to safeguard her life by precautions that would shut her off from sympathetic touch with her subjects. In her own person she showed her lofty conception of what the Royal Family owes to the nation : the lives of the people are pledged to safeguard the Throne; the lives of those who sit on the steps of the Throne should always be at the service of the people.

During years in which it became fashionable to associate intellectual development with emancipation from religious scruples, high station with immorality, and the domestic virtues of our mothers with feebleness of character, the Queen has ever stood at the head of society a noble example of the purity of womanhood and the dignity of maternity. In an age that prides itself on complexity of feeling she has always been simple and natural, and has shown that wealth, culture, exalted rank, and great mental power can be associated with motherly duties, domestic pleasures, and humble recognition of the Creator. No tarnished name was admitted to her Court. No taint of the vulgarity and moral coarseness of contemporary society penetrated her home. She could not try to reform the world, but she showed it how to be great by being just, and happy by being good.

When the Queen died, aged eighty-one, the Empire was plunged into mourning. And mourning, in the Victorian age, was deep and widespread. The anonymous author of the 'Interest to Women' column of 24 January, 1901 – thirty-six hours after the Queen's death – commented :

It only needed a most casual observation even in the early hours of yesterday to see how absolutely universal will be the adoption of mourning for our late Queen. One haberdasher alone sold over 1,000 black neckties on Tuesday evening after the sad announcement had been made, and not only were the windows draped with black and dressed with mourning goods, but the shops were crowded with sad, but busy buyers from the time of opening while the country orders were pouring in with every delivery.

By 26 January, eight days before the funeral, London and other cities presented a sombre prospect. Women were shopping frenziedly :

In the execution of orders naturally the stores gave preference to customers whose names are on the books. Others have to wait, try elsewhere, or remain content with ready-made dresses.

Ready-made costumes, of which one large mail order firm sold as many as 300 in one day, are at a premium, six and a half guineas being required yesterday for costumes priced at four and a half guineas two days previously.

Another firm has sold £3,000 worth of black fabrics to dressmakers and tailors since the announcement of the sad event.

To replace exhausted stocks buyers are hunting in Bradford and other manufacturing centres for more black.

From Roubaix during the last few days more than 140 tons of black dress material has been forwarded to England.

For a man, the donning of mourning is not a formidable task.

A black tie to be bought – the hosiers have a tale to tell of record outputs – a black coat, and a pair of quiet coloured trousers, which most men's wardrobes boast, and perchance a pair of dark hued gloves, and a man is in mourning.

Even the poor man wears his sign, be it in the form of a crepe armlet on a snuff-coloured suit or, as in the case of many a road-navigator, a dingy-hued choker about his throat.

With women it is different. To them the question of what to wear for mourning assumes the proportions of a serious problem.

Women of fashion are dressing in silks and satins, in fine-face cloths, in silk and wool poplins, and in clinging materials of the crepe-de-chine order.

For trimmings they are ordering jet, lace, chiffons, braids, silk strappings, tulle, guipures, and glace silk. Astrakhan, too, and dull passementerie are greatly in request.

Sealskin and sable are the favourites among the furs. Those with less money in their purse are buying cashmeres, alpacas, serges and ready-made blouses.

Overwhelmingly pathetic is the way in which women of the poorer classes are endeavouring to give visible signs of their grief of their dead Queen.

Many of these are availing themselves of dyers' offers to dye in forty-eight hours.

On the morrow of the Queen's death, an *Express* roving reporter recorded :

The news spread swiftly through the vast wilderness of the East End, borne by the shouting newsboys as they toiled eastward along the Mile-end road and other main thoroughfares.

From the better classes of East London down to the dregs of its hopeless slums, everyone mourned the Great Mother, who loved all her children alike, whether they were born to purple or to rags.

In the Whitechapel-road a street preacher held an open-air service, and spoke words of comfort to a large congregation, who listened with unwonted reverence.

From Houndsditch to Blackwall, the beneficence of her long reign and her weight as a moral factor in affairs of the Empire were discussed yesterday by rough men and women and hobbledehoys with an intelligence that would have astonished those who regard the East Ender as a blend of child and savage.

The squalid Irish in Ratcliff and St George's discussed the latest bulletins – one evening paper served a whole court – in voices whose tones were a lamentation. The squalid English were less demonstrative, but there was a sullen sadness in each grimy, half-starved face.

Even the polyglot Jews of Whitechapel, fresh from Russia, Germany, Poland and Europe generally, to many of whom the Queen of England is but a name imperfectly heard, looked sad.

A measure of the nation's grief was the extent of the floral tributes. Florists in the capital and the major cities reported, three days before the funeral, that their stocks were totally exhausted. Wreaths, thousands upon thousands of them, poured into Windsor. So many people – 20,000 – crushed into the Northampton Town Hall to view their town's tribute that 150 women fainted.

Properties along the route from Buckingham Palace to Paddington Station (from which the train left for the Royal Mausoleum of Frogmore) fetched extraordinary high prices.

'Brisk Demand' was the heading for a story which reported :

'Can you let me have first-class window for fifty guineas?' wired a provincial client. The reply was, 'No; the price is a hundred guineas for the lower windows and fifty guineas for those above.'

Roughly speaking, the scale for the best position is as follows : best windows, 100 guineas; upper windows, fifty guineas; single seats – best places in shop windows, ten guineas; second best, eight guineas; back row, five guineas. A few places on the roofs in St James'-street are being offered at two and three guineas each.

Some very wideawake ladies fixed upon Buckingham Palace-road as a street through which the procession would pass whatever alterations in the route were made.

They managed to secure standing room for twenty on a roof at 7s 6d per head. This is probably a record for cheapness.

A greengrocer in London-street let his first floor, overlooking the station, for £170, and sold thirty-six seats in the shop of £5 each.

At the opposite end of the street a corn chandler early in the day disposed of twelve seats in the shop for four guineas each. He afterwards learned that these had been immediately re-sold at £8 each.

But if florists and householders flourished, there were others whose pockets suffered severely. More than 3,000 people were laid off work in London's theatreland alone during the entire period from the

Queen's death until a week after the funeral – fifteen days in all. They were not paid for their involuntary absence. Hundreds of orders for jewellery were cancelled as balls and routs and functions of all kinds were abandoned. Some restaurants went out of business altogether.

The drapery trade was much relieved by this announcement from the Earl Marshal's office :

'In pursuance of the order for a general mourning for her late Majesty Queen Victoria of blessed memory, which was announced in a supplement of the *Gazette* of the 24th instant.

'These are to give notice that after the 6th day of March next it will not be desired or expected that the public should appear in deep mourning, but that half-mourning should be worn until the 17th day of April next.'

A prolonged period of mourning would have had a disastrous effect upon the enormous number of hands employed in the dressmaking trade.

Preparations for the funeral dominated every aspect of the newspapers. The *Express* could spare only one line to announce 'Signor Verdi is dying.'

Of all the ceremonial honours heaped on the dead monarch none was more significant than the naval review in the Solent when hundreds of warships lined the seven miles of the passage between Cowes (Victoria died on the Isle of Wight) and Spithead.

Accompanying the Royal Yacht *Alberta* which bore the body of the Queen was the Imperial German yacht *Hohenzollern*. Throughout Victoria's last days and during all the sombre ceremonial following her death her grandson Kaiser Wihelm II was at hand. He did play a leading part but by the nature of his relationship rather than as a result of his born theatricality. Wilhelm really loved his grandmother. He was stricken by her death and behaved very well. This protocol-bound man even surrendered his precedence at one point, so full was his family feeling. Strange that, years later, he was to remark that his withered arm was the English blood in him.

The Kaiser rode on the right of the new King Edward VII at the funeral procession and an escort of men and non-commissioned officers of the German Army brought up the rear of the procession : a remarkable demonstration of the closeness of the British and German ruling dynasties.

Victoria was, of course, the mother or grandmother of most of

Europe. Wilhelm II was her grandson. Alexandra, wife of Tsar Nicholas II of Russia, was her grand-daughter. Another grand-daughter was wife of the Crown Prince of Sweden, another was married to the King of Spain, another to the future King of Norway, another to the ruler of Roumania.

The parade of aristocracy that followed the gun carriage read like the *Almanac de Gotha* :

HRH The Duke of Connaught	THE KING	HIM The German Emperor	King's Equerry Capt Holford Silver Office
The Master of the Horse, the Duke of Portland KG	Gold Stick Field Marshal Viscount Wolseley KP	General von Scholl	

HM The King of the Hellenes   HM King of Portugal

HRH Prince Henry of Prussia	HRH Prince Christian of Schleswig-Holstein	HRH The Grand Duke of Hesse
HH Prince Albert Schleswig-Holstein	HRH Prince Arthur of Connaught	HRH The Duke of Saxe-Coburg-Gotha
HRH The Crown Prince of Roumania	HI & RH The Crown Prince of Germany	HRH The Duke of Sparta
HRH Prince Charles of Denmark	HRH The Crown Prince of Denmark	HRH The Prince Hohenlohe-Langenburg
HRH The Crown Prince of Sweden and Norway	HI & RH THE Archduke Francis Ferdinand of Austria	HIH The Hereditary Grand Duke Michael
HRH The Duke of Aosta	HRH The Crown Prince of Siam	HRH The Duke of Saxony
HRH The Hereditary Grand Duke of Baden	HRH Prince Arnulf of Bavaria	HRH The Duke Robert of Wurtenburg
HSH Prince Waldeck Pyrmont	HSH Prince Ernest Hohenlohe	HRH Prince of Hohenzollern-Sigmaringon

HRH the Prince Philip of Saxe-Coburg

HRH The Duke Adolphus Frederick of Mechlenburg-Streilitz

HH The Hereditary Prince of Saxe-Meiningen

HSH The Prince Adolph of Schaumburg-Litte

HH The Duke Ernest Gunther of Schleswig-Holstein

HH The Prince Frederick Charles of Hesse

HSH Prince Francis of Teck

HSH The Duke of Teck

HH Prince Leopold of Saxe-Coburg

Mehemet Ali

HSH Prince Ernest of Saxe-Altenberg

HH Prince Henry Reuss XXX

The Duke of Fife

HSH Prince Alexander of Teck

The Crown Equerry
Major General Sir H Ewart

Deputation of Officers of the Germany Army

Officers of the Suite of the German Emperor

On its way bearing the royal remains to Victoria Station, the train's passage allowed ordinary people a fleeting opportunity to pay their last goodbyes.

Dorking may be taken as a typical example. The Royal train passed through at about thirty miles an hour, the sudden curves which had to be taken just before entering the station rendering it necessary to slow down. Rain was falling heavily as the train rushed through, but a considerable number of the townspeople had assembled, and as the train passed the men among them reverently bared their heads. At the embankments and bridges and, in fact, at all points of vantage the people gathered, this being also the case in the rural districts where the population turned out in their thousands to pay all possible respect to so beloved a Queen.

The Royal platform at Victoria Station was near the central carriage road, and was covered with purple carpet. The roadway itself was strewn with golden sand as yet untrampled by a single hoof. In the centre of the platform stood the Royal pavilion covered in regal purple with white surmountings.

Here the mourners were to rest in the brief interval before passing

into the street. The interior was magnificently furnished in Louis
XVI style, and French and Windsor tapestry hung from the walls
with all the Imperial splendour of a palace apartment.

The scarlet of the Staff blazed with orders and the multi-coloured
garments of European princes and officers added an effective
colouring and splendid contrast.

Every staff uniform in the world was represented in that mingling
of the Kings and Crown Princes of the earth.

Japan chatted with Siam, and the scarlet breeched Austrian
learned things from the fezzed Egyptians. Imperial Germany linked
up with the Republican West and the Turk and Anglo-Indian
fraternised with Russia. For in all that varied throng one common
sentiment filled every breast – unqualified homage for the Greatest
of all Queens.

The light blue and crimson of the Germans, the mauve and yellow
of the Jap, and the grey of the Russ shone with jewels and chains
of gold. Plumes of every hue fluttered from stately busby and
burnished helmet, and pronounced among all stood the Grand Duke
Michael in light blue and red, with a crimson order sashed across
his breast.

London's streets had witnessed an unbelievable silence for Victoria's
funeral procession 'overpowering and oppressive . . . scarcely a footfall
or a spoken word broke the almost intolerable dumbness of the city.'
Now when the full mourning period was over, the country prepared
to relax under the benign guardianship of Good Old Teddy. Edward
VII who was nearly sixty when he came to the throne and was already
a well-liked figure though held in nothing like the awe bestowed on his
mother.

Edward had lived under her shadow for so long – even as a man
of fifty he would stand outside the dining-room door in a blue funk
if late for dinner – that many wondered if he could possibly measure
up to the duties of kingship.

Moreover, Edward had achieved no little notoriety, much of it
unfair, for his love of wine, women and horses. Society, which was
scorned by Victoria, was happy to open its doors to the rotund Royal
whose jaunty gusto added fun and lustre to any event.

As it turned out, Edward confounded the pessimists utterly. His
abundant good nature still found the odd eccentric outlet : he would
press an MVO (Member of the Victorian Order) into the hands of an
astonished chef who had pleased his gourmet taste – and forget to

tell the registrar of the order that it had a new adornment. Yet along-side the full-blooded life went a shrewdness, an innate sure footedness in dealing with politicians and an instinctive 'way' with the French amounting to genius.

As a child Edward had fallen in love with France. He was taken there by his parents during the early years of Napoleon III and, sad-dened at the thought of leaving, asked the Empress Eugénie to be allowed to remain. She replied that his Mama and Papa would miss him. 'Oh no,' riposted the young Prince, 'there are six more of us at home.'

His mother had a more proprietorial view of England's closest neighbour. She wrote to her Prime Minister, Lord Salisbury, urging a settlement with France over Siam lest she be embarrassed by being caught by the outbreak of a war while she was holidaying in Nice 'where they are most kind and considerate to us'.

Edward had none of Victoria's egocentricity. He had what is now called 'empathy'. He could put himself in other people's shoes, under-stand their plight and motives. That quality was to stand him in good stead when he came to handle the grave political crises of his reign. It helped too in bringing intellectual and literary outsiders into the establishment.

Just as Victoria had instituted the Royal Victorian Order for personal services to the monarch so Edward was to introduce the Order of Merit for outstanding achievement and thus to end the alienation of a section of brilliant men who felt aggrieved at the lack of recognition while others swarmed into the charmed royal circle by virtue of birth alone.

In 1902 the promise and fulfilment of Edward the King lay in the future. Meanwhile great preparations were put in hand for Edward's coronation in June 1902. Unhappily the King fell ill with appendicitis and the ceremony had to be postponed for two months. This led to considerable inconvenience and occasionally to ructions:

RUSTICS RUN RIOT

The picturesque village of Hemel Hempstead, which lies on the borders of Hertfordshire and Bucks, in the heart of the Chiltern country, has been the scene of an unseemly riot.

The postponement of the King's dinner to the poor, and the sale of the food which had been prepared, was the cause of the disturb-ance.

A mob of over a thousand persons gathered about premises owned by Alderman Gray, who was reported to have suggested the post-

ponement of the dinner, and with shouts of 'Who sold the poor's
puddens?' 'Who robbed the poor man of his beer?' and a running
accompaniment of bucolic witticisms, proceeded to demolish the
contents of the place – a glass and china store.

Stones were thrown with more persistence than precision. One
man was injured, and subsequently removed to hospital, and a youth
a seventeen was arrested.

The Alderman, a strict teetotaller, has made himself very unpopular during the last two years by trying to prevent the inmates
of the workhouse having the barrel of beer at Christmas which has as
always been given to them by Mr Elliott, the brewer.

When the King recovered the real celebration began with a dinner for
500,000 London poor, paid for in part by Edward himself who contri-
buted £30,000 to the cost.

Each dinner consisted of the following:

> Rump steak and kidney pies
> Veal and ham pies
> Roast ribs and sirloins of beef
> Pressed beef
> Boiled round of beef. Hams
> Hot potatoes
> Fruit tarts
> Bread, butter and cheese
> Bass beer. Lime juice

The cost to the authorities was a fraction under 1s 2½d. Invitation
cards were sent to all half-a-million guests, who were accommodated
in halls – including the Guildhall – private houses, chapels and churches.
Each ward had its own team of entertainers, who favoured the borough.
Westminster did well with Little Tich and the ladies' choir of Clare
Novello Davies (Ivor Novello's mother). Stepney had Dan Leno, Vesta
Tilley and Marie Lloyd, this East End district being given the strongest
contingent of all, rightly so, considering that the best comics and music
hall stars came from there. Wandsworth had Chirgwin 'the White-Eyed
Kaffir' and Arthur Rigby. All the artists gave their services free.

King Edward and Queen Alexandra were gregarious and popular
throughout the country as this report of 31 July, 1903, indicates:

The farmers who escorted their Majesties had ridden miles for the purpose. The escort kept behind the carriage because its members decided among themselves that a King should ride before everybody, which ruling his Majesty laughingly accepted.

Beside the carriage walked a royal footman who, for the first time in his life, wore the King's livery, with a high yachting cap and a row of medals. On arriving at the quarry the process of quarrying was explained by the foreman, the King and Queen meanwhile asking many questions.

The crowd followed the King and Queen through the quarry without restraint. A barefoot urchin walked beside Princess Victoria, and the Queen was always surrounded by admiring women.

'Sure,' said an old man who stood on a rock and puffed his pipe as the King re-entered his carriage, 'sure and he's as foine a man as any of us.' The King laughed as heartily as anyone.

For a time the natives were content during the return journey to merely pull back on a rope which was attached to the rear of the carriage as a brake. But when the level road was regained they insisted upon unharnessing the horses.

So anxious were they to draw the King's carriage that his Majesty silenced all signs of dissent, and the proud villagers pulled in the shafts lustily.

A woman who had walked fifteen miles to see the Queen approached her timidly on the hotel porch.

'Might I shake hands with your Majesty?' she said. 'Most certainly,' replied the Queen, holding out her hand with a gracious smile.

The only surprising element about this account is that these events took place in Connemara, one of the most staunchly Republican parts of Southern Ireland, then, of course, part of the UK.

No British monarch, at least until Elizabeth II, enjoyed horses and horse racing so much as Edward VII. A charming picture was given of him by a special correspondent in October 1904:

Let us spend a typical day with the King at Newmarket, such a day as any he has passed there this week.

First of all there is Ibrahim, the black man from the Nile, with his wonderful coffee. King Edward is very partial to a cup of coffee either before or with his breakfast made by Ibrahim, the tall, lithe, smiling, white-toothed, curly headed coffee-maker, deft of hand, quick of eye, and nimble, even cat-like, of movement.

A simple breakfast over, a glance at any pressing correspondence, a word to his favourite dog, and King Edward, who for the being might be a 'Mr Blankshire of the Hall' rides up to the heath. You might rove England through for sweeter or more invigorating air than he has the joy of breathing o'mornings on that gentle hill, with its fringes of rich autumn foliage and its sweeping views of that Eastern Anglia where once roamed Hereward the Wake.

So thoroughly is the idea of the simple life carried out, that there is no mobbing or crowding of the King when he is at Newmarket. The men with the long strings of racehorses exercising on the heath know of the King's desire for peace and quiet, and they respect it.

To such lengths does his Majesty sometimes carry his temporary aloofness from the trammels of Court life that on occasion Newmarket has witnessed the spectacle of a polished gentleman from Scotland Yard going about full of suppressed anxiety trying to find out whither the King had gone! King Edward had actually gone without informing the detectives who were charged with the special duty of protecting him.

The afternoon, of course, is spent at the races. Sometimes using a pair of powerful field-glasses, at other times gazing down the course with his keen eyes, the King stands up in the Royal box during each race, and follows the fortunes of the various horses with the zest of an experienced racegoer.

The racing over, the King drives down to the town in the ruck of vehicles of all descriptions. He has instructed the police to let the traffic go on as usual, and there is no ceremonial clearing of the road, no cry of 'Room for the King!' Now and then he actually gets 'held up' by the police in company with others when the regulation of the traffic becomes difficult.

Worldly, witty, and very wise, Edward's popularity increased as his reign advanced. He early won golden opinions for his State visit to France which did much to win over the Parisians and so further the cause of the emerging entente cordiale. He kept his head when all about were losing theirs in the constitutional crisis over the power of the House of Lords in 1909 and by utilising the Crown's prerogative to advise, warn and encourage he kept political passions within bounds. When he died in May 1910 the country's grief was genuine. Some 3,000,000 people turned out to witness the funeral cortege pass in measured beat. Due to the heat 15,000 fainted. Nine kings of Europe followed the coffin, the last grand assemblage of the high born.

Within nine years almost all of them were swept away by war and revolution. The following quarter century saw the disappearance of five emperors, eight kings and eighteen minor dynasties.

Although the pomp and circumstance of King Edward's final journey was as impressive as that attending Queen Victoria's funeral, there were subtle differences. The awe was missing. The tolerance and twinkle of the Edwardian age was rubbing off on those who had lived through it.

Selfridges, the large London store rather cheekily took much space in the Press to record their 'profound regret' at King Edward's passing and then announced that in token of their sorrow they were cancelling that day's press publicity.

The *Daily Express* published a kind of scrap book of Edward's sayings to encapsulate the character of the dead monarch – a thing the paper would never have dreamed of doing in Queen Victoria's day.

His favourite hymn was 'Nearer My God to Thee'. His favourite flower the rose, his favourite name Louise, and his favourite novel *East Lynne*.

Edward's humour and humanity also shone out of this pot-pourri :

Once asked what he would do if his family were deposed, he replied: 'No doubt if it really did occur I could support my family by lecturing on the Constitution in America.'

'I have a horror of gambling,' King Edward wrote to Archbishop Benson, 'and should always do my utmost to discourage others who have an inclination for it, as I consider that gambling, like intemperance, is one of the greatest curses which the country could be afflicted with.'

'I am happiest,' he wrote in the Duchess of Fife's album before he ascended the throne, 'when I can forget that I am 'Your Royal Highness'; when I can smoke a really good cigar and read (must I confess it?) a good novel on the quiet; when I can, like plain Mr Jones, go to a race meeting without it being chronicled in the papers the next day that 'His Royal Highness the Prince of Wales has taken to gambling very seriously, and yesterday lost more money than ever he can afford to pay'; when I can shake hands with and talk to Sir Edward Clarke without it being rumoured that 'the Prince of Wales is violently opposed to the present war'; when I can spend a quiet evening at home with the Princess and my family.

'I am unhappiest,' he wrote, 'when I have to attend some social function where I must smile as pleasantly as though I never had a pain in my life.'

In a confession album belonging to the Queen of Greece his Majesty thus described his 'Pet Aversion' – 'The most objectional being in the world in my opinion is the man who will insist on pointing at you with his umbrella and shouting out, 'There he is!'

King Edward had been an exceptionally good-natured father. He imposed none of the strict upbringing on his own children that he had suffered. Paradoxically, the new monarch, George V, was not so easygoing. He demanded that standards be upheld, as a small news item of June 1911 demonstrated:

A little incident occurred recently which shows how very particular the King is with regard to the training of his boys. Two of the younger ones were riding near his Majesty when the cavalcade passed some men who were working on the road.

The men removed their hats, and the King at once doffed his own hat. His Majesty noticed that the boys, in the enthusiasm of their gallop, had not followed his example.

He immediately called a halt, took the Princes back to the workmen, and ordered them to remove their hats. This was, of course, done, and the royal boys are not likely to forget their duty in this respect again.

Duty was as an integral part of George V's character as it had been of Victoria's – at least after she married Albert. It had not been so much drummed into him as soaked up by him from an early age. His mother had read the Bible to him every evening when he was a child and he made a point of reading the scriptures every day as an adult.

He had not been trained for the throne. His elder brother, Clarence, died in 1892 and he was suddenly catapulted into the position of heir apparent. By the extraordinary good fortune which appears to have attended the Royal House since the days of Victoria's accession he was to prove ideally suited to the demanding tasks of monarchy which poor weak Clarence would have found beyond him.

George's philosophy was summed up in the definition of the qualities required of a naval officer written at the conclusion of fifteen years' service in the Royal Navy: 'Truthfulness – without which no man can gain the confidence of those below him; obedience – without which no man can gain the confidence of those above him; zest – without which no man is worth his salt.'

George lived by those simple, consistent rules. He married his dead elder brother's fiancée, Mary of Teck, who shared the same undeviating beliefs, and whose 'middle class morality' exactly matched the mood of the bulk of her subjects.

Both George and Mary accepted absolutely that they had been called by the Almighty to serve in the station to which He had called them. They did not question Providence and they did not expect others to do so.

Yet George V was far from being a prig. His language, as befitted a former naval person, could be salty. He enjoyed hearty, simple humour. He detested hypocrites, devious courtiers and politicians who were too clever by half.

In a sense he was a throw-back to Victoria, almost deliberately standing in awe of his papa who did not seek to impose the severe regimen on his son that had been enforced on him. Gradually George adopted a more relaxed attitude to his father and to others. Thus, on St George's Day 1900 he wrote to his wife : 'William [Kaiser Wilhelm II] is the only one who has been decent towards us during this [Boer] war and I myself am quite ready to be decent towards him.'

Decency, kindliness and rectitude were to mark his reign and the royal couple had already been taken to the people's heart by the time he came to be crowned.

King George and Queen Mary's coronation was, as expected, a glorious and gorgeous occasion. But it was the second within nine years. Something entirely different was the investiture of the King's eldest son as Prince of Wales. Since Edward I had introduced his son to the Welsh in the thirteenth century, the custom had fallen into disuse, but the Welsh Chancellor of the Exchequer, David Lloyd George, saw in its revival a way to assuage Welsh national feeling and also do no harm at all to the political prospects of David Lloyd George.

Consequently there gathered a mighty host of Welshmen at Caernarvon Castle on 13 July 1911, a boiling hot day. Percival Phillips, by now one of Fleet Street's Royal commentators par excellence, set the scene :

'I, Edward Prince of Wales, do become your liege man of life and limb and of earthly worship and faith and truth.

'I will bear unto you to live and die against all manner of folks. . . .'

As Edward Prince of Wales stood with bowed head before his
father's throne in the inner bailey of the royal Castle of Caernarvon
this afternoon and repeated this ancient pledge of fealty the ten
thousand people who encompassed him were stirred with deeper
emotions than mere admiration for a scene of splendour.

The slender boy in the trailing purple mantle appealed to all
hearts. His simple dignity, with just a tinge of embarrassment, his
determination to go through the first great ceremony of his life with
honour to his father and himself, and, above all, his unaffectedness,
made such an impression as must have gladdened his parents as they
stood above him listening to his words of homage.

He had entered one of the greatest assemblages this generation
has ever seen, wearing the jacket of a midshipman in the Navy of
the King. He had come forth from his robing room in his purple
surcoat to hear the words of his Investiture, and now he stood before
his Sovereign wearing the robes of his heritage, a very princely
figure, but still the gravely eager boy whose youth seemed the more
accentuated by his coronet and mantle.

He looked wonderingly from time to time at the tiers of people
that rose almost to the battlements.

The sight of that sea of faces stretching upwards on either hand,
the blazing masses of uniforms and the decorations, the strangely
impressive choir of women in tall hats, the Druids swathed in their
mysterious robes, all set within the walls of the great ruined castle,
under a burning sun, was enough to awe any boy.

Wherever he turned every eye was fixed on him. But for all the
scrutiny and the solemn silence that followed the first thunderous
applause, the boy bore himself well. He read his reply to the people
of Wales in a clear, deliberate voice. His words were distinct in the
galleries above him.

Unfortunately the Prince's promise went unredeemed. Edward, Prince
of Wales, as Edward VIII, was the only British monarch to abdicate.

The other great Royal occasion, the like of which had not been seen
before, was the Durbar at Delhi on 12 December 1911 where the
King-Emperor presented himself to his Indian subjects. Benjamin
Disraeli had persuaded Victoria to become Empress of India. Her son
had visited the country but on his accession his Durbar had been held
in London because of his illness. George V's was the one – and, as it
happened, only time – that a British King received in homage the
representatives of all the people of what is now India, Pakistan,

Bangladesh, Burma, Sri Lanka, but were then simply the Indian Empire. Once again Percival Phillips described the pageantry :

It is difficult to give an adequate impression of the splendour, richness, and dignity of the scene arrayed on the Plain of Delhi today when the Emperor presented himself, crowned and robed, to the people of his Empire.

The sight of that concourse of 85,000 people was almost painful in its brilliance. It stirred the hearts of his subjects as it must have stirred the Emperor himself as he sat on his high golden throne in the pavilion between the two great amphitheatres listening to the words of the historic Proclamation read by the Viceroy standing at his feet.

Such spectacle few rulers of the earth have enjoyed and few people witnessed even in this country of pageantry. It was a spectacle which aroused profound emotions and swept the people in a gust of loyal enthusiasm almost overpowering in its intensity for the grave, bearded man in ermine and purple who sat there in lonely state and bowed his head.

Imagine their Majesties seated on a lofty white many-tiered pedestal sitting on two golden thrones under a twenty-foot purple-and-gold canopy supported by twelve slender bronze columns and surmounted by a dazzling gold dome. Imagine a great crescent of uncovered amphitheatre filled with spectators in serried ranks on the steep terraces.

It was at the Durbar that the King-Emperor announced the transfer of the capital of India from Calcutta to Delhi, where it has remained to this day.

The last glittering cavalcade of the old Royal world took place in Berlin in 1913 when the Kaiser's only daughter, Princess Victoria Louise, married Prince Ernest Augustus. The newspapers waxed joyful over the family atmosphere of the wedding : 'Three of the world's greatest rulers, King George, the Kaiser and the Czar will sleep under one roof in the Imperial Palace in Berlin.'

Symbolically, the remnants of the old world were flung away when Princess Louise's garter (in fact small pieces of silk ribbon emblazoned with the names of the newly maried couple) were scattered among the female guests.

Within the year the European web of personal attachments was broken and Europe was plunged into bloody conflict.

Yet long before war brought down sceptre, orb and crown, a group of fanatical men and women had been working for the downfall of monarchy, religion and the whole social order – the anarchists.

CHAPTER TWO

Hi-Jack !

In January 1909 two Russian anarchists hi-jacked a London tram-car !

Following the theft of £80 from the premises of Schnurmann's rubber processing works in Tottenham, eye-witnesses told the *Express* representatives :

Albert Keyworth, a junior clerk employed at the rubber works, returned from the bank, and in his hand he carried a bag, containing £80, the employees' wages.

At the same moment two men, obviously foreigners – one tall, sinewy and powerful-looking, the other equally powerful, but shorter and stouter – stepped hurriedly from the opposite side of the road. As the clerk stepped mechanically towards the factory gates the tall man suddenly dashed at him and flung the lad to the ground, while his stouter companion snatched the money bag and attempted to make off with it. Keyworth clung like grim death to the legs of the thief who had attacked him, almost tripping him up and making flight impossible. Then the struggling thief whipped out his Mauser pistol, and the five barrels were emptied at the courageous clerk. But the clutch on his legs and his endeavours to free himself had made the man's aim unsteady, and fortunately none of the shots told.

The sight of the pistol, however, was sufficient to make Keyworth release his hold, and the two ruffians took to their heels.

When the hunted men reached Ferry-lane they doubled once more, and, skirting Lockwood's reservoir, made a mad spurt towards Billet-road, which leads to Chingford High-road. Here occurred one of the most exciting episodes of this marvellous chase.

As the flying miscreants turned into the road they heard the clang of an electric-car bell. In a moment the daring idea of commandeering the tram car was devised and carried into execution. They ran towards the car, sent several shots at the driver, and at the same time called on him to bring the car to a stop. The terrified driver brought the car to a standstill, and clambered to the upper deck. The men mounted the car at the back, and at the point of the pistol forced the conductor through the car to the driving handle.

An elderly man and a woman with her little girl were the only passengers inside, and the sight of the desperadoes forcing the conductor to drive the car filled them with terror. The car rang with the woman's screams, while the glass, splintered by the bullets of the pursuers, clattered to the floor.

What happened next is best told in the words of Conductor Wyatt to a representative of the *Express*.

'When I saw Driver Slow make for the top and felt the warm muzzle of a recently fired revolver at my cheek I thought that the end had come. "You have got to drive the tram," said a man with a foreign accent pressing the barrel against my cheek.

'At first I told him I knew nothing about driving but there was something in his eye which told me that the only way to save my life was to take the handle. I hope I shall never have to drive a car again under such conditions.

'We went slowly at first, one of the men keeping his pistol at my head, while the other stood on the footboard firing at the crowd, who were gaining on the car and shooting as they came.

'All the while the woman and child in the car were screaming, and I was expecting every minute to be struck by a shot intended for the man who stood so determinedly by my side. I wondered what Slow was doing on top, and began to tremble for fear he should take it into his head to detach the trolley-bar. If he did I knew that I would suffer.

'By this time we were going at a furious pace, but I had to slow down as we approached the loop to let another car pass. I thought we should have to pull up, for an advertising cart belonging to the Palace Theatre in which I think there was a policeman overtook me and began to draw in front of me. But the man, whose pockets seemed filled with ammunition, shot the pony with a couple of cartridges, and the people in the van were tumbled into the road.

'At last an idea to get rid of them struck me. As the car drew near to the junction with Forest-road, I told the man that we were nearing a police-station, and that he had better alight.

' "I know better," said the man, "there is not." "All right," I said with my heart sinking within me, "then we'll go on". At that moment the old man in the car, who must be over sixty years of age, crept towards the man and jumped on his back. For a moment there was a scuffle. But the passenger's plucky attempt was of no avail. The man turned his pistol over his shoulder and shot the old man in the neck.

'We were close to Kitt's Corner then. The man at the back of the car, under cover of the iron stairway, was still firing at the crowd behind. The man who stood beside me caught sight of a greengrocer's cart standing against the kerb and shouted to his companion. They both jumped off and boarded the cart, taking a shot at the greengrocer, who was on the pavement, as they did so.'

The murderers with great cunning doubled again, this time turning into Kingsley-road and zig-zagged in the hope of out-manoeuvring the pursuing motor-cars, pushing the horse without mercy they rattled down the road, the motor-cars gaining on them rapidly. Then they realised that escape that way was impossible. They pulled the frightened horse on its haunches, and leaping out of the cart, dashed for the fields near Highams Park and Hale End Station.

The end was approaching quickly, for the strain was beginning to tell on the desperadoes, and the pursuit was as hot as ever. The way across the fields led the fugitives to the railway bridge which, on powerful brick buttresses, crosses Ching Brook. The bank of the brook is enclosed with heavily barbed wire while the arch of the bridge is fenced with a barricade made from discarded railway sleepers.

One of them breathless and exhausted, essayed to climb the fence. His hands made a futile grip for a hold. But he had not the necessary strength to draw himself up, and fell backwards.

The anarchists – 'Yakob' and Paul Hefeld from Riga were killed. Hefeld died by his own hand. The policeman who led the chase, Constable Tyler, was shot dead; so was a little ten-year-old boy, Ralph Jocelyn, who got in the path of the anarchists. Yet despite the tragedies, the Keystone Cops aspect of the affair is enhanced by the description of how the police were armed for the fray.

The police arrangements for dealing with the dramatic emergency which so suddenly arose were most complete.

Within a few moments of the first shots and the flight of the assassins the police had notified every surrounding district.

The news of the desperate fight was clicked out on the private tape machines in all police stations round, and Woodford, Walthamstow and Chingford were told by telephone of the crisis.

A hundred policemen on foot and cycles, and many mounted men were quickly occupying all the road and cutting off the escape of the fugitives.

The first policemen who leapt out of the windows of Tottenham Police Station were, of course, unarmed. An armoury of loaded revolvers is, however, kept at every police centre for use in case of emergency, and policemen on bicycles and on horseback were sent out with weapons for the pursuers.

Mounted policemen carry service revolvers in their holsters, and these were loaded and sent on to the firing line in front. Within ten minutes a Tottenham gunsmith had offered to put his stock of guns and pistols at the disposal of the police, and twenty men were thus armed in addition to those who had the station firearms. A dozen local residents also hurried out with weapons.

Sergeant Hale was one of the first to lead the chase, and although unarmed he kept the men in sight until the end. Constable Cater on a bicycle hurried after him with loaded revolvers which he gave to those policemen who were unarmed.

*

Two years later, on 3 January, 1911, London was treated to the Siege of Sidney Street, an event so inconceivable that newspapers devoted front page pronouncements to mark its unique character:

The long history of London contains no incident so sensational as the desperate battle fought yesterday round a tenement house in Sidney-street, Mile End, between two desperate Russian Anarchists barricaded in the attic rooms and a force of about 1,000 soldiers and policemen, who had taken possession of all the positions commanding the house, and entirely isolated the area of which it was the centre.

The men were believed to be 'Fritz' and 'Peter the Painter', who have been wanted for the murder of the policemen who surprised them in the attempt at breaking into a jeweller's shop in Houndsditch nearly three weeks ago. They were found at No 100 Sidney-street at 7.40 o'clock yesterday morning when they immediately opened fire from their attic fortress, seriously wounding a detective sergeant.

For seven hours they remained under cover, keeping up an intermittent fire on the police and troops which were brought up from all parts of London. A tremendous rifle and revolver fire was directed on the attic windows for many hours, until the last chance of escape had gone.

At one o'clock after all attempts to drive the men out had failed, after several persons had been wounded and the most astounding scenes had taken place in the area round the house, a fire broke out on the floor in which the desperadoes had fortified themselves.

The house was burned to a shell, and after a while the remains of the two men were taken out. The inquest will definitely reveal whether, driven to the last extremity, they took their own lives, or whether they were slowly burned to death. The probabilities are that they shot themselves when the flames cut off all possible means of escape. The latter theory is accepted by the police.

Thus ended a crime drama the like of which London has never seen – from the midnight discovery of the armed burglars in Houndsditch, the shooting of five policemen, the flight of the assassins with their wounded comrade, the discovery of his body next day in a squalid room in Mile End, the long hunt by the police for the other criminals through the labyrinth of the foreign quarter of the East End, to their discovery, and their end in the burning house in Sidney-street.

Mr Winston Churchill has sent the following message to the *Express*: 'There is no truth in the report that the house was fired by the authorities.'

Mr Churchill did not escape censure. He turned up to view the siege, and urge on the besiegers, but the press tartly pointed out that he had been a fierce opponent of the Aliens Act of 1905 which, if it had been effectively administered by the Radical Government, would have excluded undesirables like the Houndsditch murderers.

During its stormy progress in the Standing Committee of the House of Commons on Law, Mr Churchill constantly attacked the measure, and his gibes and methods of obstruction roused great indignation.

In a letter written in December 1906, Mr Churchill held that the naturalisation fee of £5 10s should be reduced and added that the Aliens Act 'shuts the door with a slam in the face of a poor man, however honestly and high-mindedly he may have lived'.

Britain was castigated in practically every Continental journal for its toleration of terrorists. *L'Instrageant* of Paris summed up the views of the French, Russian and Austrian papers – for it was principally against the rulers of these lands, notably the last two, that the assassins' plans were aimed – by declaring :

> Until now Great Britain was Anarchy's pot-house. The knights of the bombs lived in perfect safety in the United Kingdom and prepared their plans for the destruction of society. We have often complained of the monstrous egoism of our friends of the entente cordial in permitting this state of affairs. Now the situation has changed, and the British Government will unite with the rest of the powers in suppressing the odious propaganda of the Anarchists.

Berlin's political police announced that they had long known of the Houndsditch anarchists who belonged to the Kavaross group, a particularly dangerous strain of anarchists, and had informed London about them, but the British police had ignored the warning. Much satisfaction was felt in Berlin that Britain had not, after all, purchased immunity by providing a haven for terrorists.

A close parallel exists between the anarchists of the Edwardian era and the European terrorist groups, such as the Baader-Meinhof gang, of the sixties and seventies. Both sets were soured idealists whose hatred of the establishment had overborne their love of humanity. They followed 'the light that never was on land or sea', a wondrous Utopia of their own imaginings. Anyone who, wittingly or unwittingly, got in their way while they were gathering resources for the cause (even so pitiful an amount as £80) had to be gunned down. Policemen, as servants of the 'Boss class', could expect no other; innocents like children and pregnant women were casualties of war. It was a pity if they died but their deaths were of small importance in the mighty struggle . . . etc., etc.

Such fanaticism could till the soil for highly-organised socialists with their ready-made, universalist solutions *provided* the soil was ripe.

In Britain, diversity, tolerance and acceptance of the status-quo provided an effective antidote to revolution.

CHAPTER THREE

Contrast without Envy

The England of 1900, when the *Daily Express* was born, was going through a period of placid tranquillity. True, the country was fighting a war in South Africa (still regarded as a fairly simple affair, though before the end it was to draw in 400,000 Empire troops) but *socially* the nation was at one with itself. There were enormous differences in wealth, work, living conditions. Such welfare as there was, was confined to parish outdoor relief and the workhouses. Yet as the columns of the newspaper make plain there was a notable lack of envy. There was general acceptance of the class structure, widespread interest in the doings of Society – and a mere two Labour Members of Parliament.

Few would have forecast that in the decade to come the community would be riven by violent political controversies over free trade, a major constitutional crisis, near civil war in Ireland, a furious onslaught on property by women demanding the vote, the most savage strikes in our history and the end of the great Pax Britannica which, under the benign folds of the White Ensign, had held the world more or less at peace for a hundred years. The vicarious pride in ruling the largest Empire the world had ever seen, the confidence engendered by the unchallenged might of the Royal Navy, totally supreme since Trafalgar, and the satisfaction of knowing that every second ship on the High Seas flew the Red Ensign and British merchant ships could circle the globe without ever touching a port where the Union Jack *didn't* fly, made up for the melancholy circumstances of many poor folk.

The contrasts in the first issue of the *Express* could hardly have been more extreme.

The Earl of Lonsdale was most disturbed to read that he wasn't at the front in South Africa with his cavalry unit because of the enormous premium on his life demanded by his insurance company. He got his man of business, a Mr B. Clarke private secretary, to write :

His lordship desires me to say that this statement is absolutely incorrect and calculated to cause a great deal of mischief, for, as a matter of fact, the reason he did not accompany the W. and C. Yeo. Cav. Contingent was that he had been appointed assistant adjutant-general to assist the Imperial Yeomanry organisation here.

The idea that someone might not go off to fight because the insurance premium on his life would have been prohibitive would not have caused undue surprise, even if the report had been correct : money was a talisman, to be used as its owners thought best. In a deferential hierarchic society private expenditure was private business. When Sir Edward Payson Wills, a director of the Imperial Tobacco Company, died, he left £2,531,207. The amount of estate duty paid was £37,968 (in 1977 duty would have taken nearly £2,000,000). It was cause for modest pride that eight millionaires died in the last year of the century and the total of their wealth had reached £20 million. The rich were becoming richer as trade and investment picked up and the aristocracy had a further source of finance : American heiresses. In October 1907 the *Express* New York correspondent reported :

More than 500 American girls have married titled foreigners. The following table, which was compiled by a New York newspaper, shows the estimated fortunes of ten Americans who have married English noblemen in the past twenty five years :

Duchess of Marlborough	£2,000,000
Lilian, Duchess of Marlborough	800,000
Duchess of Roxburghe	2,000,000
Duchess of Manchester	400,000
Lady Curzon	1,000,000
Cora, Countess of Strafford	200,000
Countess Craven	209,000
Countess of Donoughmore	100,000
Countess of Yarmouth	200,000

The total dowry of the American girls who have married titled foreigners is estimated at £33,000,000.

Other American wives of titled foreigners are the Princess Colonna (Miss Mackay), the Countess Festetics (Miss Haggin), Princess Hatzfeldt (Miss Huntington), each of whom had a dowry of £200,000.

Miss Margaret Taylor married Count Imperatori of Italy, while the latter was playing in an orchestra at Sherry's Restaurant, New York, and Miss Emily Moekel, of Brooklyn, married Count Ferrari, also of Italy, when he was a waiter at the World's Fair, Chicago.

The most melancholy case was that of the Baron Takace de Kis-joka, of Hungary, who married the daughter of Mr Charles Hart, of Cleveland, got only £80 for his honeymoon, and was afterwards put on an allowance of £16 a month.

The 'life style' of the nobility and the wealthy captivated a popular paper like the *Express*, which was read by the lower middle class – clerks, small shop-keepers, teachers and skilled artisans – and it gave great play to the pleasures of the rich. The more opulent the setting, the more highborn the guests, the wider the publicity.

In June 1912, the *Express* devoted two columns on the front page (despite hundreds of thousands of workers in half-a-dozen trades being out on strike) to what it decreed 'The Ball of the Century':

More stately, more brilliant, certainly more costly than the great Waterloo gala which Byron immortalised, the 'Hundred Years Ago' Ball at the Albert Hall last night in aid of the Soldiers and Sailors Help Society, provided a spectacle which a hundred years hence will still be a landmark of magnificence.

Even the royal personages who watched it – Princess Christian, Prince Henry of Battenberg, Prince Arthur of Connaught, Prince and Princess Alexander of Teck, and others – all seemed dazzled as they stepped to the front of the royal box to take their first view at the ballroom.

It was almost indescribably lovely before the dancing began. Imagine the Albert Hall transformed into a perfect lawn of moonlit, dewy turf. That was the effect when the cunningly contrived lights flashed from fourteen blue-draped arc lamps over the floor. Above – surely the roof had been removed? – they seemed real stars that peeped from the darkened sky. Yet over those stars was the roof of the hall, and below that roof there were galleries of spectators, all hidden from the view of the dancers below.

The band played Weber's 'Invitation to the Waltz' – itself nearly a century old – during the programme. But who needed an invitation, with such a floor as this?

And when the floor began to fill, no Court or country in Europe – a hundred years ago or at any other time – could have shown you such a company. They came, these guests in their great-grandfathers' clothes, from all Courts and all countries.

Tall Hussar, pelisse and sabretache and sword, all swaying with his stride, rivalled his ancient enemy, the Cuirassier of the Imperial Guard, for the privilege of scribbling his name on the programme-fan of a London lavender girl. Jane Austen maidens looking not half so timid as they would have done a century ago though, danced with smart young men-about-town from Almack's.

Such gowns, too! Had Lely's beauties stepped from their Hampton Court frames, and Knellers and Gainsboroughs, too, they could not have made a fairer show.

Half the dresses, indeed, did come straight from Old Masters. In the 'Ancestors' quadrille, which Lady Sarah Wilson arranged, all the dancers' dresses were copied from the paintings and prints at Blenheim.

The Duchess of Wellington ransacked Apsley House to provide her friends in the 'Waterloo' quadrille – the feature of the evening – with fans, ornaments, and arms contemporary with the Iron Duke. She herself wore a brocaded kirtle which formed part of the bridal dress of the great general's consort in 1806.

And when they all came out from under the mock stars of 1812 the real stars had flown. It was five o'clock this morning – and 1912.

The glories of an English summer afternoon, amid the unhurried grandeur of Lords, sharing the unbought grace of life was captivatingly described by old Harrovian J. Malcolm Fraser in July 1902.

'Oh, well caught, sir! – well caught!' A shrill cry of delight burst from behind innumerable cornflower buttonholes, as the Harrow captain neatly catches a ball and flings it triumphantly into the air.

Our stand is a regular stronghold of dark blues. On the front bench sit a cohort of Harrovians intrenched behind the most spotless of white waistcoats and the shiniest of patent leather boots. They are all picked men of fourteen and under, whose leathern lungs and clarion voices may be relied on to strike terror into the hearts of our enemies the light blues. But the Eton cheer runs us close, and it will need skillful judging to decide whose paeans of praise are the more penetrating. Behind our cohort sit reinforcements of fathers and uncles, whose minds for a few brief moments turn back to when they too sat like rows of little white-breasted birds, and cheered their elevens on to victory. Relieving the monotony of black coats and silk hats, the sun-lit muslins of mothers and sisters look invitingly cool.

Our party consists chiefly of innumerable Harrovians and a delightful little girl, whose life is torn between the onus of newly put-up hair and the inconvenience of newly lengthened dresses.

'It was a splendid catch,' she remarks, with the air of a connoisseur. 'But it must have hurt,' she adds with true feminine compassion.

'Not it; he's got awfully hard hands,' says her brother decisively.

'How do you know?'

'I'm his fag,' comes the reply, with Spartan brevity; and for a while the conversation lags.

Never had Lord's cricket ground looked so gay. Not even the Oxford and Cambridge match brings out so many smart gowns and pretty women. Lord's, on Eton v. Harrow days, becomes the drawing-room of London.

Under the trees, behind the coaches, long white-clothed tables groan beneath bowls of lobster salad, salmon, chicken, tongue, strawberries, and quails entombed in golden jellies. At the gates of the private grounds behind, black-lettered cards proclaim the owners who are entertaining their guests beneath the shady may and chestnut trees.

'Well bowled, sir – well bowled!' Harrow's demon bowler has eclipsed himself. The ball has pitched just right, skimming the stumps and carrying the bails a good two yards behind the wicket-keeper. Our young barbarians have been saving themselves up for this. They have not cheered for at least two minutes by the clock. Now six wickets are down for a paltry fifty runs, and the small throats open in a shrill rapture of shouting. Mere sound seems hardly able to express delirious joy of the moment, and the stands fairly rock to the stamp of many feet.

The boy in the light blue cap takes this disaster stoically enough. He walks half-way up the pitch examining the ground, wondering how on earth he misjudged the ball as he did; then finding no clue to the mystery, turns towards the pavilion and drags off his cap in acknowledgment to the cheering ground. True sportsmen that they are, Eton and Harrow join in praise to their rivals, especially if the innings has been 'jolly good'.

Approval of robust young public schools boys was echoed in this 1911 account of the public schools boxing championships:

Those who dislike bloodshed and object to seeing people carried away more or less insensible should make it a point to avoid the Public School boxing championships.

The public schoolboy, when fighting for the honour of his school, is a particularly fierce person. He is there, if possible, to knock his opponent out, and is not troubled with any false notions about making it easy for the other fellow, more especially as, if he slowed up at all, the other fellow might very well recuperate and knock him out.

Some of the bouts yesterday were certainly rather strong meat, and gentle mothers and sisters who had come up to see their sons and brothers perform, wilted visibly as they gazed on the object of their interest smothered in blood from head to foot or carried insensible from the ring by the callous 'Tommies' who were deputed to act as seconds.

But there was not a spark of ill-feeling or temper throughout the many bouts, and as soon as ever a decision was given or a knocked-out hero had sufficiently recovered consciousness, the erstwhile deadly foes would shake each other warmly by the hand and beam. The English public schoolboy may be a bloodthirsty little animal, but he is a sportsman right through.

The keynote of the whole proceedings was struck by one badly battered youth, who, hopelessly outboxed, and mercifully ruled out in the second round, looked wistfully at the judge and gasped, 'Can't we finish it?'

While applauding the Roman stoicism and pluck of the scions of the well-to-do, the *Express* did not hesitate to publicise attacks on the stupid well-to-do. The story of the drugged babies suggests that life for some toddlers behind the beech hedges and trimmed lawns was positively gruesome. The account comes from the issue of 29 April, 1910:

The ignorance of mothers, not so much in the poorer classes but among the well-to-do is the subject of a striking article by Mrs Enid Campbell Dauncey in the *Contemporary Review*.

She points out that it is usually the very poor who are quoted and spoken of as needing lessons in the care of children: whereas among the middle classes and the rich an ignorance of babies' diet and other matters exists which is incredible.

One of Mrs Dauncey's most remarkable charges against well-to-do mothers is that the children are drugged by sedatives given to them by ignorant or lazy nurses. She says :

'Said a fond though fashionable young mother to me a few days ago : "My new nurse is a treasure. Baby never cries at night now. He sleeps without waking once. I am so thankful : it made us miserable to hear him cry. Oh, no, of course, I don't nurse him myself. What an idea! I can't give up my friends and my life for that. Besides babies do much better, really, on bottles.'

'Well, before I left I was privileged to see the sleeping marvel who, at two months old, did not cry in the night after a heavy meal of almost pure starch.

'As I left the house he returned from an airing in the charge of his ogling, smiling nurse, his tender spine subjected to the frightful strain of sitting propped up in a perambulator, and his poor little puffy, greeny-white face and curiously shadowed, dull, fixed eyes saying to me, as plainly as a shouted voice, Opium !'

Anybody who knows the traces of opium in an infant's face, Mrs Dauncey declares, can see it on a hundred little white faces in Kensington Gardens any day.

The children of the very poor might have welcomed opium : dreams being infinitely preferable to the reality of their home lives.

Throughout the Edwardian era the columns of the popular newspapers were sprinkled with items like these. On 31 July, 1903 :

The St Pancras Borough Council is making a determined raid on the cave-dwellers within its boundaries.

These wretched creatures are numbered not by hundreds but by their thousands. They haunt basements in slums, which are literally underground dwellings to which the light of day scarcely ever penetrates.

Now, as a result of a two years' survey of the whole borough, the law is to be put in motion.

There are no fewer than 1,151 of these underground dwellings in St Pancras. All these are condemned, and by stages will be emptied by their occupants. Whole streets have to be tackled, and this week the first batch, 130 in number, have received notice that they must quit within a period of three months. In these 1,151 cells probably not fewer than 5,000 persons exist.* The night population is vastly in excess of these figures.

*According to a report by Sir Edwin Chadwick, every week an average of 6,000 children are born in Greater London and 1,000 of them do not live to be a year old.

Sometimes, these cave-dwellings are mere boxes – rooms so situated that there is absolutely not even a window in the cell. Being right underground, a spluttering candle affords the only light in which the people live.

Yesterday afternoon an *Express* representative by the courtesy of the St Pancras officials, paid a visit to several of the people under notice to quit.

One of the best of these dens was in a wide and spacious street in Camden Town. The house was old-fashioned, and as the door opened there was a rush of bad air. Below, down a flight of narrow rickety stairs, was the underground basement. It was the one dwelling place of a whole family, consisting of a man and his wife and their two children, a boy and a girl.

For some time the eye could only dimly distinguish objects. This one room bore traces of being used as kitchen, living-room, and bed-room. There was no possible privacy, no possible comfort, no possible ventilation. From a sink in the corner a nauseous smell emanated. Five shillings a week was paid in rent.

1 July 1909

Death from starvation and destitution owing to inability of the parents to provide food, was the verdict returned at the inquest yesterday on Charles Leaning, the three-year-old child of an out-of-work scaffolder living at Westmorland-lace, Hoxton.

The father said he had been unemployed for nine weeks. His wife made boxes, earning five shillings or six shillings a week, and on this he, his wife and five children lived.

As four shillings a week was paid for the rent of two rooms, the family's weekly budget was as follows:

To rent .... 4s.
To living .... 2s.

Seven living on 2s a week allows an average expenditure of $3\frac{1}{2}$d per week for each.

When the child died the mother was at the police court, where she was fined five shillings for not sending one of the children to school. As she could not pay, her husband was sent to prison.

3 April 1903

The drama of London's rat plague was further elaborated yesterday at the inquest at Greenwich on the body of the child who was gnawed to death at Lewisham.

On Monday night Mrs Brookes, of Riddington's Yard, put her baby, Rosina, to bed, leaving her in charge of a ten-year-old boy, and went to the Park Hospital, Hither Green. On her return she found the child dead – bitten to death by rats.

Dr Donnellan, who was promptly called in, said yesterday that there was an irregular surface on the left jaw, measuring 3 ins. by $2\frac{1}{2}$ ins. and another on the scalp an inch square. This had been gnawed by rats, which had bitten into the bone; other parts of the face were also bitten.

Death, continued the doctor, was due to shock and loss of blood; a rat, would suck at a wound made by its own teeth.

Dr Oswald, the coroner, said it was a dreadful thing that in these days a child could be done to death by rats. The house in which the people lived was unfit for habitation and should be seen to by the sanitary authorities.

In returning a verdict of 'Death by misadventure', the jury cautioned the mother and asked the coroner to draw the attention of the borough council to the house in which the incident occurred.

Insecurity at work matched and often caused these bad social conditions.

In 1904 there was a trade recession brought about partly by increasing German competition and partly by the end of the short lived 'peace boom' that followed victory in the Boer War. The London docks suffered severely and the dockers aggravated their plight by an ill-timed strike.

The *Express* headed a story quite simply 'STARVING DOCKERS':

In the grey dawn of yesterday morning a crowd of gaunt and half-starved dockers stood outside the great gates of the docks. Not five per cent of them found the work they sought, for there was none to give, and the disappointed labourers turned sadly away.

When the announcement was made that no more men could be taken on, some blasphemed, others with pinched faces shortly afterwards returned and hung about in the hope of finding even an hour's work, which meant four pounds of bread and an ounce of tea for their little ones at home.

'Why are you not working?' asked the *Express* representative of a docker yesterday.

'Why don't I work? you ask; give me work, that's all I ask,' was the reply. 'I have not done an hour for three weeks. I can't get parish relief, and I will not go to the workhouse.

'I have been off and on at work at the docks for twenty-seven years, but I have never been in such a plight before.

'At the docks there are a number of regular hands who get all the jobs in slack times. They are the "red ticket" men. Then come the owners of the "blue tickets" who get the jobs the "red tickets" cannot take on, and after them come the casuals like me. When there are no leavings, I and men like myself starve.'

About the same time a regular dock labourer named Arthur Gollard, fearing that an attack of scarlet fever, then raging in the capital's East End, would destroy his work prospects, tried to hang himself. He failed in his bid. The breadwinner's fear of losing his job was a palpable thing in many households, while fear of running into debt was so strong that the most astonishing articles were put up for sale, well illustrated by this classified advertisement in 1904 :

Old artificial teeth bought : good prices given; money sent return post : if price not accepted teeth returned – V. Pearse, 10 Granviile Road, Hove, Brighton.

General Booth, leader of the Salvation Army, was much in favour of the practice – with the proviso that if the teeth belonged to a dear departed and the family was not poverty stricken then the dentures should be given to the Salvation Army (which could raise cash on them) rather than be sold to middle men.

Why did these conditions, especially when contrasted with the opulence of the few not provoke a violent reaction, rather than the reforms which ushered in the Welfare State ? A host of reasons may be adduced : from the phlegmatic character of the British people to the counter attractions of sport. But surely the strongest bulwark against revolution was the belief held by the great middle class (more an attitude of mind than an income bond), that many of the poor had brought their poverty on themselves by reckless drinking and breeding. Churchmen, nonConformist no less than Anglican, gave credence to this view.

'Beer drinking is no less than a religion to the average East Ender.'

In these words the Rev Richard Free, of St Cuthbert's, Millwall epitomises a terrible indictment of the condition of the East End of London.

'The besetting sin of the East Ender is intemperance,' he writes in his new book *Seven Years Hard*. 'The drink habit is universal.

'Christmas is the thankfully acknowledged time for the most glorious "drunk" of the whole year. Then our friend the working man will go to the public houses and lay his golden sovereigns on the counter with instructions that he is to have drink as long as the money lasts.

'When he becomes incapable, he reels home, or is carried home, and sleeps it off. On returning to consciousness back he goes and repeats the process. If there is still a balance on his deposit account he will go at it again and again until it is exhausted. Many a man has five or six bouts during the Christmas holidays.

'Worse still, mere children of from thirteen to sixteen years old will be seen in the open streets, in the glare of the morning, maudlin and utterly helpless.

'On Christmas Eve the factory girl will draw out of her wine club every penny she has been saving for weeks past, and will spend the whole of it on a cake (a little) and liquor (much). I have known her to knock off work at one, and be dead drunk by five.'

It is not unusual, says Mr Free, for the bridegroom to present himself at the altar rails 'fuddled', and funerals are 'frequently scenes of sottish revelry, forcibly reminding one of those Irish wakes of which we used to read in childhood,' and the drink on these occasions, 'not infrequently degenerating into swinish debauchery, goes far into the morning.'

The 'undeserving poor' got short shrift from those who, in many instances, earned less than the shiftless but who foreswore drink and gambling and accounted for every penny spent. Early in 1907 the *Express* held up for approbation a remarkable old woman in Dorking, Widow Roffey, aged 92, who had kept a diary recording all her expenditure – and money spent on her since childhood. She computed the total as £1,913.12s, an average expenditure of 8s a week.

She made out an inventory of a life-time's clothing :

Dresses	41	Stockings	274
Petticoats	47	Bonnets & Hats	163
Shoes & Boots	80	Shawls & Wraps	34
Aprons	53	Gloves & Mittens	30

Such exactitude prompted loud hosannas from the thrifty readers of the *Express*. A City clerk wrote:

'My income is only £130. I am thirty years of age and have a wife and two children. We live in a six roomed villa, and I offer the following budget, showing my average weekly expenditure:—

		s d
Rent	....	£0.9.6.
Housekeeping	....	1.0.6.
Fares to City	....	0.8.0.
Lunch	....	0.2.0.
Wife banks	....	0.7.6.
I bank	....	0.5.0.
Wife's pin money	....	0.2.6.
Total	....	£2.10.0

'Out of the 20s 6d allowed for housekeeping we put by weekly 1s for coal, 1s for clothes, 1s for boots, so that when any of these is needed the money is ready.

(sgd CITY CLERK)'

A father of 19 children (ten more had died), Mr Thomas Arthur Stack of Purley, remarked in an interview: 'It's all rubbish to say people can't afford children. If a man has no children he spends his money in ways less profitable to the nation.'

Commenting on workers' dwellings a committee of the London County Council declared in its report of 30 June, 1903:

'The persons who occupy these cottages insist on having one room in their tenement which can be set apart for occasional or ceremonial use only.'

The average workman's parlour is 'a mausoleum of wax fruits, family Bibles and dusty antimacassars, and the only persons admitted to it are the doctor, the undertaker, and the insurance man.'

Against such implacable respectability, what chance had revolution?

Board of Trade statistics, published in February 1907, revealed a wide spread of income among the deserving working class. Omnibus drivers could earn £2 12s for a working week up to 100 hours. For the same hours, a greengrocer's assistant could receive only 15s, although it is to be remembered that the assistant was probably a youth.

To help the housewife on slender means to budget for her family the *Express*, in 1908, printed a pamphlet from Mr Rowntree's Reform Association; the pamphlet listed a weekly diet sheet for a family of five – mother, father, and three young children – that would not cost more than 12s 9d a week. The Tuesday's menu read :

'Breakfast : Porridge and milk, tea, bread and dripping, herrings (3).
'Dinner : Broth re-heated with dumplings and bread.
'Tea : Tea, brown bread and treacle.
'Supper : Cocoa, bread, dripping, cheese.
'Quantities : 8 ozs oatmeal, 1 qt skim milk, 3 lbs white bread, $\frac{1}{2}$ lb dripping, 4 ozs barley, 1 turnip, 2 carrots, $\frac{3}{4}$ lb flour, 4 teaspoonfuls tea, $1\frac{1}{2}$ lb brown bread, $\frac{1}{4}$ lb treacle, 1 oz cocoa, 2 ozs cheese, 6 ozs sugar.'

Wages may have been low but so were prices. A cheap day ticket to Dover from London cost 5s, a week's visit to the Paris Exhibition of 1900 was on offer at £4 4s 6d, all inclusive of full board and admission. A Royal Mail de luxe cruise to the Norwegian fiords (14 days) could be had for just £1 a day.

The *Express*'s philosophy, chiming with the views of its readers, was that hard work and prudent savings could make up for life's unfairnesses. It saw nothing incongruous in reporting that : 'Mr. J. Hutchinson Driver, Master of the Ripley and Knaphill Hunt, took his pack to the grounds of Chertsey Workhouse and made a generous distribution of sweets to the women, tobacco to the men and toys to the children.'

The *Express* knew its respectable public was neither sullen nor sour but lapped up details of luxuries it would never enjoy itself. When the Carlyle Club in London's Piccadilly was opened by F. E. Smith, KC, the Tory politician, in May 1914, there was lyrical praise.

The visitor might imagine on entering it that he had wandered into an Elizabethan mansion in some far away corner of Devonshire . . . a Buccaneer smoke room . . . open Tudor fireplaces . . . horn lanterns . . . ancient pistols . . . and, with a touch of surprising modernity, electrophones fitted in the corners of the room so that members may sit in comfortable armchairs and listen to records of theatre, music hall, or concert, plus a typewriting room with typists in attendance for the busy man of commerce.

Echoes of a bygone age sound in this recital of additional services:

A buffet is open day and night, members' hats are ironed as a matter of course, clothes are taken in hand by the club valet, brushed, pressed and sent home if desired. There is also a set of apartments, for the use of members' wives, with maids in attendance, and all these services are included in the club subscription.

Another unusual privilege of membership is the introduction of a friend, if necessary by letter. The friend becomes a guest of the club – with all its services at his disposal – for a couple of days, and may remain, after that, a temporary member for a fortnight.

Messenger boys who will run to any corner of London will be within instant call.

The ordinary club dining-room has been purposely omitted, as most men prefer going to a restaurant, but the cold buffet will be supplemented at eleven o'clock every night with a Welsh rarebit, for which there will be no bill.

Wines and other liquors will, as in other clubs, be paid for, but members will be invited to 'say when' instead of having a fixed quantity served by a waiter.

But for sumptuous living and expensive dying nothing could equal the great Million-Pound will case of July 1913, to which the *Express* devoted forty thousand words.

Mr Malcolm Scott sought to set aside his brother's, Sir John Scott's million pounds will on the ground that undue influence had been exercised on Sir John by Lord and Lady Sackville. The dramatis personae, for what the *Express* called 'The greatest drama outside Drury Lane', was scintillating. For the Scott family, the plaintiffs, was F. E. Smith, KC, MP. For the Sackvilles was the big Irishman with the soft brogue who had brought down Oscar Wilde – Edward Carson, KC, MP. In politics the two were thick as thieves, operating as a partnership on the Tory benches and championing the cause of Ulster. In court they were often deadly rivals, well aware of each other's strengths and weaknesses.

The principal defendant, Lady Sackville, was a beautiful society hostess, part Spanish and French speaking. The deceased, over whose will the squabble was taking place, had been the adopted son of Sir

Richard Wallace, the art collector who had gathered together the famous Wallace Collection (now in Manchester Square, London). The *Daily Express* court reporter set the scene :

Crowds were unable to gain admission. The ushers were there at eight o'clock in the morning – two and a half hours before the performance began – receiving applications for admission and allotting seats. Hundreds of persons gathered outside the door of the court like the struggles that used to be seen at the gallery door of Drury Lane or the Haymarket in the far-off days before the queue was invented. But those who struggled were persons who figure in *Burke's Peerage, Baronetage and Landed Gentry*.

There were scores of ladies in lovely dresses, and they all happened to be round the door when it was opened. They did not wish to scramble; they merely wished to get in early; so they all moved forward together and met in a crush which frightened some nearly to tears and others to anger. There were calls to ushers for help, and cries of alarm.

Parasols went down in the squash and were trodden under foot. The men stood back smiling but the women, who were clearly unused to the fierce delights of fighting for places, tried in a body to edge past each other, all astonished that the rest did not give way.

But it was worth losing a three-guinea parasol to secure a seat. No cross-examination ever seen on the stage, of a beautiful sparkling woman by a skilful, practised KC was ever so entertaining, or so thrilling as the cross-examination of Lady Sackville by Mr F. E. Smith.

It went from one extreme of human emotion to the other – from leaping laughter at the drollest 'demonstration' ever perhaps given by a witness, to a flood of tears from the witness herself – tears that were wrung from her by the production of a private letter written to one of her dearest women friends; never, of course, intended for any other eye, and now read aloud by the cross-examiner, who insisted on knowing what it meant.

The tears were provoked by Mr Smith's ungallant suggestion that Lady Sackville had not been the disinterested friend of the timid, shy Sir John Scott that she had pretended to be :

'Would you have liked him as much if he had not been rich?' asked Mr Smith in a silken voice, as if he quite expected the answer Lady Sackville made – 'Absolutely the same.'

'Not the slightest difference?' added the agreeable cross-examiner gently.

'Not the slightest,' said Lady Sackville.

'Not the slightest,' Mr Smith echoed in a honeyed tone of agreement. He added, by way of inviting confirmation, 'You were attached to him for his own sake?'

Lady Sackville, of course, said, 'Yes'. She fell in with Mr Smith's suggestions that if Sir John had been poor she would have been as hospitable to him. Certainly.

By this time the crowded court was listening with a curious attention. Mr Smith looked reflectively at the piece of blue notepaper, and framed a new line of questions.

'It would not be correct,' he asked, 'to say that for the last ten years of Sir John's life you were wearily waiting?'

'For what?' exclaimed Lady Sackville in astonishment.

'For all his death would bring you?'

'Not a word of truth!'

'Not a word,' repeated Mr Smith quietly. Then he stood up, picked up the blue paper, and held it out.

'Is that your handwriting?' he asked, and Lady Sackville, having been handed the letter, said, 'Yes.'

Mr Smith, in reply to the President, said that the letter was written by Lady Sackville to Mrs Ralph Cook, and was noted as having been received on 21 October 1911. He began reading it :

'Dearest Ann, S. [Sir John] wrote to me that he had made his new arrangements about his will, which will be made afresh and signed tomorrow, leaving everything he had dangled before my weary eyes for ten years away from us three. . . .'

'Did you write that?' he asked.

'Yes,' said Lady Sackville warmly. 'Mrs Cook was one of my very best friends, and she behaved like that.'

'Therefore, you would write the truth to her?' said Mr Smith quickly.

The cross-examiner held on his way.

'Was it,' he asked, 'the inheritance your eyes had been weary about?'

Lady Sackville seemed to pay more attention to her own thoughts than to the questions. She shook her head and in an absent way said, 'I cannot tell you.' Her eyes filled with tears.

'I am sure I don't understand what you mean,' she said with emotion as the voice of Mr Smith hammered away. A copy of the letter was handed to her. She read it. The tears in her eyes fell down her cheeks. She sank down in the chair behind her, laid her head in her hands and wept bitterly. The court looked on silently.

Sir Edward Carson seemed troubled by the scene. He said, in his Irish voice, as soft and soothing as it is sometimes rasping and hard, 'Ye need not mind, Lady Sackville.'

'But there has been a whole week of these lies,' she burst out, amid her tears : 'it is dreadful to listen to these lies. I do mind.'

The laughter concerned the stout, round-cheeked elderly Walter, brother of Sir John, who, along with other Scotts, was contesting the will. According to Lady Sackville, Walter, far from disliking her and distrusting her motives, had been in love with her.

'I said, "Mr Walter, if you go on like this, I shall have to tell my husband and Sir John." He said, "If you tell Johnnie you will ruin my life." He added, "I love you! I love you! and I want to be your friend and not Johnnie's. If you ever want a friend, you must come to me."

'Of course, I have always found him very objectionable, and I said, "I will ring the bell for you to be shown out." Then he followed me on his knees across the room. I went out of the room, leaving him there in that ridiculous position.'

The *Express* court reporter excelled himself in recounting the reaction to this :

Every eye in court glanced from Lady Sackville to the stout and elderly man and back again. Lady Sackville's eyes shone with enjoyment as, in a twinkling, she exclaimed, 'Yes, like this,' and, doubling the first and second fingers of her right hand at the second knuckle, she ran her two fingers along the edge of the witness-box, as quickly as if she were making a run on a piano.

Her hand was perfectly fitted with a lemon-coloured chamois glove, and the two chubby half fingers did their trot along the edge of the witness-box in a manner so completely ludicrous in their life-like suggestion of a stout man hobbling on his knees that the effect on the court was electrical in its sudden explosiveness.

Everyone gave a shout, a yell, a shriek, a scream of laughter at the same instant. It was like an electric battery being applied unexpectedly to a mass meeting of Central Africans. The audience was convulsed. The President fell back in his chair, and his sides shook. Tears came into the eyes of the briefless barristers.

People rolled about in laughter, and the laugh had to exhaust itself before the law could pick up its solemn threads. For a quarter of an hour afterwards the spectacle of those two hobbling fingers rose in the mind's eye, and made the onlookers again and again nearly explode with laughter.

That was the triumph of Lady Sackville in her gayest mood.

Her sense of humour showed itself even when she indignantly declaimed against the 'tissue of lies' which she said had been told by witnesses on the other side.

'I don't like to say that the lady is lying,' she said, with a shake of the head and then a little shrug of the shoulders, and a rising of the corners of her lips, she added, gently, 'but she is, really.'

Two or three times she turned the laugh against Mr Smith altogether, as when he asked if she considered Miss Davidson, the elderly maiden lady who gave evidence on the other side, attractive.

Lady Sackville put her head a little on one side, as if she were just a little bit shocked at the laying of a trap for her, and with a look of reproach at Mr Smith she told him with mock gravity that he really ought not to ask her questions like that !

When she was being questioned about Mr Walter Scott's love-making, she looked across at the jury with a smile as she said that she 'gave the man a chance' – a chance, she meant of getting over his folly.

At lunchtime on the last day many fashionably dressed men and women remained in court during recess and had a picnic lunch on the benches vacated by counsel and witnesses.

After an absence of less than ten minutes they found for Lord and Lady Sackville. Sir John Scott's will, said the jury, had been duly executed and there had been no fraud or undue influence by either Lord or Lady Sackville. Mr Malcolm Scott was ordered to pay costs.

The will disposed of property to the net value of £1,180,000 (about £13 million by late nineteen seventies values) and just half that amount went to Lady Sackville. The remainder was divided among Sir John's brothers, sisters, cousins and friends. The legacy to Mr Malcolm Scott was cancelled because he contested the will.

Thus ended the greatest society case of the pre-First War era. The sums of money so nonchalantly tossed about were astronomic and even those described as a 'paltry legacy' – £2,000 per annum – were ten times greater than the yearly earnings of well-paid office employees. Yet far from there being demonstrations of envy, the Strand was cleared by police because of the intense public interest in the verdict and the passionate partisanship of the crowds in favour of Lady Sackville.

CHAPTER FOUR

Upstairs, Downstairs

Society court actions may have given the commonality a cheerful earful of what the Lady said to the suitor, but for the *bon mot*, the glittering epigram, they had to look to Society and especially that part of it that joined up with politics.

Margot Asquith, the sharp-featured, sharper-witted wife of the Liberal Prime Minister, provided a glimpse of the grandeur of 'Upstairs' in a celebrated court case in 1911. She was appearing as a witness in the suit of Mrs Horace West who was suing her father-in-law for slander. Sir Algernon (the father-in-law) had been going round saying that the reason for the break-up of his son's marriage was Mrs West's extravagance. She claimed that these malicious tales had caused her to be excluded from Court and social gatherings. Among the functions denied her were Foreign Office receptions, to which, as the Premier's wife, Mrs Asquith was allowed to take many of her own friends. Counsel for Sir Algernon cross-examined Mrs Asquith :

'Is there the slightest pretence that anything that passed between you and Sir Algernon affected the question of your receiving this lady [Mrs West] ?'

'No.'

'Have you heard of a lady being excluded from Society because she was extravagant ?'

'Extravagance,' replied Mrs Asquith with raised eyebrows, 'is usually a passport to society.'

Extravagance was duly recorded but, in the readership of the popular press at least, roused no envy. Quite casually *The Idler*'s Society's Doings column of October 1900 (during the Boer War) reported :

Mr W. K. Vanderbilt has just presented his daughter, the Duchess of Marlborough, with a cheque for $500,000 to celebrate the safe return of her husband from the Transvaal. The Duke and Duchess of Marlborough are at present in Paris, where they are making considerable purchases of artistic furniture and old tapestry, destined to adorn the new home which the Duke is having built in Mayfair.

The savour of the social scene at the start of the century is captured in this column, crowded as it is with as many names from *Debrett* and the *Almanac de Gotha* as it was possible to encompass. Thus :

A very successful dance was given last week by Sir Henry and Lady Tichborne at Tichborne Park. The house party included the Maharajah of Kuch-Behar, Lord and Lady Mowbray and Stourton, Lord Southwell and others.

The Duke of Saxe-Coburg-Gotha, with his mother, the Duchess of Albany, has gone to Reinhardsbrunn Castle near Gotha.

The Grand Duke of Hesse has taken a house near Paris, where he is living in the strictest incognito.

The Duke and Duchess of Orleans [the duke has just escaped expulsion from St James's club for misbehaviour] have arrived at Palermo where they are staying at the Palais d'Orleans.

Lord and Lady De La Warr are going on a yachting tour to the West of Scotland, and will go up the Caledonian Canal.

Sir Gilbert and Lady Clayton-East, who have been on a cruise in their steam-yacht, return this week to Hall Place. Miss Clayton-East has been to Schwalbach.

Sir Gerald and Lady Edeline Strickland have left Sizergh, Cumberland, for the Villa Bologna, Malta, where they will pass the winter.

Lord and Lady Jersey intend to spend the winter in Egypt.

Mrs Mackinnon has taken No 5, Pont-street, for the winter months. Colonel Mackinnon, who went out to South Africa in command of the CIV, is expected home at the beginning of the month.

Captain and Lady Margaret Spicer are expected in London shortly from Arndilly, Craigellachie.

Ten years later the column had lost its pseudonym, and was retitled 'In Society'. The foreign element was eliminated – but the 'names' were dropped in thicker clusters than ever :

The Duke of Somerset has arrived at Claridge's from the country.

The Duchess of Wellington has arrived in town from Ewhurst Park.

The Marquis of Salisbury, who had intended to leave yesterday for the Riviera, has postponed his departure.

The Marquis of Lansdowne will leave Bowood today to fulfil political engagements in Liverpool.

The Earl and Countess of Harrowby have returned to Sandon Hall where they will stay for the remainder of the winter.

Lord and Lady Wolverton have been staying at St Moritz.

The Hon Thomas Cochrane, MP and Lady Cochrane, with the Misses Cochrane, have left Crawford Priory, Fifeshire, for the Pavilion, Ardrossan, Ayrshire, where they will remain until after the general election. Mr Cochrane is busy addressing meetings of the electors of North Ayrshire.

Society and society's code also cropped up in much more unlikely places than the gossip columns.

In a divorce action – prompted by the wife's suspicion that her husband was up to no good because after a visit to Harrogate he never touched an onion – the defendant, Mr Herbert Greenwood Teele, a Leeds solicitor, took this oath : 'I swear on my honour as a gentleman and as an old Wykehamist – you know how much I think of the old school – that I have never been unfaithful.'

The public schools were very much part of the social fabric and much admired. Although it is doubtful if one in ten thousand of its readers had been to Eton, the *Express* in March 1907 published a column of reminiscences of one Mary Fraser who had helped to run the local tobacconist's. The Department of Health would today look askance at Mary's activities (and at those of King Edward VII, who frequently attended smoking concerts) but she was proud to recount them :

Eton boys, of course, like other boys are not supposed to smoke, but there! like everything else 'where there's a will there's a way.'

In the shop in my time, there was a peculiar wire blind to the upper glass half of the door. This had the advantage of allowing a customer to see out into the street, but a master could not see inside the shop.

I used to put my head out to see if the coast was clear, and then a boy could slip out without fear of being caught and 'swished'.

Very few of my customers got birched, I am sure. . . .

One boy I knew had an income of £45,000 a year, in trust, while he was still at school and he ran up a bill of £100 for smoking materials.

When he left he ordered a magnificent silver cigar box – a model of Paddington Station, a perfect piece of work, which was made specially for him. He gave it to a lady afterwards as a jewel case, I believe.

It was not considered 'playing the game' for a master to look back or hang about the shop, but there was one who did and he became unpopular and had to leave.

When older Etonians and other former public school boys got together, as at Henley Regatta, newspaper writing became a lyrical paean of praise :

Looking up the course, one saw this afternoon a sight that can only be seen at Henley, and once a year. There was a mile and a half of flannelled Englishmen afloat.

The Englishman never looks as well as in flannels and shirt sleeves.

A somewhat less euphoric view of England was taken by the first Rhodes scholars to arrive in Britain from America :

Thirty-five young men, representing all that is best in American university life, from the points of view of erudition, athletic attainments, and personal character, arrived in Liverpool yesterday from Boston by the Cunard liner *Ivernia*.

They are America's Cecil Rhodes scholars who, under the will of the South African Colossus will complete their studies at Oxford University, where they will spend three years at a cost of £300 each per annum.

They sat for examination at their various universities – Yale, Harvard, Princeton, Pennsylvania, Columbia and other educational centres.

They are very American. Eager, sallow, brimming over with energy and enthusiasm, and dressed in the free-and-easy style affected by the American student, they are likely to cause a decided stir in the select circles of the university on the Isis.

It will be long before they attain to the Oxford manner. So pronounced is their nasal twang that the prospects of their rising to the Oxford drawl are poor.

'What are you going to do on the completion of your three years at Oxford?' asked the *Express* representative. 'Will you become English citizens?'

'Not likely!' chorused the thirty-five. 'We are not going to desert the greatest country on earth for the smallest in extent.'

These Yanks at Oxford ardently endorsed the reply of an eminent, though humbly-born, Jewish scientist to a peer's question about his 'family'. 'I am descended from the illustrious blood of Abraham.' The Americans, even those from the Ivy League universities, were the apostles of equality, coming as innocents to the land where everyone – well, almost everyone – knew his place: and none more so than that large and admirable body, the servant class.

Domestic service claimed far more employees, 2,500,000, in the years before the First World War than any other occupation. They seem, on the whole, to have been a contented lot and the newspapers frequently reported examples of fidelity. One of the most touching concerned Charlotte Elizabeth Eardley. The story was told in the coroner's court at Wood Green, London, on 11 October, 1904:

Charlotte Elizabeth Eardley had been in service of Mrs Leath at Ribblesdale-road, Hornsey, for seventeen years. On Wednesday evening last she served dinner as usual and then, to the astonishment of the family, collapsed on the dining-room floor.

'Oh, I have burnt my hands,' was all she said then. Later a doctor was called, and found that her body and limbs were terribly burnt. Her injuries were considered so serious that she was taken to the Wood Green Hospital. She died there from the effects of the burns.

In hospital the full story of her courage came out.

Early in the day on which she collapsed, her clothes caught fire while lighting a gas ring. She fought the flames without assistance, not wishing to worry the family. Before she had torn off the burning clothing she was badly injured. Nevertheless, she went upstairs and put on another dress.

In spite of the fact that she was suffering almost unendurable agony, she went about her housework and performed all her duties as usual. The accident happened at nine o'clock in the morning, and she kept on working without complaint until dinner time.

'I did not say anything to my mistress as I did not want to upset her, as she was not well,' she told a nurse in the hospital. 'God only knows the agony I was in.'

After the coroner had remarked on the woman's devotion, the jury returned a verdict of 'Accidental death'.

Devotion called forth reciprocal loyalties from the employer as this item from the issues of 22 April, 1909, illustrates:

The family of Mr S. N. Carvello, of Hamilton House, St John's Wood, has just lost by death an old and respected servant whose period of service covered seventy-five years, which is one of the longest records of domestic service in one family.

Her death is recorded in the following paragraph, which appeared in yesterday's *Times*:—

COOK – on the 18th April at 8 Hamilton House, Hall-road, Hannah (Jane) Cook, in her ninety-third year, for seventy-five years most faithful friend in the service of the late Mrs John Abraham of Clifton and her daughter Mrs Carvello.

Miss Cook entered the service of Mrs Carvello's mother at Clifton when she was seventeen years old; afterwards became Mrs Carvello's nurse, and subsequently, when her little charges grew up and married, came to London with her as parlour maid, and remained with her until she died.

For many years she had been regarded almost as a member of the family rather than a servant, for her long and devoted service endeared her to those with whom she had lived for so many years.

Miss Cook's record, although one of the best, was excelled by Susan O'Hagan of Lisburn, near Belfast, who died in January at the age of 107, after ninety-seven years in the service of three generations of the Hall family of Lisburn.

Three years ago the Domestic Servants' Benevolent Institution brought to notice the instance of Miss Caroline Chipp, then ninety-eight years old, one of its pensioners who saw Queen Victoria crowned in Westminster Abbey. She was still in service, and said to be the oldest living domestic servant.

Other servants were not so fortunate. Stern standards were imposed in some of the stately homes. Mary Mercer was cook to Lord and Lady Norreys at a salary of £38 a year. The husband of the Norreys' char-woman wrote a letter to Lord Norreys:

LIFE STORIES ILLUSTRATED.

A Busy Housemaid.

THE COMFORTS OF HOME are, as everyone will admit, greatly increased and intensified by the diligent service of that much criticised person, the Domestic Servant.

AN IDEAL MISTRESS is possessed of the womanly appreciation which recognises that there are occasions when the numerous details of Household Duties accumulate beyond the capacity of even the most industrious maidservant, and such a mistress has a sympathetic consideration for the Vexatious Hindrances which prolong the labours of the day many weary hours beyond nightfall.

My Lord, – I beg the kind liberty to write to you a few lines for the honour and respectability of your house, the other servants, and my wife. I think it is my duty to inform you that yesterday, when my wife went into the pantry to get a spoon there was nobody in the pantry. Then a door opened and the butler and cook came out under suspicious circumstances. It is disgraceful and I feel most disgusted about it.

The subsequent events were recounted in court in June 1905 when cook Mercer sued for wrongful dismissal and the following dialogue was recalled:

'Lord Norreys: Mrs Mercer, why did not the charwoman come this morning?

'The Cook: I do not know, my Lord.

'Lord Norreys: I will tell you the reason. The charwoman says that you and the butler have misconducted yourselves.

'The Cook: My lord, I have always conducted myself properly.

'Lord Norreys: Will you ring for the butler?

The butler, having arrived in the drawing-room, also denied the charge. On the following morning the charwoman called and saw Lord and Lady Norreys and subsequently the cook was summoned to appear before her employers in the smoking-room.

On her way to the smoking-room, however, she met Lord and Lady Norreys in the hall. Lady Norreys called her a bad woman and added, 'I give you half an hour to get out of this house. The streets are the place for you. A respectable house is not the place for you. Get out of my sight, you contemptible creature.'

Upon hearing these words, which were partly endorsed by Lord Norreys, said Mr Powell, counsel for the plaintiff, Mrs Mercer asked for the family doctor to be called in order that she might clear her character, but this was refused.

'Well, if the doctor won't bother with me there are others who will,' replied the cook.

After this the woman was dismissed summarily, without her wages in lieu of notice. On her way out she met Lady Norreys who remarked: 'The best thing the man can do is marry you.'

Lord Norreys justified the woman's dismissal, said Mr Powell, by alleging that she:

1) Had remained in the kitchen with the butler after the other servants had gone to bed.

2) Had passed a great deal of time alone with the butler in the pantry.

3) Had been alone in a cupboard in the pantry with the butler.
4) Had let the butler pinch her arms.

When cross-examined by Mr Dickens, KC, Mrs Mercer said the butler was a stranger to her when she entered Lord Norreys' household. She was never in the pantry with the butler with the door locked, and the French maid had never complained that she had misconducted herself with the butler. She had remained downstairs after the other servants had gone to bed because she had work to do, but she had never sat up till midnight.

'What did the butler call you?' asked Mr Dickens for the defendants.

'Either Mrs Mercer or Cook,' replied the woman.

'Did he call you "My little darling?" ' was another question. Mrs Mercer replied with a dramatic 'Never'.

'Did he call you "My little Mary?" ' continued Mr Dickens. Mrs Mercer gave a most emphatic 'Never' and said it was no laughing matter.

'The butler always treated me with the respect due from one servant to another,' she continued.

'I have always led an honourable and respectable life, and the charge is a wicked and cruel one.'

The butler, George Dawe, was the next witness. He was a red-faced, well-set man who wore two South African medals with clasps. He repeated Mrs Mercer's denials, and in answer to a question as to whether he called the cook 'Little Mary' he said: 'No. I've sung the song of that name, but I never thought it would be brought up against me. I have kissed the housemaid, but not the cook. I did "smack" my lips in imitation of kisses behind the cook's back.'

The jury found for cook Mercer and awarded her £6, one month's board and wages.

Another servant who won an award, this time for 15s, was Miss Lily Grant, who refused to carry parcels for her mistress, Mrs Wolfus, on the grounds that she, Lily, had been engaged as a domestic, not an outdoor servant. Miss Lily fell into the bracket for which there were a score or so advertisements in a daily newspaper of 1914: 'Between maid required for Kensington, £14-£22 p.a. according to experience, excellent place. Three in family, six servants.'

Waiters were a lot less well looked after than house servants, and they too rebelled on occasion:

William Thomas McCulloch, once a cloak-room attendant at the Carlton Hotel, sued his former employers for £83 19s which he said was his share of tips given to the attendants by visitors, and which, he asserted, the Carlton authorities had appropriated to themselves.

In the course of the evidence the fact came to light that a large proportion of the tips given to waiters really goes to swell the dividends of the company.

McCulloch was engaged at a salary of 5s a week. He trusted to the benevolence of visitors to make a living wage from tips. He was put with nine other attendants in the cloak-room. The system in vogue at the Carlton, as explained by counsel, is for the whole of the tips received by members of the staff to be paid into a common fund, which is subsequently shared out by the employees in certain specified proportions.

When the division came, Mr McCulloch found to his dismay, that the management deducted £13 a week from the total cloak-room tips. He was told that this was for 'uniform money' and the 'benevolent fund'.

McCulloch computed that all the time he was in the cloak-room £380 was received. He now claimed his tenth share of this on the ground that when he was engaged he was not informed of the system of deductions.

During the eighteen months he was at the hotel he said he received an average of £2 5s to £2 10s a week as his remuneration, including his wages of 5s a week. His hours were from 10.30 one morning till 1.30 the next.

The jury awarded McCulloch £50, and judgment was given accordingly.

As is the case nowadays, many of the waiters were foreign. There were 140 Frenchmen, eighty of them cooks, at the Savoy. But at least one suggestion, in 1900, for solving the servant problem – by a mass migration of Chinese – was not implemented:

It has been seriously proposed that Chinese should be imported to serve in various household capacities and flattering remarks have been made upon the yellow man's utility for general purposes. It is, however, to be feared that hopes of relief from this quarter are foredoomed to disappointment.

There are two big stumbling blocks in the way of the proposal. Chinese in large quantities are as difficult to transport over here as camels. No purpose would be served by bringing here single specimens.

To begin with John* would require to be personally selected and similarly conducted hither, at a cost per head, say of not less than £20, thus involving a cash outlay of £10,000 to start with a batch of five hundred. On being landed he would have to be lodged and fed while the farming-out process was in motion. Being totally ignorant of our language (save a scanty, doubtful vocabulary acquired in the forecastle), it is probable that his services for the first year or so would not command more than £15 on an average.

Meanwhile a large sum would have been sunk in him, to systematically recoup which would necessitate an office, a staff of clerks or inspectors, and the acceptance of sundry other risks by whosoever ran the show.

Whether the Chinese of 1900 would have been altogether happy with the severe restrictions on service in the UK is another matter. Shopgirls, let alone domestics, were required to conform to near-military regulations. When the Shopworkers' union ran a campaign for more freedom in 1909, this report described the position of out-of-town girls who served in big city stores and boarded under supervisors:

In most West End houses the regulations of those who live in are of the strictest character. When a girl wishes to remain out beyond, say, ten o'clock at night, or wishes to remain out all night, she has to fill up the following form:

SLEEPING-OUT PASS
- - - - - - -

Assistants wishing to sleep out must in every case deposit one of these Notices in the Box near the Timekeeper's desk.

At any other time than Saturday this notice must be countersigned.

Assistant's Name ....

Sleeping at ....

Date .... Countersigned ....

The manager of one important firm told the *Express* representative that he insisted, if a girl wished to visit a theatre, on knowing who were her companions. 'I do this in her own interests,' he said.

*A common nickname for a Chinaman at the time.

The general manager of Messrs Dickins and Jones said : 'Girls from the country are placed under our care. We regard ourselves as standing in the position of parents. If, then, they come to London it would be unwise for them to look about for lodgings themselves. It is much better for them to live in.'

The manager of Messrs D. H. Evans said that many of their women employees expressed themselves in favour of living in. They seemed quite satisfied and contented.

He could give no opinion concerning fines, since they had none. He added, however, that he had worked in one prominent business house where fines existed for seventeen years and no one was ever penalised.

The manager of Messrs Barker, Kensington, said : 'I think that the living-in-system is by far the best for girls – not for men. It is a safeguard and makes for their happiness and welfare.'

The moral protection afforded shop assistants was matched in July 1907 by physical insurance for domestics through the Workers' Compensation Act which obliged employers to compensate household servants for accidents. After a year's operation, the Press reported :

Millions of pounds in risks have been accepted by the leading London insurance offices, and already the actuaries are finding that the present premium of 2s 6d a head is too low.

The figures were fixed a year ago, before the insurance offices had learned by experience how very unfortunate Mary Jane, the cook, and James, the butler, could be. All the estimates had to be fixed by guesswork.

The unluckiest indoor servants, according to the figures are :
1) Cooks, who run hourly risks of burns and cuts.
2) Housemaids, who are liable to fall downstairs or out of windows.
3) Butlers, who are frequently cut while opening bottles.

A surprising fact is that chauffeurs have escaped scathless. A comparatively heavy premium of £1 has to be paid in most cases for insuring chauffeurs, but it has seemed as though they are more fortunate than even scullery-maids.

Mr Hearn, the manager of the Employers' Insurance Department of the Ocean Accident Corporation, told an *Express* representative : 'We have had many curious claims. Among them have been :

'A housemaid who caught a cold in her eyes by sleeping with the window open.

'A cook who was kicked by a boy seven years old.

'A cook who got a bit of coal in her throat while in the cellar breaking up coal.

'A servant scratched while catching rats.

'Underkeepers shot by poachers.

'We get dozens of cases of servants slipping on soap left on the stairs or getting badly burned after lighting fires too quickly with kerosene.'

The Provident Clerks' Guarantee and Accident Company which does a large business in domestic risks, has also found how numerous are the claims.

'We have had several curious claims among the thousands we have settled. Servants have claimed for the loss of their false teeth, for housemaid's knee, and all sorts of mishaps. One wanted compensation after drinking a mixture of gin and gunpowder by mistake.'

In 1913 the *Daily Express* decided to take a hand in raising the standards and prestige of domestic service by introducing a servant-finding scheme for prospective employers:

The advantage to the mistress and to the maid is obvious. The full requirements of the former appear in the *Express* and the girl is therefore prepared for every condition of service expected of her should she obtain the situation. She cannot say at the end of a month that she did not know that 'no followers were allowed', or that the mistress insisted on deducting the maid's share of the insurance contributions from her wages, a right to which of course the mistress is entitled.

Two months later, in March 1913, the paper began a series of essay competitions for servants on a county basis:

> *Do domestic servants make better*
> *husbands or wives than business*
> *or factory employees?*

The *Express* £5 prize this week is offered to the domestic servant living within the County of

BERKSHIRE

who can write the best essay giving his or her reasons in reply to the above question.

Competitors need only write down just what they think on the subject, without bothering about correct spelling or punctuation, but no essay is to be of more than 200 words.

Every domestic servant, man or woman, employed indoors or out-doors, living within the district specified is eligible, except those employed casually.

The winner of last week's essay is Alfred Sheppard, butler to Lady Haliburton, 57 Lowndes-square, SW, whose six reasons illustrating the chief points which go to make domestic servants happy in their situations are the best and most clearly expressed of all the hundreds of essays sent in.

The following is the winning essay :

'I consider the following six points most important to ensure the happiness of domestic servants :

'(1) Regularity and punctuality in the household. Where the reverse of this exists servants are generally harassed and uncomfortable.

'(2) Sufficient food of good quality, with reasonable time to partake of it.

'(3) A good bed to lie on in a healthy room.

'(4) Reasonable and sufficient outings, cheerfully given. Generally speaking, domestic servants have less liberty than any other worker, and it is impossible for them to be healthy and happy unless they get sufficient relaxation from the monotony of the daily routine.

'(5) Permission to ask a friend to the house under reasonable and proper restrictions.

'(6) Last, but not least, mutual sympathy between the employer and servant. Where this exists friction seldom arises, and when it does it soon is smoothed over. Where a master or mistress is sympathetic a good servant will not quibble over extra work. Neither will he or she betray a trust or abuse a privilege.'

Spurred on by the example of the Press, the Government opened the world's first ever trade school for servants at Newcomen in June 1913.

While newspapers, Ministers and employers gave attention to the well-being and training of young women employees, voluntary organ-isations were formed to defend working girls against the peril of the White Slave traffic. On 4 January, 1913 pamphlets from the National Vigilance Association were issued by the Post Office to girls working in telephone exchanges :

Girls are warned:

'Never to speak to strangers, men or women, in the street, in shops, in stations, in trains, in lonely country roads, or in places of amusement.

'Never ask the way of any but officials on duty such as policemen, railwaymen, or postmen.

'Never loiter or stand about alone in the street.

'Never stay to help a woman who apparently faints in the street.

'Never accept a stranger's invitation to join a Sunday school or Bible class, even if the stranger wears the dress of a sister or a nun, or clerical dress.

'Never accept a "lift" offered by a stranger, in a motor-car, taxi-cab, or any vehicle.

'Never enter any house, restaurant, or place of amusement on the invitation of a stranger.

'Never go with a stranger, even if dressed as a hospital nurse, or believe stories of relations being suddenly taken ill, as this is a common device to kidnap girls.

'Never accept sweets, food, or a glass of water, or smell flowers offered by a stranger.

'Never buy scents or other articles at the door, as so many things may contain drugs.'

The emphasis on the danger of scent as a means of rendering the victims unconscious was dramatically illustrated in the *Express* six days later:

Is it possible for a girl to be drugged by a stranger by means of a pocket handkerchief in broad daylight in a busy City street and to be taken away without the suspicion of a single onlooker being aroused?

The alarming experience described by a pretty London working girl to an *Express* representative indicates that it is possible and suggests an explanation of many strange disappearances.

The girl is Miss Katie, aged twenty, of Wood Green, one of the 700 members of the Girls' Guild of Good Life, which has its headquarters at Hoxton Hall, and her veracity is vouched for by Mrs Sarah Rae, the honorary president of the guild, who has known her for nearly seven years. She has worked for many years in a Hoxton factory and lived with her grandmother in a quiet square near Wood Green.

'Peace hath Higher Tests of Manhood than Battle ever knew.'—WHITTIER.

QUEEN VICTORIA'S PRIZE—TO THE FAITHFULLEST!

Not to the Cleverest! nor the Most Bookish! nor the Most Precise, Diligent, and Prudent; But to the

NOBLEST WORK OF CREATION.

In other words, 'His Life was Gentle, and the Elements so mix'd in him, that Nature might stand up and say to all the World,

THIS WAS A MAN!'—SHAKESPEARE.

NOBILITY. 'It was very characteristic of the late Prince Consort—a man himself of the purest mind, who powerfully impressed and influenced others by sheer force of his own benevolent nature—when drawing up the conditions of the annual prize to be given by HER LATE MAJESTY QUEEN VICTORIA at Wellington College, to determine that it should be awarded *not* to the *cleverest* boy, nor the *most bookish* boy, *nor* to the most *precise, diligent,* and *prudent* boy, but to the NOBLEST boy, *to the boy who* should show the most promise of becoming a LARGE-HEARTED, HIGH-MOTIVED MAN.—SMILES.

We shut our eyes, the flowers bloom on;
We murmur, but the corn-ears fill;
We choose the shadow, but the sun
That casts it shines behind us still.

And each good thought or action moves the dark world nearer to the sun.

A POWER THAT CANNOT DIE!

REVERENCE IS THE CHIEF JOY OF THIS LIFE.

INFINITE.

THE
BREAKING OF LAWS, REBELLING AGAINST GREAT TRUTHS.

Instincts, Inclinations, Ignorance, and Follies.

Discipline and Self-Denial, that Precious Boon, the Highest and best in this Life.

O BLESSED HEALTH! HE WHO HAS THEE HAS LITTLE MORE TO WISH FOR! THOU

'It must be so—Plato, thou reason'st well! else whence this pleasing hope, th's fond desire, this longing after immortality?'—*Addison.*

'There is no Death! What seems so is transition; this life of mortal breath is but a suburb of the life elysian whose ports, we call death.'—*Longfellow.*

'INTO MAN'S HANDS IS PLACED THE RUDDER OF HIS FRAIL BARQUE THAT HE MAY NOT ALLOW THE WAVES TO WORK THEIR WILL.'—*Goethe.*

SUBSTANCES IN THE BLOOD THAT ARE HURTFUL AND INJURIOUS TO HEALTH AND LONGEVITY.

We quote the following from a well-known writer on Pathology:—

'Now a word on the importance of the regular and proper action of these excretory organs and of the intestinal canal. The former separate substances from the blood that are hurtful if they are kept in the blood. The waste substances that are got rid of by the intestinal canal include the parts of the food that are not digested and certain secretions from the intestinal canal, especially from the large part of the intestine. These substances are injurious if left in the body, as certain portions of them are reabsorbed into the blood, especially the foul organic matter in them, so that if these various excretory organs do not perform their functions in a proper manner, waste substances are either not separated from the blood or are reabsorbed into it and poison it, and as the blood is distributed to the various tissues of the body they are not properly nourished and they become degenerated, weak, and incapable of performing their proper functions, so that the regular action of these excretory organs of the body is of the greatest importance with regard to health, for not a single tissue of the body can be kept in a proper condition if the waste substances are not got rid of in the manner they should.'

Were we to mention the many and various diseases caused or produced by blood poisoning, it would require more space than we have at command. To hinder the poison from gaining admission, you must sustain the vital powers by adding to the blood what is continually being lost from various circumstances, and by that means you prevent the poison being retained in the body. The effect of Eno's 'Fruit Salt' is to take away all morbid poisons and supply that which promotes healthy secretions only by natural means. The chemical nature or antidotal power of Eno's 'Fruit Salt' is to expel the foreign substance or render it inert (by natural means only). If we could maintain sufficient vital power we could keep the poison from doing any harm. That power is best attained by following the Rules for Life (see page 10 in Pamphlet), and using, according to directions, Eno's 'Fruit Salt,' which by its healthy action keeps the secretions in perfect order only by *soothing* and *natural laws,* or in other words it is impossible to overstate its great power in preventing unnecessary suffering and disease.

THE JEOPARDY OF LIFE IS IMMENSELY INCREASED WITHOUT SUCH A SIMPLE PRECAUTION AS

ENO'S 'FRUIT SALT.'

It rectifies the Stomach, and makes the Liver laugh with Joy!!

(OR IN OTHER WORDS, ITS NATURAL ACTION IS TO EXHILARATE—NOT TO DEPRESS).

It is not too much to say that its merits have been published, tested, and approved literally from Pole to Pole, and that its cosmopolitan popularity to-day presents one of the most signal illustrations of commercial enterprise to be found in our trading record.

CAUTION—Examine the Capsule, and see that it is marked *ENO'S 'FRUIT SALT.'* Without it you have the *sincerest form of flattery*—IMITATION.

PREPARED ONLY BY J. C. ENO, LD., 'FRUIT SALT' WORKS, LONDON, S.E., BY J. C. ENO'S PATENT.

'A few days before Christmas,' she said, 'I left the factory early and contrary to my usual custom alone.

'Immediately in front of me, but a few inches to my left, was a well-dressed man, in a long stylish-looking overcoat, with the collar turned up, a Trilby hat, and carrying gloves in his hand. He had a heavy black moustache, and a rather pale face, and gave me the impression of being a foreigner – why I cannot say.

'I had just been standing there only a few seconds before this man took a large linen handkerchief from the left inner pocket of his coat, turned partly around and flicked me with it in the face. I thought it must be an accident until he repeated his action twice. I immediately became giddy and felt the whole pavement going round and round.

'I smelt a peculiar pungent scent, quite different from the scent people use on their handkerchiefs. I thought I was going to faint and fall to the ground. Fortunately I had previously noticed a confectioner's shop near by, and to this I made my way as best I could, intending if a policeman came in sight, to tell him about the man with the pocket-handkerchief.

'I managed to get into the shop, where one of two women assistants at once noticed my condition and brought me a chair. I felt then that I was safe. I sat there for a little while, and ordered a soda and milk, which made me feel better.'

'If Katie had fainted,' said Mrs Rae, who was present during the interview, 'how easy it would have been for the stranger to have claimed her as a relative or friend who had been suddenly taken ill, and to have taken her off in a cab, without a single person who had witnessed the affair being any the wiser, using the handkerchief again if she showed any signs of recovering.'

One of the aims of the Guild of Good Life in which Queen Mary and Queen Alexandra take an active interest is to guard its girl members from the white slave and similar perils.

Police files indicated that perhaps 200 girls a year were transported to brothels abroad, though how many went willingly and how many were abducted is impossible to say.

What comes through very strongly in the news columns of the time is the sense of responsibility for women. It may have been occasionally feudal, often paternal or even patronising – but it *was* caring.

CHAPTER FIVE

The Gentle Sex

In 1900 women did not have the vote and to judge by the comments of the, alas, anonymous women columnists did not seem particularly interested in the vote and would not have known what to do with it if they had got it.

An item from the second day's issue of the *Daily Express* under the heading 'THINGS A WOMAN WANTS TO KNOW' said bluntly:

The higher education of woman is in itself an admirable thing, but the highest education of woman will be to show her how to become a good mother, and how best she may work for the perfection of the race. Mothers too often appear to believe that the mere fact of motherhood conveys a sort of instinct as to how best to rear their children, and seem to think it an insult to suggest that study, and deep study is necessary if they would save the beloved from danger and death.

As an example of the ignorance that may exist even among the well-educated, on a hot July day I once heard a young married woman complain that her baby seemed to be 'quite ill' from the heat. On inquiry I found that it was wearing two thick rollers, one of flannel and one of cotton, bound tightly round its abdomen, in addition to the ordinary old-fashioned clothing of infants, the errors in which I hope to point out later on. When I asked why the little one, though old enough, was not short-coated, she replied that she had bought the clothes, but neither she nor any of the servants knew how to put them on, and she was waiting till the baby's grandmother returned to town!

Returning to womanly duties the following day, the authoress of 'Things a Woman Wants to Know' had some choice advice for neglectful maidservants:

No doubt the signature of our beloved Sovereign has been written in many things, but once at any rate it was written in dust by the Queen herself. One day, passing through a somewhat unused suite at Windsor, the Queen noticed that the housemaid had neglected her duties, and a table was white with dust.

As a silent rebuke the Royal Mistress wrote Victoria R across it. The next day the name still remained, so the Queen inquired the housemaid's name and wrote that below her own signature. Needless to say the third day both names had disappeared.

Nor were censorious columnists and disapproving Sovereigns the only people young women were supposed to defer to. Aristocratic mamas could – and did – bring down their formidable wrath upon the heads of attractive, wilful wenches with ideas above their station : Lady Francis Cecil and Miss Jessie Bain of Belfast, for instance. The *Daily Express* of 1 October, 1901, reported :

It is twelve months since Lieutenant Richard William Francis Cecil, of the Antrim Artillery Militia, second heir-presumptive to the Marquis of Exeter, and prospective inheritor of the Brooks millions, arrived at the historic Carrickfergus Castle for a course of gunnery training. He resided at Greenisland – a pretty suburb of Belfast, overlooking the waters of the lough, and commanding a view of the fine coastline of Antrim and Down. Here resides also Miss Jessie Bain, a charming and accomplished brunette, of about the same age as the lieutenant.

The pair frequently met at local functions of a social and sporting character, and an attachment sprang up. They were often seen together cycling, driving or walking, and their engagement, when announced, caused no surprise in the district.

All went well with the young couple for a time. The banns had been twice published on the Sundays of 15 and 22 September, and were to have been finally published on Sunday last.

Then unexpectedly entered Lady Cecil, with the remarkable advertisement in the local newspapers, giving notice to ministers of all denominations, registrars, and others whom it may concern not to publish any banns or issue any licence for the proposed marriage, 'my said son being an infant of the age of nineteen years'.

Authority could descend, in another way, on prospective married couples, as a report of the same date made clear :

Messrs J. Irvin, Con and Co Limited, a firm of grocers and provision merchants at North End, Liverpool, issued the following manifesto, addressed to all their young men assistants:

Matrimony – A Warning

'We fear that some of our assistants are entering into marriage contracts without realising the trouble they are getting themselves into. It is a most serious step for any man to take, and especially so for one who hopes to be his own master some day.

'His first object should be to save at least £200; after that enough to furnish a cottage, as when marriage is entered into before these two objects are attained there is absolutely no hope of saving as the whole earnings must go for housekeeping, etc.

'We ourselves have set our face against any man marrying before he is a manager, and, indeed, we do not even then approve of it except he has money saved; and so strongly do we feel this that we shall not in future retain young men who marry without our consent.

'We earnestly trust that our young men will lay this matter to heart, and act upon our advice.'

Editorially the paper took the view that women, bless their lovely, silly little heads ought, like small children, to be seen and not heard. Commenting on the visits paid by fashionable ladies to South Africa during the Boer War, the *Express* thundered:

Women have been thought a nuisance before now by godless men, but never stigmatised as 'a plague more pestilent than flies'. Yet there is every reason to believe that the eminent surgeon, Mr Treves, in denouncing them was speaking by the book. The fashion, and it is no more than a fashion, like crinoline and cartwheel hats, cannot be deprecated too strongly. It has been in the last degree inconvenient; it has imported an element of intrigue and gossip quite out of keeping with the portentous business of war. To flirt and philander with young men who have other work to do; to hang about the hospitals offering help for which they are unsuited and entirely untrained has been their sole occupation.

It may be remarked in passing that female philandering had a lot less to do with the British Army's appalling performance in the early days of the war than British generalship.

A little later, Dr R. P. Rentoul, addressing the Institute of Hygiene, chided men for neglecting our greatest national asset, woman's health.

'Man,' he declared, 'by failing to give the order of merit to the right woman, has produced a type of female who is a compound of the hysterical, neurotic, degenerate, and sometimes the criminal. The child-hating married woman (a not insignificant quantity), whose demoralised desires are limited to a rich husband, a flat, a poodle dog, and a male hanger-on, is a product of our modern civilization and a menace to our race.

'The woman who deserves the order of merit is the physically and mentally healthy woman, who represents the best thing in life – motherhood.'

He suggested that if the law raised the age of marriage to twenty-five years in the man, and twenty-one in the woman, required a pre-nuptial medical certificate of good health, made it illegal for the diseased to marry, abolished actions for breach of promise where existing disease could be proved, prohibited paupers and vagrants from marrying, taxed bachelors and reduced taxation to those of small income who had large families, it would go a long way to increase the sum total of human happiness and there would be fewer separations, fewer squalid homes, and fewer degenerate children.

Another doctor, about the same time, remarked that 'The bicycling girl does not take kindly to the duties of motherhood. She is accustomed to cycle before marriage, and she wants to keep up her cycling afterwards.'

Yet as early as 1900, the revolt against treating women as enchanting creatures of fashion or healthy receptacles for children was growing. The protest was muted, even genteel, but it was there all the same.

Mrs Fenwick Miller, a lady of esteem and aristocratic connections, wrote a signed piece – very unusual for those days – on the subject of daughters-who-don't-count :

By custom and by law, daughters are obviously held among us to be less the children of their fathers than sons. The polite Englishmen in China are shocked when a Chinese father replies to the question of how many children he has, by giving the number of his sons only; or declares that he is childless although half-a-dozen little girls call him father.

But is there sufficient difference between this frame of mind and that of the English practice of making title, landed property in settlement, and the same sort of property under an intestacy, skip over the daughters of a man, and pretending that he has died childless, go a-hunting among his distant relatives for a male descendant of the blood to take and enjoy what the father of perhaps many daughters has left behind?

The question has been brought to mind by the announcement the other day that Queen Victoria had determined to make the Duke of Fife's daughters eligible to succeed to his dukedom in the event of his having no sons.

Up to the present time the Duke and his wife, Princess Louise of Wales, have only daughters in their family, and, according to the chivalrous laws and customs above referred to, the Duke of Fife is described in peerages as having, as regards his dukedom, 'no heir'. Not so different from the Chinese as British women might desire, me seems! The Duke of Fife's eldest daughter will henceforth be his heir; but it is by special favour of her Royal great-grandmother only.

If the father himself sometimes seems to forget the fact, and to count as nought his possession of a whole houseful of clever, affectionate, and well-built daughters, it is because he is not allowed to look upon his girls as his children and heirs in the same way that a son would be counted his child.

This custom of the setting aside of daughters in the peerage as not the natural heirs of their own parents, and making them give place to more distant males, or behaving as if the fathers of daughters were, in fact, childless, reacts on society as a whole. Nobody can say how much mischief it does to women, in keeping them poor, and therefore powerless, and in making the welcome of a girl child less hearty, and the training of her for life less careful than that of a male one.

Mrs George Corbett, authoress, went straight to the heart of the matter with a simple, carefully-argued, oh-so-reasonable plea for the vote: the first time (October 1900) that the question of female suffrage appeared in the *Express*:

To say that women do not want to vote is to voice an error, which can only be believed by those who have not sufficient intellect of their own to comprehend the enormous strides that have been made by women of late years, and the tricky way in which several of our Franchise Bills have been shelved only proves that we are feared as equals in brains and possible influence, not despised as irresponsible inferiors.

Is there a benighted individual left who dares assert that when a woman is able to canvas votes for candidates, to support herself by means of an occupation requiring intellectual capacity, to be the means of giving employment to numbers of men, and to contribute handsomely not merely to the local rates, but to the Queen's taxes, she is still less capable of registering a sensible vote, and less deserving of it, than is the agricultural labourer whose knowledge is bounded by the limits of the village in which he lives, or the drunken loafer who is a burden upon the community from childhood to old age?

Round about our docks, and scattered about the Marshes, are numbers of men who can't spell 'c-a-t, cat' much less a longer word. Their ignorance is only equalled by their degraded mode of life. Their earnings are chiefly spent in public houses. And their political knowledge is entirely derived from tap-room oratory or the Anarchistic utterances of men who covet the proceeds of other people's industry and brains.

On the other hand, there are in Western London and elsewhere, many women who control large business establishments, and I know of one who has over one hundred branch shops, employing an enormous number of men. There are also numbers of professional women whose usefulness to the community in which they live is enormous.

Take my own case. I can honestly claim to have provided wholesome entertainment for millions of readers and employment for thousands of workers. I am compelled to pay the same rates and taxes as if I were a man, and I am also compelled to do my share towards paying for the free education of children, who are thus enabled to compete with those of the professional and highly-taxed classes.

Yet anything in the shape of a man is privileged to vote. And anything in the shape of a woman is presumed to be unfit to do so. Brains and general usefulness don't count, that is clear.

It is also quite clear that women of education want to vote very badly; that they have petitioned for it in their thousands; that failure does not daunt them; that they mean to have the vote and that the time will come when Universal Adult Suffrage will be recognised as the only just method of acknowledging the growing usefulness of women's work and influence.

New Zealand, in 1900, had enjoyed universal suffrage for seven years and from there a Mrs Constance Barncoat gave British readers the benefit of her experience of this strange, new, and rather frightening development :

Women's suffrage has not unsexed women and made them leave their homes to run about canvassing and addressing meetings and generally meddling all day long; nor has there been since its passing any appreciable increase of scraggy, sexless spinsters, that type of woman being still chiefly to be found in the pages of illustrated comic papers. And many indeed are the prophecies falsified by these two negative results of women's suffrage.

But far more serious is the argument that it is at least question-able whether women's suffrage has produced any positive good result. It is difficult to argue that it has tended to raise the moral standard of members.

A more serious argument against women's suffrage is the fact that in Wellington alone at last year's election in New Zealand two members were returned who were about as notoriously disreputable characters as are to be found out of gaol in the place.

It is inconceivable how any self-respecting woman could have voted for either of them on any ground whatever : but as it is quite certain that numbers of men would never have been induced to give them their support, there is no other conclusion but that numbers of women must have helped to swell their large majorities. The only possible explanation to me is that their wives and daughters, against whom nothing could be said, may have gained them many women's votes – out of pity.

Until 1903 the debate on women's suffrage was conducted in an amiable, demure fashion. This movement for reform had been founded – at Sheffield – in 1857. The members carried on their cam-paign with the utmost decorum, for it was a cardinal principle with them that intelligent women who asked for the vote would at all times remain ladies. In 1903, however, the formidable Pankhurst family – Mother Emmeline, daughters Sylvia and Christabel – emerged as the leading force in a new organisation, the Women's Social and Political Union. Now began the period of militancy which lasted until the open-ing of the Great War and included bombs, martyrdom (Emily Davison flinging herself in front of the King's horse at the 1913 Derby) and the imprisonment of a number of high-born and gently-reared women.

The case for female suffrage – that women were quite as capable as men of exercising the vote – had been strengthened in the 1890s and early 1900s by the granting of Parliamentary voting rights to their cousins in New Zealand and Australia. Women in the UK had also been municipally enfranchised as far back as 1869. Why then were they denied the Parliamentary vote?

Well, the anti-Suffragettes claimed that most women didn't want the vote anyway and that the whole disturbance was got up by wealthy females with time on their hands who had been educated beyond their manners. One of the most eloquent speeches against giving women the vote came from that enlightened Liberal statesman, Mr Herbert Henry Asquith. Speaking as Prime Minister on the Women's Suffrage Bill – a private member's measure on a free vote – at the height of the agitation in 1913 he adumbrated several reasons for denying women the Parliamentary vote.

There was no mandate for the bill (it had not been part of the Liberals' election policy).

There was no evidence of a general demand by women.

The sex was not fitted, by nature, for the function.

The House ought to think twice before making the largest addition to the franchise ever made.

There was no truth that the woman employee had been neglected by man-made laws.

Extension of the franchise would not be in the best interests of either women or the community.

It would not enrich our social or domestic life, raise the standard of manners, chivalry or courtesy or refine the reciprocal dependence and reliance of the two sexes.

Mr Philip Snowden, the little crippled, blazingly forthright spokesman for the Labour Party, argued that 'women want the vote in order that by the exercise of political power they may be better able to serve their sex. All this talk of the mental inferiority of women is only an instance of the colossal conceit of man. You can't argue with conceit. You can only pity it.'

Sir Edward Grey, the Liberal Foreign Secretary, breaking with his chief Asquith for the only time in twenty-five loyal years of close political partnership pleaded for the bill:

'I ask you whether you consider that women are responsible beings. If you answer no, there is an end of it. Unless you answer no you have to find some other reason for not giving women the vote at this time of day.

'There are five million women in employment which is as essential to the life and well being of the State as that in which men are employed. Why should they be deprived of a vote when the greater part of politics deals with questions in which women are intimately concerned?

'It appears to me that in all these matters the woman who makes the home is in no inferior position for the study of politics to the man who supports the home.'

The bill was defeated by 266 votes to 219. Mr Lloyd George joined Sir Edward Grey in voting for the women, which was very gallant of him considering he had been a target for termagant fury on numerous occasions being hit over the head with a case, jumped on in a golf bunker and having his Walton Heath house blown up. Mr Birrell, another prominent Liberal, also lined up with women's suffrage which was somewhat foolhardy as his wife had warned him that once women got the vote they would tend to vote Conservative. She was right. Women got the vote in 1918 and the Liberals never gained power thereafter.

The vocal minuet in the Commons bore little reality to the turbulence outside. For eight years prior to that debate the suffragette extremists had been stepping up the tempo of violence. One incident, in 1905, when Miss Christabel Pankhurst and Miss Annie Kenny (one of the comparatively few working class girls involved in the movement) were imprisoned, was followed by four major outbreaks – including raids on Parliament – in each of the three succeeding years; seven big attacks in 1909 and no fewer than thirty-five in the first half of 1913, twenty-four of which were arsonist or bomb attacks – one an unsuccessful attack on St Paul's Cathedral.

The *Daily Express* was a male chauvinist of the first order. It dubbed the militant suffragettes 'fooligans' and malignants. Full rein was given to this pugnacious bigotry in the paper's account of the women's attempt to storm Parliament on Wednesday, 25 October, 1906:

This army of raucous fooligans made a feline raid on the peace of both Houses of Parliament and were repulsed by the police with heavy loss of dignity, drapery, and millinery, as well as deprivation, temporarily, of liberty.

Ten of the fooligans were arrested, and they will be charged at Westminster Police Court this morning with using threatening and abusive language.

The raid was begun on a well-ordered plan. Looking properly demure, the fooligans went in twos and threes into the central lobby, and quietly asked for various MPs. This was a ruse adopted for the purpose of getting a large assembly of fooligans into the Palace of Westminster unnoticed.

Suddenly, just as the peers were assembling for their afternoon sitting, and many MPs were passing to and fro, three fooligans sprang upon a settee near the statue of the late Lord Iddesleigh, and began to yell. It was a well-chosen spot. Past this point the peers had to walk to the inner entrance of the House of Lords. Near this point MPs coming from the Commons' Chamber pass on their way to various reading and other rooms.

The three standing on the settee were a female named Montefiore, in glowing red attire, another named Sanderson, in black, and a third.

'We want our privileges! Give us our due as Englishwomen! Votes for women!' they screeched. The spacious lobby, quiet a moment before, was now all noise, shrieks, turmoil. A broad-shouldered policeman, who has a short way with fooligans, went up to one of the screeching women and embraced her. He put a pair of mighty arms around her, lifted her off her feet and carried the shrieking, spluttering, shaking bundle of costume and vibration bodily into the street. The other two, screeching with cat-like shrills that set all teeth on edge, were led out, and three more fooligan 'orators' sprang upon the settee and took up the yelling.

Meanwhile, several of the ill-behaved persons made a desperate attempt to get into the inner lobby, and these, too, were seized and carried, many of them kicking violently, into the street.

Two of the amazons, however, managed to crawl under the barrier, and were making a wild dash to the floor of the House of Commons when they were caught by the skirts and held back.

When they were seized, they screamed like hysterical servant girls, clutched the barrier, and had to be detached by main force.

The struggle with the police made them look even more ridiculous. Their hats and cloaks came off, and these articles of wearing apparel were left on the floor, as the stupid owners were bundled into the street.

A knot of peers and a throng of MPs as well as a crowd of visitors gathered round and smiled.

'Keep these brutes off' cried the rank and file of the fooligans. 'Here, you men,' appealing to the peers and the MPs, 'save us from these policemen.'

The 'you men' laughed. 'Can't you put forward a hand to protect

British womanhood?' cried several fooligans, casting spit-fire glances at the smiling legislators, who laughed all the more.

Meanwhile, Chief Inspector Scantlebury had brought up re-inforcements of constables from the halls and corridors of the great palace. He showed his men what to do. He grasped a tigerish looking 'lady' round the waist. With superb ease the giant inspector carried her off and with a look of professional gravity he returned to the scene of the fray.

'Cowards!' 'Brutes!' 'Votes for women!' 'You monsters!' 'Give us our rights!' screamed the fooligans. One fooligan escaped from the too tender grasp of a constable. With a wild shriek of half-insane joy she screamed out, 'Done again! Brutes! Cowards! Protect our womanhood!'

Here and there a tiny white hand, clenched in defiance, shook itself in anger from under the arm of a policeman.

Altogether, it took the police a quarter of an hour to clear the lobby, and many of them bore marks of the affray, their faces being scratched and buttons wrenched off their tunics.

Innocent bystanders occasionally suffered at the hands of militant feminists. Take the case of the unlucky Baptist Minister, the Reverend Forbes Jackson. He bore a passing resemblance to Lloyd George and happened to be on the station platform at Aberdeen about the time Lloyd George was due to leave that city, having addressed a meeting there.

Suddenly – as the *Express* account had it :

He was attacked by an infuriated suffragist who, brandishing a whip shouted : 'I see through your disguise, Lloyd George. You cowardly hound. I'll punish you.'

With that she proceeded to lash Mr Jackson across the face with the whip, stigmatising him all the while as a cad and a coward.

Mr Jackson, bewildered and dazed, could at first only raise his hands in the hope of warding off the blows, but after a few moments he sought to pacify his assailant and to assure her of the mistake.

It was all to no purpose. The lash descended as violently as ever, and severe injuries were inflicted, the blood pouring down the face of the victim.

The station officials, astounded at the suddenness and ferocity of the attack, and failing at the moment to realise what was meant, were not able to intervene in time to prevent serious consequences.

The first person to grapple with the assailant, who was still in a flaming passion, was a Caledonian Railway official, and from his grasp she managed to escape, making another dash in the direction of Mr Jackson.

Porters now came running from all parts of the station, and they pushed the woman down on the platform and held her there until the police arrived.

She was taken to the police office in the prison van, to the accompaniment of shouts or encouragement and approval from the other suffragists, who were apparently still under the impression that it was the Chancellor of Exchequer who had been so cruelly whipped.

Outbreaks of this kind prompted the Mayor of New York to issue a statement to newspaper reporters on the difference between American and British womanhood :

'I do not think that American women will ever resort to the violence of the English suffragettes,' he said.* 'There is reason for it over in Great Britain. There are about a million and a half women who have no man, and they are rather desperate.

'We are not in such a condition here. As soon as every woman has a man the women become very peaceful.

'If they are allowed to vote, voting will not get them husbands. They will be as badly off in that respect as ever.

'If English militants should come here I would not have them imprisoned. I think I would try to get husbands for them. That would quiet them wonderfully.

'You ask me what is the weak point of the British way of dealing with the militants. When you come to dealings between men and women, the weak point is always the same. A man does not like to hurt a woman. That's the whole story.

'I am in favour of women voting if they want to, but I am certain very few want to. They like their husbands and children so much that they do not want to be bothered with other matters.

'They would say, "Let father attend to this matter. It puzzles our little heads too much." '

Mayor Gaynor was typical of many men, perhaps the majority, in being humorously dismissive about the suffragettes. But the cause of

*Untrue. At that very moment militant female temperance supporters were burning down saloons in Massachusetts, Missouri, and Kansas.

women's liberation was not without its male champions. In January 1912 a fashionable wedding took place at the Chapel Royal, Savoy, London, of Miss Una Stafford Dugdale to Mr Victor Duval, secretary of the Men's Political Union for Women's Enfranchisement. The bride had no intention of pledging her obedience to her husband who had no wish that she should do so. But a snag arose. The Savoy, being a Royal Chapel, any change in the wedding service could be construed as a slight to the King. So bride, groom and officiating clergyman agreed on a compromise, contained in the Reverend Hugh Chapman's statement to astonished guests and expectant newsmen :

'Before the beginning of the service, I wish to state that, owing to the publicity given to it, I have been compelled at the last moment to take advice as to the legality of a wedding with the omission of certain words which may not commend themselves to those concerned.

'Having been informed that the omission of these words is sufficient to render its validity at least doubtful, more especially in a Royal Chapel which belongs exclusively to the King, we have agreed among ourselves to read the service throughout as an act of loyalty to his Majesty, while we sincerely hope that before long there may be an amended form of service which shall render it possible for Christian people to receive the blessings of the Church without hurt to their susceptibilities and, as we believe, in the true spirit of the gospel of Christ.'

When the criticised passage in the service – 'to love, cherish, and to obey' – was reached, the bride's voice was too low for the congregation to hear the actual words, but those near the altar afterwards declared that Miss Dugdale had not pronounced the word 'obey'.

The bridgegroom confirmed the statement. 'The chaplain,' he said, 'used the words "and obey" but the bride did not repeat them after him.

'We consider that we have made our protest.'

Light-hearted moments did occur in the crusade, and one such concerned the puckish Henry Labouchere, MP. Mr Labouchere adored espousing unlikely causes and then dropping them when they became popular. He was a natural-born prankster who, in his university days at Cambridge, bluffed an angry parent with sublime audacity.

Young Labby, who always boasted that he never allowed his studies to interfere with his pleasures, ran up to London in search of fun and sex. Alas, his father spotted him in the Strand and upbraided him furiously, at which Labby hotly denied his identity and informed a bemused parent that the whole business was a case of mistaken identity. Rightly anticipating that the parent might recover his wits, Labby hastened back to Cambridge to be followed half-an-hour later by an irate father who was both amazed and relieved to discover his son, head swathed in a wet towel, deep in his books and intensely interested to hear that someone his absolute double was apparently walking round the Strand.

Such levity made him the darling of the clubs – and the lawyers (for he made a hobby of libelling people and paid out £250,000 defending himself in court) – but his merry wit did not at all impress the suffragettes.

He talked out an enfranchisement bill to come before Parliament, in 1905, remarking :

'I voted for women's enfranchisement thirty-seven years ago and every successive year since then has made me more and more regret that vote.

'As a penance, I have opposed the bill tooth and nail whenever it has been brought forward.

'Women cannot discharge the duties of citizenship. Women are nervous and emotional and have very little sense of proportion.'

Two hundred suffragettes who were lobbying the House tried to capture Labouchere. However, he made good his escape and soon afterwards decided to quit politics – at the age of 74.

Another touch of humour, albeit unconscious, was delivered by the Poet Laureate Alfred Austin (who once penned the immortal lines about the Prince of Wales :

> Across the electric wires the message came
> He is no better, he is much the same.)

He wrote to the paper asking :

Will any one deny that, in great emergencies, men are, as a rule and collectively, calmer and more submissive to sound judgment than women, whose virtues reside rather in another direction? Give women the franchise and it is conceivable that war might be brought about by women against the effort of men to avert it.

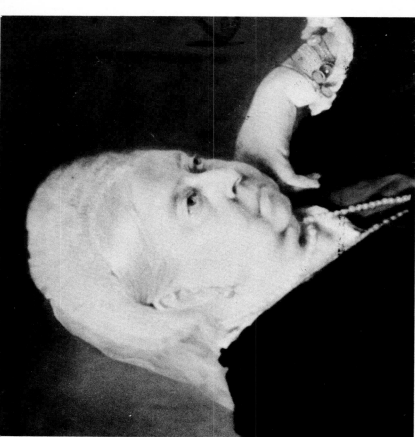

(*Above*) When the white races ruled the world they had one Great White Queen – Victoria.

(*Right*) More than 3,000 people were laid off work in London's Theatreland during the period – 15 days – of deepest mourning for Queen Victoria. King Edward VII and Kaiser Wilhelm of Germany lead the funeral procession.

Asked what he would do if ever his family were deposed Edward VII replied: 'No doubt if it really did occur I could support them by lecturing on the British Constitution in America.' A royal gathering at Sandringham.

A future king – George V – with the monarch of the roads, an early Rolls Royce driven by the Hon C. S. Rolls.

Yet it is the sombre and shocking side to women's liberation of Edwardian days that remains enduringly in the public conscience.

Mrs Pankhurst gave a clear warning of her intentions when she addressed a Caxton Hall rally in February 1907. She told her followers that if the Government failed to respond to the suffragettes' demands another meeting would be held, 'for the purpose of deciding what further sacrifices are necessary.'

'We may have to face the possibility of loss of life. If that is demanded, we must prepare ourselves for it. If it is necessary we will not shrink.

'We will not be afraid if they bring out hose-pipes, if they bring out the Horse Guards, or if they bring out the soldiers and fire on us. We are not playing.'

A new suffragist song was sung at the meeting, of which the following are two verses:

Come march with us to victory; come join the battle song, of women chained to labour, who are suffering grievous wrong.
In a free land we are free not; mid equals have no place.
Men treat as merest playthings the mothers of their race.

We teach the little sons of men; we help the direst poor;
We nurse the wounded soldier, and fight the evil doer;
Yet in the Council of the State we have no voice or say
No voice in making cruel laws we may not disobey.

Under the green, white and purple banner of the Women's Social and Political Union the militants threw themselves against the entrenchments of the Establishment. Outrage followed outrage. Shop windows were systematically smashed along London's fashionable shopping streets. A rash of fires swept through unoccupied schools and sports club pavilions. Golf course greens were cut up (presumably because golf was a favourite pastime of such leading opponents of suffrage as Mr Asquith and too-tepid supporters like Mr Lloyd George.) The contents of post boxes were destroyed.

By far the noisiest demonstration occurred on the evening of Friday, 12 March, 1912, when windows in Downing Street and eleven other famous thoroughfares in the capital were shattered. The following morning's *Daily Express* described it thus:

The attack began at the Premier's residence, at 10 Downing Street, shortly after five o'clock, when a private motor car containing Mrs

Pankhurst, Mrs Emily K. Marshall, and Mrs Mabel Tuke, evaded the police who were in the street at the time and proceeded leisurely to No 10.

Immediately a crash of glass was heard, and before the police knew what was happening four windows on the ground floor of Mr Asquith's house had been smashed by the occupants of the car.

The three women in question were promptly arrested and taken to Cannon Row Police Station, where they were subsequently charged with causing wilful damage, in company with six other suffragists.

Meanwhile this outrage in Downing Street had been the signal for window-wrecking operations elsewhere.

Hundreds of plate-glass windows were smashed by bands of hysterical women who, armed with small stones, weights, and other missiles, flung them at the windows as they marched along.

A feature of the campaign was the use of small hammers, which the women carried in their satchels, and used with great effect on the plate-glass windows.

Shopkeepers, hearing the revolver-like reports, rushed into the street, only to find that their windows had been hopelessly wrecked.

At once the entire trading community was up in arms, and police and other protection was summoned, but it was too late to stop the devastating march of the women, who continued their career of destruction through street after street.

The operations were too well planned to prevent further damage being done, for each band of women had its area carefully mapped out beforehand.

One hundred and twenty women were arrested. Seven thousand pounds worth of damage was inflicted in two hours.

Three days later a warrant was issued for Mrs Pankhurst's daughter, Christabel – the one least desirous of accepting martyrdom.

'We are busy here keeping the flag flying', said Mrs Drummond, one of the suffragette organisers. 'We must get on with our work. Miss Pankhurst will, we know, do what is best in our interest and in her own.'

Miss Pankhurst concluded that her own interest was best served by remaining in Paris, to which city she had flown, but scores of her fellow crusaders were sent to jail. Their lot in prison was described to the *Express* by a Home Office official :

The sentence is intended to be – and actually is – a real and severe punishment, particularly for a delicately nurtured woman who endures it for the first time.

Hard Labour – although the actual labour involved is not 'hard' to those accustomed to manual work – is a trying ordeal to those who, in addition to the loss of liberty and the deprivation of accustomed luxuries, find themselves set to work which is strange to them.

At Holloway the hours of labour required are sternly enforced. The women prisoners have to make their own beds, clean and scrub out their cells, and polish their food tins to the satisfaction of wardresses.

The hard labour must be put in at one or other of the following useful domestic activities :

> Washing in the prison laundry
> Sewing and making clothing
> Bead working.

The governor is responsible for seeing that the labour of all the prisoners is made use of to the best advantage of the public service, and he is not permitted to employ any prisoner in any private work whatever for himself or any other officer of the prison.

For the first seven days a woman prisoner who is under-going a sentence of, say two months with hard labour, is put on 'Diet A'. The daily menu is as follows :

Breakfast

Bread .... 6 ozs
Gruel .... 1 pint

On Sundays there is porridge in place of gruel, and again on Tuesdays, while on Mondays the breakfast is varied with 8 ozs of potatoes.

The dinners are as follows :

Bread .... 6 ozs
Suet pudding .... 6 ozs

Supper, which is the same each night, consists of :

Bread .... 6 ozs
Gruel .... 1 pint

After the first week, the hard labour prisoner is placed on 'Diet B', which is rather more sustaining.

Suffragists who, under sentence, find themselves for some infraction of discipline classed as 'idle of ill-conducted' are liable to be placed on 'No 1 diet'. This is :

1 lb of bread per diem with water.

This diet cannot be ordered for more than three days at a time, and no task of labour is enforced on any day on which bread and water constitutes the sole food supplied to a prisoner.

When some of the women went on hunger strike they were force-fed. This, however, had a bad effect on public opinion so the authorities had recourse to a cat and mouse ploy whereby a suffragette was released 'on licence' and then arrested – and given a much heavier sentence – if she resumed violent activities. Sometimes the Home Office used the cat and mouse technique to release suffragettes who had collapsed under the stern prison regimen. Mrs Pankhurst told a rally in the Pavilion Theatre, London, (which, by discrimination-in-reverse was banned to men), that one of her followers, Miss Lenton, had been freed because she had contacted pneumonia after having been forcibly fed. The Home Office, claimed Mrs Pankhurst, did not want the responsibility of having a sick woman on their hands so they freed her as a humanitarian gesture. 'Our women,' cried Mrs Pankhurst, 'are still being forcibly fed. My daughter [Sylvia] is being forcibly fed.'

That punishment was not enough for criticis of the suffragette militants. An *Express* leading article in March 1913 demanded that the malignant feminists should be transported!

The Suffragette women insist on saying that they should be treated as 'political' offenders. Any hooligan may follow this line of argument in his defence. 'My Lord,' he may say to the judge on the bench, 'I claim immunity. I do not agree with Mr Lloyd George's Marconi investment policy, and as a protest I battered in this wayfarer's head and took his watch and purse. I am a political prisoner, and if you sentence me I shall hunger-strike.'

And the judge will probably sentence him to penal servitude; and if he hunger-strikes he will get the cat. 'Equal justice for men and women,' cry the Suffragettes. Let them have it then.

Mrs Pankhurst's 'political' past is modelled much on the lines of the Tammany politician. She is the widow of a professor at Owens College, Manchester, who was himself something of an agitator. When he died his widow received a lucrative position as registrar of births, deaths, and marriages at a salary of between £300 and £400 a year. This 'job' she 'farmed out' so that she could best prosecute her work for the 'cause' which appreciates her so well that she is in receipt of £1,000 a year and a motor-car. Many a high-souled 'cause' can be led with such emoluments.

The sands have run out. It is time to cry a halt. The Suffragette criminals must go. St Helena is the place for them.

Readers went even further :

'These neurotic women clamour for a vote. What they need is a fire hose.'

'Hard labour and salts and senna would soon quench the ardour of these notoriety-beating females.'

'The hand that rocks the cradle rules the world, but women who smash windows need the birch.'

'Their place is Bedlam, not Parliament. They need strait-jackets, not the franchise.'

'Every real woman should wear an anti-suffrage badge, so that men could know whom still to respect. These mad creatures make their sex ashamed to walk in the streets.'

'Why not put them in a room, one at a time, say for about an hour, with half a dozen mice ?'

Even Queen Victoria was enrolled into the anti-suffragette ranks :

That the greatest woman in public life in England during the last century was unalterably opposed to 'Votes for women' is shown by a letter by her and quoted by Mr Sidney Lee in his biography of Queen Victoria.

In 1870 Queen Victoria wrote :

The Queen is most anxious to enlist every one who can speak or write to join in checking this mad, wicked folly of 'Woman's Rights,' with all its attendant horrors on which her poor feeble sex is bent, forgetting every sense of womanly feeling and propriety.

God created man and woman different – then let them remain each in their own position.

Tennyson has some beautiful lines on the difference of men and women in 'The Princess'. Woman would become the most hateful, heartless and disgusting of human beings were she allowed to unsex herself : and where would be the protection which man was intended to give the weaker sex ?

The bitterness that had characterised the last phase of Suffragette agitation went very deep, yet it vanished with extraordinary rapidity when the Great War broke out in 1914. Mrs Pankhurst turned her whole, splendidly organised movement over to national service.

Suddenly women were wanted as nurses and auxiliaries, on the land and in the munition factories, in the shops, and on the buses and trams to replace the men who had left for the Front. Divisions between women – those on the Suffragette side and those against – were forgotten. None were for the party and all were for the State. When the war ended women (over the age of thirty) went to the polls at the Parliamentary General Election and the *Daily Express* proudly recorded the fact and duly exulted in the Conservative triumph brought about in no small measure by the women's vote – just as Mrs Birrell had prophesied those many years before.

CHAPTER SIX

Welfare and Socialism

In its biographical sketches of victorious candidates in the 1900 election – comfortably won by the Conservatives – the *Express* had this to say of Mr Harold Tollemache, MP for Eddisbury :

> Few of the devotees of golf are more ardent than Mr Tollemache, who has varied the monotony of fifteen years' experience by prominent participation in the Parliamentary handicaps. Cricket also claims him.
>
> He is a land magnate with an intimate knowledge of farming.

The Tories had been elected for a successive term on their pro-khaki appeal as the party which had crushed Boer resistance to British Imperialism in the Afrikaaner Republics of Transvaal and the Orange Free State. In celebrating they were being somewhat premature as the Boers were to keep up a successful guerilla war for another two years. But as a staunchly Tory and Empire paper the *Express* was jubilant at the election outcome.

It had already given some publicity to a rising young star – son of a former Chancellor of the Exchequer – who had become something of a national hero by escaping from Boer imprisonment, having been catpured while serving as a war correspondent on an armoured train : a certain Mr Winston Churchill.

An *Express* reporter gave this account of Churchillian electioneering at Oldham in October 1900 :

> He began in the true Randolph style, (his father is Lord Randolph Churchill.) He spoke of 'my constituents' with the blush of a bridegroom talking of 'my wife'. He said that everything in the garden was lovely. He likened the Liberal party to a hornet, with the head biting the tail and the tail stinging the head. He said the brains of

the party were all in the tail, and he supposed the Union Jack on the Liberal placards was that which they pulled down at Pretoria in 1881.

The new member was getting along very nicely, in a speech that was half his father and half debating society, and one began to forget his sibilant lisp.

Then he lost his temper. In the midst of flowery passage about the hoisting of the flag at Pretoria, a stout lady in the gangway clenched her fists, became red in the face, and demanded to know what about the Dublins and what about the Irish Fusiliers? She was very excited about it, and she caused a disturbance.

Mr Churchill replied that he never was in favour of women's suffrage, and that the incident showed the folly of entrusting women with votes. The lady with a grievance was hustled out.

Churchill had even harder things to say about the Radicals, the Left-wingers among the Liberals: 'a squabbling, disorganised rabble. . .' 'The radical reminds me of hoary headed profligate overtaken in his old age by the results of the sins and follies of his youth.' When, four years later, Winston was to turn coat and join these radicals, the *Express* gloatingly reminded him of what he had called his new-found friends. This worried Winston not one whit. He remarked later, when he had returned to the Tory fold that anyone can rat, but it takes someone special to re-rat.

Coverage of the 1900 election campaign was substantial and reasonably impartial. Even the Socialist John Burns – who refused to link up with the two official Labour MPs – got a pretty good press. This remarkable man, sixteenth child of a Scottish engine fitter, who was wholly self-taught and had once known a man who knew Karl Marx, was now, by 1900, a well-established member of the Commons, but he could not be said to have the wherewithal to enjoy the facilities of the best club in Europe.

John Burns neither drinks nor smokes; he lives on Spartan fare; wears cheap clothes; and is a complete stranger to an overcoat. He rides a bicycle, but not mainly for enjoyment; he got it so that he could save tram fares to and from the House of Commons.

There is not a more polished speaker in the House than Burns. His diction is as perfect as his syntax, and his speeches are attentively listened to by every member. The fact is, he talks up to his audience.

Far otherwise is it in Trafalgar Square, or in Battersea, for that matter. He talks down, indulges in braggadocio, swears threats on the 'bourgeoisie'; he throws diction and syntax to the winds; he rants, gesticulates, and all to please his audience – his employers.

John's employers are many. And, of course, he tries to please them all. He gets £100 a year from the Amalgamated Society of Engineers, and his weekly income, which he told me is £5, is made up by other workmen's societies. He works hard for his money.

In those days MPs weren't paid and it wasn't until he got into the Cabinet –as a Liberal in 1906 – that Burns started to earn what, by any standard, was the high salary of £5,000 p.a.

The *Express* could afford to be magnanimous to the likes of John Burns, for the Socialist movement as a whole, broken up as it was into mutually hostile factions had made virtually no impression on the voters. The weary disdain of the utterly sure of themselves was echoed in St George's division of London :

This aristocratic region preserved its wonted outward calm yesterday, though many Unionists who had come up from the country to record their votes said unkind things about Mr Everitt, the daring Radical who put them to so much inconvenience and expense.

Some electors could exercise their choice in a number of constituencies, depending on where they had property, which then constituted a qualification for the franchise.

The *Express* instanced the case of Mr Joseph Baxendale, senior member of the removal firm, Pickfords, who had 43 votes :

'Mr Baxendale is undoubtedly entitled to his votes,' a representative of the firm said, 'for the property in London alone is worth half a million, and is all rated up to the full value. As the votes are scattered from Falmouth to Cork and West Hartlepool, it would hardly be possible for Mr Baxendale or his partners to vote in all of them.'

Though Mr Baxendale has so many votes, there are probably others with more.

Sir Thomas Lipton, and other businessmen with many branch establishments ought to be in the running for the credit of being 'the champion pluralist'.

In the end, Mr Baxendale didn't vote at all. He was too busy chasing red deer in the Highlands where presumably, not even Pickfords had a property.

Plural voting may have been an anomaly (it was not finally abolished until 1950 when the university seats disappeared) but it does not appear to have been a cause of burning grievance, possibly because the Liberals, who had strong support among businessmen, were no more keen to dispense with the system than were the Tories. Electoral reform is rarely promoted by those who benefit from the unreformed state.

In the political reports of the time there is a curious, old-fashioned acceptance of things, even by those who, one would have thought, would have been most likely to criticise the distribution of wealth and the plight of the disadvantaged.

Mr Will Crooks, the Labour Mayor of Poplar, was to be presented to King Edward VII in March 1902. The trouble was that, to match other dignitaries, he needed court dress:

'The fact is,' said Mr Crooks, 'I have too much respect for the King either to ask to be excused wearing Court dress or to go in a dress which I must either borrow or borrow the money to buy.

'My constituents would be delighted to know that I had been presented: but they would not care for me to go in a hired Court dress, and I should not care to go in ordinary dress unless His Majesty expressly commanded me to do so.

'It has been suggested to me that I should write to the Duke of Norfolk, and ask that an exception should be made in favour of a Labour member; but I decided that that course would not add to, but detract from, the dignity of the office I hold.

'The youngsters at home,' continued Mr Crooks, 'asked me if I was to be presented to the King on Thursday; but when I said that I should want a Court dress, they merely said "Oh!" They knew that meant money.

'No, it is out of respect for the King that I shall not join the mayors on Thursday. I would not ask for an exception to be made in my favour. But I appreciate the courtesy of the invitation, all the same.'

A little later, as MP for Woolwich, Mr Crooks proposed a modest measure to make it obligatory on all railway and steamship companies to afford, free of charge, to all members of both Houses travel between their places of residence and London for the discharge of their Parliamentary duties. In the case of members of the Commons, his bill proposed free passes to their constituencies as well. His revolutionary proposal got nowhere. On the same day that Crooks' bill was published – 4 August 1904 – a five-line paragraph appeared at the foot of page 5 of the *Daily Express*:

MINERS' WAGES REDUCED

Miners' wages are to be reduced 5 per cent, the reduction dating from the first making up day in August. This is the decision at which the Coal Conciliation Board arrived yesterday by the casting vote of the chairman, Lord James of Hereford.

There was not a cheep of protest.

But a year later, there were roars of protest about practically everything. Politics had become passionately alive and partisanship of the most violent hue stalked the land.

What happened to transform the electorate? First the Tories, in office for more than nine consecutive years, started to show their age. Their judgement went. Mr A. J. Balfour, having succeeded his uncle, the great black-bearded Salisbury, did not enjoy the prestige and automatic loyalty bestowed on his predecessor. Moreover, Mr Balfour was an intellectual who tried to reason things out instead of following his instinct and damning his principles. Bad luck played its part too. There was a trade recession – hence the cut in the miners' pay.

The campaign for Tariff Reform (putting duties on foreign manufacturers while permitting Empire products to be imported duty free) launched by the popular and populist Tory chieftain, Joseph Chamberlain, created a terrible furore, inside and outside the Conservative Party. Many Tories – their official title was Unionist to proclaim their belief in the union of Ireland with Britain – were free traders. The Liberals joyfully proclaimed that tariffs would mean 'dear bread'. But more than economic arguments, trade depressions or political blunders, the event that gave moral uplift to the Liberal campaign and sealed the Tories fate was Chinese slavery.

There were no Chinese slaves, of course, but the Liberals made a mighty emotive appeal over Chinese indentured apprentices who had been brought over to South Africa to rebuild the ravaged townships and communications of the now-annexed Boer republics. Liberal candidates toured their constituencies accompanied by slant-eyed actors playing the part of Chinese 'slaves' who were occasionally battered about the head with mock cat-o-nine tails. All the resentment that was bubbling up at the Government anyway found a pharisaical outlet in the alleged – and largely mythical – oppression of the poor Chinese in South Africa, while Liberal sympathies were also engaged for the downtrodden Afrikaaners. There was no mention then of the Black population of South Africa.

The sound of the hustings blotted out all else as the *Express* social diarist lamented on the last day of 1905, three weeks before the poll :

The social world is in a state of disruption owing to the near approach of the general election. For the next three weeks entertaining will not be worthy of the name.

Politics are the order of the day and night, for even dinner parties – gatherings of friends arranged on the spur of the moment – are all of a political character, and the after-dinner talk is of candidates and chances.

The political situation at home has had a disastrous effect on the season at Cairo and on the Riviera. Earlier in the year arrangements had been made for the usual winter invasion of the south, but all this has been knocked on the head by the events of the last month. Villas at Mentone and San Remo have been placed hurriedly in the agents' hands, with instructions to accept the first offer, while arrangements with Biarritz hotels have had to be cancelled at the last moment.

Electioneering threatens to become quite a fashionable pursuit with many women who are not ordinarily interested in political matters. With husbands, brothers, cousins, and nephews in the field, they feel it incumbent on them to offer their services as canvassers.

With mornings given up to political correspondence and to electioneering by motor car, and evenings spent on political platforms, the society woman has not a minute to spare for social engagements. During the last week, it is true, a partial truce was tacitly called in the constituencies, and electioneering was forgotten in the round of Christmas festivities, but the struggle will begin in earnest next week.

Country houses during the first three weeks of the New Year will be used as hotels, where politicians can put in a night after a strenuous day's electioneering, and rush off by the morning train to distant parts of the constituency.

Great county magnates like the Marquis of Londonderry and the Marquis of Zetland are remaining at their country seats until the end of next month, where they are at the call of their party. But the ordinary country house party is the merest farce. Even bridge has been ousted for the more fascinating work of vote-catching, and hosts are finding it very difficult – if not impossible, in fact – to get men to shoot for three days running during January. One short day's shoot will, in the majority of cases, be followed by a wild stampede to the next constituency on the list.

The campaign was furious, pursued with zeal and passion. When debonair, monocled Joe Chamberlain, the ex-radical from Birmingham who had become the gleaming hope of the Tory stalwarts of Empire, visited the City to give a two-hour speech on Tariff Reform 10,000 people turned up to hear him : 7,000 in secondary halls to which his speech was relayed by electrophone.

Chamberlain's triumphal entry can hardly be imagined today. 'At the bottom of Gresham Street,' reported the *Daily Express*, 'a procession of stockbrokers, four deep, joined in and preceded Mr Chamberlain's carriage waving Union Jacks.'

The nub of the Chamberlain message was that the City of London could only remain the financial centre of the world, and the clearing house of international banking so long as it remained the heart of a united Empire protected against foreign competition.

'Why', he cried, 'is the bill of exchange on London the standard currency of all the world's commercial transactions? Because,' he answered, 'of the productive energy and capacity behind it, constantly creating new wealth through our special relations with the colonies, dependencies and India. . . The prosperity of the City is intimately connected with the prosperity and greatness of the Empire of which it is the centre.'

City energy was matched by advertising acumen. The makers of Bile Beans – derivative of an Australian herb for curing constipation – got in on the act. Their advertisements in the *Express* blazoned :

'Have you not been struck with the fact that during the whole of Mr Chamberlain's fiscal campaign, he might have had in his eye the benefits which this country has reaped and is still reaping from the introduction of the great Australian medicine, Chas Forde's Bile Beans. You only need to glance at the following extracts to see this :

'Mr Chamberlain said : "People want better prescriptions than have been given to them in the past."

'That is so. As soon as Bile Beans were known to be a better prescription for liver and stomach disorders than any others, their sale increased enormously, and is still increasing.

'Mr Chamberlain said : "I am like a physician offering a prescription to a sick country."

'So are we. The prescription is Bile Beans.'

While Tories cheered and sang 'Rule Britannia' (it was another year before 'Land of Hope and Glory' appeared), the Liberals and their radical and Irish nationalist allies were advancing throughout the country. Ten years of jubilant jingoism and Imperialism were about to give way to a decade of social and political change, driven forward by political calculation no less than by humanitarianism.

Joe Chamberlain apart, the Liberal-Labour alliance had all the best speakers and writers : Winston Churchill, who had now joined the Liberals, Herbert Henry Asquith, John Burns, George Bernard Shaw, H. G. Wells ('voice like a squeaky door but the pen of an avenging angel') and, above all, the Welsh wizard, David Lloyd George. They also had a friend of King Edward VII, the scintillating Lady Warwick. The *Express* duly reported her intervention :

Four or five hundred Radical and Socialist electors of hardworking South West Ham sat in a board school last night and gazed on the Countess of Warwick.

Outside there were hundreds of other electors, who stood on tiptoe to try to get a glimpse through the windows of the celebrated society beauty.

The idea of the organisers of the meeting was that the Countess should set the local heather on fire with a burning revolutionary oration. She had whizzed down from the West End in her red motorcar after an early dinner.

She wore a lovely fur toque, with pretty feathers sticking out at the back, which must have cost ever so much money. There were beautiful large 'blobs' of something that looked like real tortoiseshell dotted round the edge of it, and the West Ham Socialist thought how nice that toque would look on Mary Ann.

Then she had the most exquisite blue cloth dress, fitting as closely as a glove, so that it showed her beautiful figure to perfection. The sleeves, cut in the very latest style, stopped short just below the elbow, and from there down to her wrists the beautiful Countess wore the most beautiful white open-work mittens.

From her neck hung a long, dainty brown gauzy scarf. Round her neck was tightly clasped a string of heavenly blue beads, and more loosely, dangling low, hung a long and costly string of large yellow stones.

In the front of her dress she had a royal bunch of crimson carnations and a spray of violets. Her left hand was gloved in the daintiest white kid, while her right hand was ungloved, so that she could safely shake hands with West Ham.

Similar sarcasm was piled on Lloyd George. The *Express* never failed to remind its readers that Lloyd George had been attacked by a lynching mob four years previously for championing the Boers against the British. He had gone to Chamberlain territory to speak at Birmingham Town Hall but 40,000 Chamberlainites made sure he never spoke. They stormed the Town Hall. They wrecked it. Two people died and Lloyd George was fortunate to get away with his life – disguised as PC 87D. The *Express* recalled how Lloyd George formed up with the police in a side room and held a dress rehearsal until he got the step and bearing of a true Bobby while the real PC 87D, Officer Stonier, didn't find it a pleasant experience to wear the politician's suit which was too small for him and put him in imminent jeopardy.

Lloyd George had a viper's tongue and the unhappy Tory Party cowered under its lash. Taking the line of a previous Liberal leader, Lord Rosebery, he declared that 'trade protection would bring us into a battle with the whole civilized world compared with which Armageddon would be a friendly jest'. (Armageddon came about nine years later and a scarcely noticed by-product was protection). Extravagant language of this kind might have been laughed out of court if the Tories had had anyone – Chamberlain apart – capable of raising dismissive humour. But they hadn't. On every platform, in every barroom argument they were trounced.

Desperately the *Express*, for the first time, introduced the German menace to swing the voters to the Tories. The paper's correspondent in Nuremberg, centre of the German toy trade which was knocking British products into a cocked hat, called attention to the Germans' attachment to the English Liberals.

I attended a private meeting of manufacturers. Almost to a man they expressed the fervid hope that the Liberal party would win overwhelmingly, because of the danger to German trade by reason of the proposed tariffs. If Mr Chamberlain were to win, the majority of the men said they would either be obliged to open works in England in order to compete on even terms with the British manufacturer, or they would have to curtail their output, which would necessarily raise the prices in Germany. In other words 'dumping' would cease.

'Throughout Nuremberg, which does an immense export trade to England, the hope is constantly expressed that the Liberal Party, which is Germany's best friend, may win.'

Despite this propaganda effort which might have brought a whistle of admiration from Dr Goebbels, the Tories were routed. The Liberals and their allies won by a landslide.

Liberals	387
Irish Nationalists	84
Labour	41
Tory	158

The composition of the new House was interesting. It bore a fairly close resemblance to the present in that there were 100 barristers (84 in the 1974 Parliament), 183 businessmen (162), 34 solicitors (24), 29 journalists (51). The really significant difference was the number of teachers and lecturers – 92 in the Parliament of 1974, the largest single group. There were 14 in 1906.

The new Government was headed by a Scotsman, Henry Campbell-Bannerman whose apparent mildness concealed a restless urge to right wrongs and redress the balance between the privileged and the poor. The year 1906 marked a decisive turn. Within a few months of the Campbell-Bannerman administration taking office the trades unions had been given legal immunity from actions by their officers which would otherwise have left them open to criminal prosecution. So long as the cloak of 'pursuit of a trade dispute' could be used as cover, the unions could do almost anything with impunity. Bannerman's Trade Disputes Act reversed a decision of the House of Lords that union funds were liable for compensation for any injury to persons or property inflicted by striking trade unionists. That the workers deserved to have the balance tipped towards them and away from the hitherto over-powerful employers was beyond question. That they should have been given quite such a degree of freedom of restraint from the law was much more open to doubt.

But the Liberals saw the writing on the wall. Labour had 41 seats. How long would it be before the rising Labour Party overtook the Liberals as the opposition to the Conservatives?

Giving the unions special privileges had more to do with politics than with social justice: it was the Liberals' way of buying Labour support.

Campbell--Bannerman's Trade Disputes Act was of significance to generations yet unborn. The publicity of the day was fixed on old age pensions and State health insurance, the beginning of the Welfare State.

This is how the *Express* presented the pension news of 8 May, 1908:

Mr Asquith introduced in the Commons yesterday a Budget which sets up an entirely new principle in this country – the responsibility of the State to provide for the aged poor.

The pensions of 5s a week at the age of seventy are to be payable, with a few necessary reservations, to every one with an income of less than 10s a week.

The scheme will cost £1,200,000 during the current financial year, and next year the Chancellor will require the enormous sum of £6,000,000 for the purpose. Where will he get it?

It is the opinion of many members of the House that Mr Asquith is acting the part of the prodigal father, and laying up a colossal burden of obligations for the successors of the present Government in office.

Mr Asquith explained his old-age pension scheme in the following terms:

'Criminals and lunatics must be excluded. By criminals I mean persons under sentence of imprisonment. The deduction under this head is about 1½ per cent.

'We propose to exclude only actual paupers – persons now actually in receipt of Poor Law relief. As to character, the less we go into that, short of actual conviction for crime, the better.

'As regards the amount of the pensions, it has been generally agreed in this country that it should be 5s or £13 a year.

'Married couples living together ought to be pensioned at a lower rate, say, 7s 6d instead of 10s a week.

'Then there must clearly be a provision for forfeiture in the case of persons shown to have been guilty of fraudulent representation or persons subsequently convicted of serious offences.

'Applicants will be supplied at the post office with a form of application, in the filling up of which it will be the duty of the local postmaster to give all the assistance required.

'The application, when filled up, will be transmitted to the local pension authority.

'The pension authority will be a committee appointed by the

county, borough, or urban district council either from within or without their own body.

'The pensioner, if his application is granted, will be furnished with a book of monthly or weekly coupons which will be payable at the post office. The pension cannot be "charged" and is payable only to the individual or his representative.

'We think it safe to assume that the maximum number of actual pensioners will not exceed 500,000 and that the maximum cost to the State is not likely to exceed six millions sterling. It will take time to adjust the details.'

In the Committee stage the Tories fought for a sliding scale to give something, at least 1s a week, to those whose income lay between 10s and 14s so as not to penalise the prudent folk who had scraped and saved and invested a little.

On the first day of payout at the post office, 1 January, 1909, more than 550,000 people queued at 24,000 counters throughout the UK to collect an average of 4s 4d, at a first week's cost to the State of £119,166 13s 4d.

Poignant scenes occurred as these old souls went up to receive something they'd never dreamed of – a payment for doing nothing.

Old-age pensions were the great topic yesterday, writes an *Express* representative.

Everyone asked everyone else, 'Have you drawn your pension?' Old folks hobbling along the streets with blue booklets tightly held in their hands were greeted by all the parish with the cheery cry, 'Got your pension?' Most of them seemed to have blue booklets, which means that they were drawing the maximum of 5s a week, having, without the pension, an income of 8s a week or less.

It was a pathetic sight – the stream of old, worn men and women, some half-blind, some bent with age and rheumatism, hobbling along with sticks, some led by neighbours, some moving along by themselves a few steps at a time, shaky and fearful but independent to the last.

The most pathetic feature of the payments was the death of several old people as they had received or were about to receive their pensions:

James Cleary, an ex-gunner of the Royal Artillery dropped dead in Bishops Stortford post office after marking his papers with a cross in lieu of signature.

Mrs Mary Burrows, of Horncastle, was found dead in bed in the morning. She had made arrangements to draw her first pension yesterday.

Emmanuel Hawthorne, of Spalding, drew his pension and dropped dead when he returned home, it is supposed that the excitement acted on a weak heart.

An old Kilkenny woman died on her way to the post office at eight o'clock to draw her pension.

A woman dropped dead from excitement in Sandwich post office at eight o'clock as she was handed her 5s.

Two other Sandwich pensioners – James Luckhurst, aged seventy-two, and Mrs Brenchley, aged ninety, also died yesterday.

The next big step in the creation of the Welfare State was National Insurance.

Basing his legislation on the promise that the 'Liberal Party has been summoned by heaven to face a nobler task . . . to see that, even in the meanest attic . . . there is no man found dying of hunger'. Lloyd George, who had succeeded Asquith as Chancellor, set about abolishing the spectre of famine. In the year of his People's Budget, 1909,* 119 people died in the UK from privation and starvation. The principle of reform was not disputed – except by the most hard-hearted who held that those who got themselves into such a plight deserved to perish – but the methods chosen by Lloyd George were manifestly disputable.

He first thought of nationalising the Prudential Insurance. (Nationalisation was quite popular among Liberals at that time. Churchill suggested nationalising the railways.) The proposal was rejected by the Cabinet, not least because of its bad effect on the Pru's millions of subscribers who were also voters.

So a straightforward State insurance scheme, based largely on the German variety introduced by Bismarck thirty years previously, was promulgated. In bare bones it required :

All workpeople earning less than £160 a year to be insured against sickness.

Premiums to be 4d a week by the employee, 3d a week by

*The Budget's proposed Land Tax provoked the House of Lords to veto the legislation and brought on a constitutional crisis. By threatening to create 500 new peers, Premier Asquith forced the Upper Chamber to accept a greatly diminished role limiting its delaying powers to two years and eliminating them altogether on money matters.

employers and 2d a week by the State, (hence the Liberal slogan 'Ninepence for fourpence'.)

In times of sickness the insured to receive free medical attention and 10s a week for three months plus 5s a week for a further three months.

Maternity grants of 30s to be provided.

One and a half million pounds to be spent building sanatoriums for consumptives – tuberculosis then being the most feared disease.

The total number of people insured, including the self-employed who did so voluntarily, totalled nearly 15 million.

Unemployment insurance for building and engineering trade workers financed by 2½d levy on employers and employees, providing 7s a week unemployment benefit for fifteen weeks.

Friendly societies, county health committees and trade unions were the chosen instruments for paying the State-endorsed benefits.

What stuck in the gullets of some people was the method of providing medical treatment for those insured under the State scheme. This was the panel system by which general practitioners were obliged to visit 'panel' patients (i.e. those insured under the State scheme) in return for a per capita payment from the National Insurance officers. As in 1947-1948 when Aneurin Bevan extended the panel system to embrace the entire population, so in 1911-1912 many doctors became apoplectic at the prospect of being obliged to attend patients – although many GPs happily gave their services for nothing to those unable to afford medical treatment.

Briefly, the anti-panel faction argued that so many malingerers would take advantage of the panel system to ask their doctors for certificates excusing them from work that the genuinely sick would suffer. In some cases this proved to be the case.

A jury found that Frederick Townsend, labourer, died of a strangulated hernia through medical neglect, his GP, Dr Hickson being unable to give him the attention required 'owing to the scandalous amount of work imposed upon him by the Insurance Act'.

Doctors, furious at what they saw as political interference with their freedom, held anti-Lloyd George rallies. Among the epithets flung at the Chancellor at one such meeting in January 1913 were 'moral leper', 'Judas Iscariot', 'Bill Sykes', 'Uriah Heep'. Those who refused to join the panel scheme, it was alleged, faced ruin because their patients were intent on something for nothing.

Platform oratory gave way to real tragedy in November 1913.

A Dr Horace Dimock, 29, was appointed a panel physician at Wisbech, a remote market town in the Cambridgeshire fen country. He was not welcomed by the local doctors who were opposed to the panel scheme. They boycotted him. He replied by writing anonymous letters to and about his fellow practitioners. Following complaints he was put under surveillance by the police, arrested and charged with criminal libel; released on bail he promptly committed suicide. Wisbech, quiet demure Wisbech, then went berserk. Six thousand people rioted against the persecution of Dr Dimock. The windows and doors of the offending medical men, led by Dr Meacock, Isle of Ely Chairman of the British Medical Association and foremost foe of the Insurance Act, were broken and only repeated charges by the police – and the reading of the Riot Act by the Mayor – prevented far worse. At Dimock's funeral hundreds of working men and women walked behind the hearse carrying wreaths. Hundreds of police lined the route to prevent a repetition of the violence. Dr Meacock and his fellow non-panel practitioners – Lucas, Gunson, and Poyser – were execrated and the local county insurance committee virtually passed a vote of censure on them. Horace Dimock became the first martyr to medical obscurantism – at least in the eyes of the Radicals.

The *Express* was not having this. Their representative interviewed Dr Harry Meacock and this was the doctor's story:

'We have been accused of persecuting the late Dr Dimock – have had our houses attacked by a mob, and been assailed by every objectionable epithet imaginable, and we think it is high time that some of these inaccuracies which have appeared in print were corrected.

'When the supply of panel doctors broke down at Wisbech, Dr Dimock was imported into the town to complete the panel. The conditions of his coming there were deemed dishonourable by the British Medical Association, and we had no other course open to us but to consult our association.

'A letter couched in the most courteous terms was prepared by the secretary, explaining the resolution passed by the council, and asking Dr Dimock to meet the local division and discuss the situation. The letter was forwarded to Dr Dimock, but the request was ignored, no reply being received from him. This being the case, we could do nothing but silently ignore Dr Dimock. Because of this we – the non panel doctors of Wisbech – and our wives and families have had to endure a virtual reign of terror.

'It was not long after Dr Dimock's arrival in Wisbech that prominent people began to receive anonymous postcards of a libellous, scurrilous, and insulting nature, and the matter was placed in the hands of the police.

Dr Dimock was observed by the police on more than one occasion to post some of these cards himself, while the report of the hand-writing expert leaves no doubt in the matter.'

Whatever the rights and wrongs of the Wisbech affair, David Lloyd George lacerated the social conscience of the nation and, in speech after speech (known as 'Limehousing' after his most rabble-rousing oration in London's East End), developed the theme of 'them and us'. He pointed to the 58,000 terminal cases of consumption per year and contrasted that with the wealthy few who were able to take their doctors' advice and pop over to Switzerland for their lungs' sake. His supporters contrasted the gap between needs and the frugal means supplied by local bureaucracy, quoting, among other documents, a letter from the Kent County Medical Officer to one Mr Hugh Story, a TB sufferer of Bexley Heath :

Dear Sir (or Madam)
Re supply of Ancillary Nourishment
Owing to the large numbers of patients receiving 'sanatorium benefits' who had applied to the Kent Insurance Committee for extra nourishment, and to the fact that the sum of money available for this purpose is limited, it has become necessary to reduce the quantity of nourishment supplied.

As you have been receiving such assistance for a considerable period, and as it is impossible to continue this indefinitely, I am compelled reluctantly to cancel any further supply in your case for the present. Accordingly I am instrucing the tradesmen concerned to discontinue the supply of such food after Saturday of next week, 22 November 1913.

Knowingly or unknowingly, Lloyd George, helped also by the 'treat 'em mean and keep 'em keen' philosophy of some employers and landlords, was seeding the soil for the class war to come. What the *Express* and its readers feared was that the beneficiaries would be the Socialist Party and Red Revolution.

The rise of British socialism in the popular press was signalled by a four paragraph report of 2 February, 1901 :

The meeting at Manhester yesterday of the Labour Representation Committee was attended by eighty-two delegates, representing 348,862 trade unionists, 94,000 members of trade councils, and 23,861 Socialist sympathisers.

The committee was specially charged by the Trade Union Conference at Plymouth with the encouragement of the election to Parliament of men in sympathy with Labour, and the delegates reported yesterday that gratifying success had attended the movement.

Councillor J. Hodge, who presided, declared that they had nothing to expect from the Liberal Party, who merely dissembled their love for the puropse of kicking Labour downstairs, and urged that they should take up a distinct attitude towards both political parties.

A resolution was carried in favour of an Independent Labour platform for the defence of the legal rights of combination, and for the passing of a law terminating the system 'under which the producer of wealth has to bear an enormous burden in the shape of rents and profits, which go to maintain large classes of non-producers.

Theer had been for many years socialist societies and one or two independent MPs propagating the general theme of equality and the forced redistribution of wealth, but the Manchester meeting marked the true beginning of a Labour movement to give the trade unions political representation in order to change the law in the unions' favour.

Between 1901 and 1906 the *Express* and other Conservative minded papers viewed the newcomers to the political scene with a benevolent twinkle. The unions, it was felt, were entitled to representation as much as the landed or manufacturing interest. We were broadening down from precedent to precedent.

But when in 1906 more than 40 Labour MPs were elected, and when, like their leaders Mr Keir Hardie and Mr Ramsay MacDonald, they began to preach the total transformation of society the *Express* sang a different tune. Until then the paper had tut-tutted over the financial sorrows of Labour members, such as Mr John Wood, the member for Stoke-on-Trent who complained :

'I have a wife and four children, and with my brother who is a navvy, have to support my mother. And beyond the fifty shillings a week that I draw from the Navvies' Union I have nothing to fall back on.

'There are what are called "the amenities of the House". Tea on the terrace? No, I am afraid that is not included. There will be no tea on the terrace for me on fifty shillings a week.'

Then came the opening of Socialist Sunday Schools in January 1906. Headlined 'Under the Red Flag', the *Express* reporter told of a different kind of Sunday school taking place above the Co-operative Stores in Tunbridge Wells, Kent. The facetiousness overlaid a deeper feeling of unease:

Fourteen mild-mannered infant Socialists sat in the room yesterday afternoon and listened to an earnest young man wearing a cycling suit and red badge delivering an address on the iniquities of capitalists.

As the ages of the little Socialists ranged from four to twelve years, the address was couched as far as possible in words of one syllable, and neat similes about puppy dogs and pussy cats were introduced to attract the infant Socialists' minds.

At the opening of the proceedings the high treble voices of the youthful Socialists chanted a verse of the 'Red Flag'. In this they were assisted by two very burly, good-natured looking Socialists of maturer years, who wore blood-red ties. Five of the very young lady Socialists wore blood-red dresses.

Part of the gospel that the young man in the cycling suit taught was 'Love your neighbour as yourself', but the doctrine was expounded on lines entirely different from the ordinary Christian method of teaching.

'If,' he said, 'you were going along the street, and met a poor little girl who was ragged and very hungry, what would you do if you loved her as you love yourselves? Would you give her your clothes and your food? Certainly not; you would love yourselves too much. Besides, it would be foolish. You would yourselves grow weak and ill if you went without your clothes and your food.

'Who, then, should provide this little girl with what she needs? Why, the rich, of course – those people who live on the workers and have a sort of after-Christmas feeling all the year round because they always have too much to eat. They are the people who should feed the poor little girl.'

Then he asked them what their rights were, and the youthful Socialists repeated in chorus: 'The right to be sheltered; the right to be fed; the right to be clothed.'

'How is this great ideal to be achieved?' the young man continued. 'Why by dividing among everybody the land which now belongs to people who get rich by making poor men work on it. That is the ideal which you little Socialists are always to keep in mind. If your poor dadda is going about out of work, you must be dissatisfied. You must tell people that we all have the right to be fed, clothed, and housed by the State.'

Following all this talk came quite a pretty ceremony. The two burly Socialists and all the little Socialists joined hands, and, standing in a circle, sang to the tune of 'Auld Lang Syne' the following so-called hymn :

> And now we'll clasp each other's hands,
> And by the dead we'll swear,
> To keep the red flag waving here,
> All through the coming year,
> We love the bold and boundless mind,
> The heart of purpose strong,
> Which feels the woes of humankind,
> And wars to vanquish wrong.

Still more worrying to the *Express* was the list of immediate reforms issued by the Social Democratic Federation on 3 October, 1907. The group was, admittedly, far to the left of the Labour Party in the Commons, but it proclaimed the stark ideals for which all socialists should be striving. The demands embraced :

Abolition of the Monarchy
Repudiation of the National Debt
Abolition of all indirect taxation
Institution of cumulative tax on all incomes and inheritances
    exceeding £300
Free maintenance for all attending State schools
Public ownership of food and coal supply
Nationalisation of the trusts
Establishment of State pawnshops
Establishment of State restaurants
Public ownership of the drink traffic
Free State insurance against sickness and accident
Abolition of standing armies
Abolition of courts-martial.

When, on the same day, the Bishop of Stepney announced that 'Socialism is the master current of life' and 'that the twentieth century will take its place as the era of socialism and co-operation', the *Express* became thoroughly alarmed.

If the Church was going to be infiltrated, then the aims of certain Socialists to remould family life by taking away children and putting them in creches (rather as was done in the early Israeli kibbutzim) would be given divine sanction. The words of Jesus Christ would be turned into Socialist propaganda. So the *Express* launched a campaign to inform the public about how trumpery and meaningless was all this talk of Christian socialism. The leading article of 4 October, 1907, declared :

> The clergy and ministers are a great help to Socialism. They introduce it to circles which otherwise it might never reach. Their support, with the unthinking, invests the creed of loot in the name of the State with a respectability and honesty that are very helpful.
>
> The Socialist Fabian Society, of which Mr Bernard Shaw is the most prominent leader, numbers clergymen and ministers among its members. But Mr Shaw's attitude to Christianity is blasphemously hostile.
>
> Mr Shaw says:
> 'Popular Christianity has for its emblem a gibbet, for its chief sensation a sanguinary execution after torture, for its central mystery an insane vengeance brought off by a trumpery expiation.'
>
> Socialism is indeed saturated through and through with Atheism.

By the end of 1907 the Socialists were holding up to 3,000 meetings a week. In those days, however, the universities were hot beds of Toryism and the *Express* gleefully reported one meeting that did not go Labour's way :

> Mr Keir Hardie went to Cambridge on Saturday, and his attempt to obtain a foothold for Socialism in the university town was met by unprecedented acts of hostility on the part of undergraduates.
>
> They stormed the 'hall, threw a bottle of sulphurated hydrogen through one of the windows, and so caused a most obnoxious odour, hurled lumps of sugar, oranges and phials of offensive chemicals at him, hissed and booed him, sang 'God Save the King' and tried in every possible way to ridicule him off the platform.
>
> But the most daringly conceived scheme was a plot to kidnap the

Socialist leader. This had its amusing side.

The idea was to capture him, imprison him in a room, and to put a bogus Mr Keir Hardie on the platform, who was to talk nonsense.

With this object, one of the undergraduates was disguised as Mr Hardie. It was a realistic disguise, so realistic in fact that a number of his colleagues mistook him for Mr Keir Hardie himself, collared him and despite his loud protests that he was nobody else but himself, thrust him into a room, locked the door, and then went away in search of further fun.

Meanwhile Mr Keir Hardie's 'double' escaped from the room by means of a rope. He at once declared himself to the leaders of the conspiracy, but by this time the real Mr Keir Hardie had arrived at the hall in safety, and so the plot to kidnap him fell through.

Sterner stuff ensued when the Conservatives surprisingly won a by-election from the Liberals in Mid-Devon in January 1908. The *Express* had sinister tidings of the length to which Socialist and radical supporters of the defeated Liberal candidate would go. Sergeant Major Rendell, who had taken a prominent part in the Tory campaign, was found dead in the mill-race that flows through Newton Abbot. He had received two black eyes and a violent blow on the head. No radical Socialist, however, was arrested and as the Sergeant Major had been in the bar of the Commercial Inn the evening he disappeared, the conclusion was that he had been involved in a pub fight and was not the victim of the Red Army of Mid-Devon.

Now the *Express* really got going: it helped to sponsor the anti-Socialist Union. It ran stories with such emotive headlines as one on 15 April, 1908:

DRIVEN MAD BY SOCIALISM — SUICIDE OF A LAD OF SIXTEEN

The reading of Socialist books was stated at an inquest at Woolwich yesterday to have preyed on the mind of a young Deptford butcher who hanged himself on a tree on Bostal Heath.

The name of this victim of Socialism was Charles William Woodward, aged sixteen, and he lived in a quiet little street in Deptford, called Glenville-grove.

'He used to read a good deal of Socialistic literature, and it seemed to have got on his mind,' the boy's uncle told the coroner.

The youth became so depressed that he seemed to think his

employment was in danger, and he was also troubled on account of his failing sight.

The jury returned a verdict of 'Suicide while temporarily deranged'.

A fuller story of this Socialist tragedy was told to an *Express* representative by Mrs Webb, the lad's aunt, with whom he lived. 'Charlie was always reading silly books on Socialism,' she said, 'He used to bring them home and read them in bed. Often he would take some out with him to read at business.

'We used to tell him how foolish it was, but he was always reading books, and it must have turned his brain.

'Last Wednesday he bought a red tie. We told him it was not at all a nice colour, but he said that was all right, it was a Socialist tie.'

To combat the Socialistic teaching of the Bishop of Stepney and his Anglican followers and the Socialists of the Free Church Council, a non-Conformist Anti-Socialist Association was established 'to unmask hideous atheism'.

It was not only in chancel, pew and vestry that the gospel according to Marx was being spread. The pantry too was not immune.

SOCIALISM IN THE KITCHEN
SPREADING DISCONTENT AMONG SERVANTS

proclaimed the *Express*:

An attempt to convert domestic servants to Socialism is being made under the cloak of a newly established Domestic Servants' Trade Union – the first that have ever started propaganda in the kitchen.

The Red Flag campaign below stairs has been organised by Miss Kathlyn Oliver and Mr Charles N. Shaw – both well-known Socialists. Their aim is to band together the housemaid, the 'general' and the 'tweeny' maid in the interests of Socialism and 'reform'.

Servants are reminded that 'the conscientious domestic worker is entitled to as much respect as the Prime Minister, who is as much a servant as any despised "slavey".'

In an article on the objects of the Domestic Servants' Union in the *Woman Worker*, Mr Charles Shaw, the Hon Treasurer (pro tem) opens his propaganda in the servants' hall.

He asks: 'Do you know of any other body of toilers who would consent to toil and moil in underground kitchens through the scorching days of summer for a mere pittance?'

Then, in case the servant is suited to her place, he says : 'A certain proportion of domestic servants are snobbish. They are, as one man has expressed it, "parasites living on parasites". One refers, of course, to those engaged in the houses of the wealthy and titled loafers.'

An official of the Anti-Socialist Union said to an *Express* representative last night :

'The formation of a trade union for servants, which has never been done before, is in itself an excellent thing, and we are not opposed to trade unions at all.

'But this organisation, to judge by its promoters and its expressed views, is intended to spread Socialism and discontent among a contented and hardworking class who have been hitherto outside the reach of agitators.'

The last great political convulsion to rack Liberal England before the onset of war was the Home Rule crisis.

Following the general election of 1910, the Conservatives and Liberal parties were evenly matched in the Commons. To continue in office the Liberals were obliged to rely wholly on the Irish Nationalists and Labour. Part of the price was a Home Rule Bill giving Dublin its own Parliament and power over all internal affairs. Theoretically this would restore the status quo-ante – Ireland had had its own Parliament until the Union Act of 1800. In fact, the first decisive step would have been taken towards an independent Ireland. However, the Protestant population of Ulster, numbering one million, objected fiercely to any scheme subjecting them to the rule of the Catholic majority in Ireland. They stated their 'fixed determination to resist to the uttermost all attempts to deprive us of our rights as subjects of our beloved King and citizens of the British Empire,' resisting to the uttermost including arming, drilling and training to fight any attempt by the Catholic South or the British Government to coerce them into Dublin rule.

The Tory Party, led now by Andrew Bonar Law, himself of Ulster descent, flung itself wholeheartedly on to the side of the Ulster Loyalists. Lord Willoughby de Broke, a Tory peer, wrote to the *Express* in September 1912 :

If the Government insists on a civil war, they can have it. There are greater calamities than civil war. The surrender and repeal of the Union would be a greater calamity than civil war.

It is difficult to see how any one who holds these views can stand aloof when other men are fighting for them. For my own part, I shall volunteer for active service in Ulster in the event of His Majesty's Government deciding to coerce men and women whose only offence is that they wish to remain inside the British Constitution, and I have little doubt that many other Unionists will do the same.

Sir Edward Carson, the barrister and Tory leader, told 100,000 Orangemen at Craigavon in July 1913:

'The Army is with us and it is with us for this reason – that the British Army was never guilty of betrayal or treachery.

'The Government has resolved to give us no quarter,' Sir Edward Carson added, 'and if they go on with that idea I tell them this – we will give them no quarter when the time comes.'

Sir Edward's confidence in the British Army was justified in a dramatic fashion nine months later; the Army mutinied and refused to march on Ulster. More precisely, Brigadier General Gough and the officers of the Third Cavalry Brigade stationed on the Curragh outside Dublin refused to march into Northern Ireland. They were immediately dismissed the Service but the War Office was inundated with resignations from other officers who refused to fight against loyal Ulstermen. The private soldiers were fiercer still in their opposition. The crisis began on Friday, 20 March, 1914, and ended on 23 March with the Government's capitulation.

From that spring onwards events moved sombrely towards civil war in Ireland and a total rupture between Liberal-Nationalist coalition and the Conservatives. The newspapers published a covenant and invited signatories from their readers:

I .... of .... earnestly convinced that the claim of the Government to carry the Home Rule Bill into law, without submitting it to the judgment of the nation, is contrary to the spirit of our Constitution,

DO HEREBY SOLEMNLY DECLARE

that, if that Bill is so passed, I shall hold myself justified in taking or supporting any action that may be effective to prevent the armed forces of the Crown being used to deprive the people of Ulster of their rights as citizens of the United Kingdom.

Among the signatories were Sir Edward Elgar and Rudyard Kipling.

A month later, at the end of April, the *Express* reported:

Thirty-thousand rifles and 3,000,000 rounds of ammunition were landed at Larne, Bangor and Donaghadee for the Ulster volunteers. They were landed in accordance with a programme that was carried out unaltered in the smallest detail, and conveyed quietly and methodically to designated depots throughout Ulster by five columns of motor transport, aggregating nearly seven hundred vehicles of all kinds.

More than fifty-thousand men were mobilised for eleven hours. Eleven thousand volunteers of the Belfast division dominated the capital as the county battalions dominated the towns and villages to the north and west.

Nursing corps were at designated posts, where field hospitals had been established and in many of the finest mansions in Ulster women were waiting all night with surgical dressings, bandages, and sterilised water for the wounded who might be carried there.

When the dawn brought assurance that the great undertaking was successful, the army of the night melted away as though by magic. Merchants went to their offices, workmen to the shipyards, farmers to their fields, without having slept, and calmly resumed the usual duties of their everyday life.

It can hardly be imagined that all these arms, shipped by the way from Germany, could have entered Ulster without the connivance of the Army and police. The argument for allowing these illegal, and deadly imports, was the arming, also from German sources, of the Southern Irish volunteers. By June detachments of what would ultimately become known as the Irish Republican Army, the IRA, were training in London. There were even Irish jokes to overlay the tragedy and make it bearable.

An *Express* representative was present at the last drill and describes it as irresistibly comic :

Over a hundred volunteers presented themselves for enrolment – some working men, but a large majority drawn from the Post Office and various departments of the Civil Service, which have an irresistible appeal for the Irish.

After the half-crowns had been collected the volunteers were ordered to 'fall in'. They fell out – fell out furiously among themselves. Tipperary and Kerry hurled hot words at each other, and a 'patriot' from Sligo thrust his lower jaw into the face of another from Cork, and told him that if he was heard again calling William

O'Brien 'a dacint man' his remains would go back to Ireland in a luggage train.

Curiously enough, no heads were broken in the next five minutes. After this interval the first speaker said he washed his hands of the company, and would form another brigade of volunteers. He was shouted down with cries of 'Stop arguin. We want t'dhrill.'

It was obvious that the section commanders knew no more about drill than they had been able to gather from a cadet's manual in the last few days. The proceedings recalled the drilling of the Donegal militia when the sergeant put a hay rope on the recruits' right foot and a straw rope on the left, and shouted, 'Hay foot, straw foot,' when he wanted them to march in step.

At the order of 'Right wheel' from the section commander, half the section went right and half to the left. Everybody bumped.

After a quarter of an hour's bumping, there was an interval for rest and discussion. Then another quarter of an hour's bumping, and the volunteers dispersed until Thursday evening next, when they will drill again in the same German gymnasium.

This gymnasium, by the way, is entirely under German control, and has a special proviso preventing any Englishman from becoming a member. It is, therefore, a fitting meeting place for the Separatists.

Ironically it was Germany, the provider of arms for the political combatants which unwittingly reunited the two Irelands and prevented the Civil War it had done so much to promote.

Just when the King's last-minute intervention had failed and the Irish Protestant and Catholic armies stood ready to open fire, a far greater conflagration brought an end (temporarily at least) to the Irish problem – and a whole way of life which was already, early in the century, being foretold by seers, scientists and cranks.

Indian officers riding in procession in London at the coronation of King George V remind the British crowds that Britain holds mastery over the mightiest Empire the world has ever known.

Change was in the air . . . the carriages that peers waited for at King George V's coronation were horseless ones.

'I, Edward Prince of Wales, do become your liege man of life and limb . . . ' Alas, Edward Prince of Wales, as Edward VIII, was the only British monarch to abdicate.

CHAPTER SEVEN

Things to Come

Asked for his views of the future on the first day of the twentieth century, George Bernard Shaw replied : 'The only point upon which I see any reason to congratulate the twentieth century is that at all events it cannot possibly be worse than the nineteenth.'

Canon Gore of Westminster was in no such flippant mood as he preached the last sermon of the nineteenth century :

> Something like awe fell upon the people as the eloquent Canon spoke in the stillness of the great Abbey of the things that might have been, and the disappointment of those who desired the glory of God.
>
> Even the literature of the day, he reminded them, was not inspired as formerly. There was no Carlyle and no Tennyson to put into melodious words the great truths of Nature. Leaders of men were lacking in the present day.
>
> Religion was in an equally bad plight, poor in moral quality, without humility or fear of God. The liquor traffic was stronger than ever. Lust stalked the street and commercial immorality was unchecked.

Sometime later the Bishop of Stepney adjured his congregation to beware of self assertion :

> 'The cry of modern life is : I want to be myself : I want to live my own life.
>
> 'The strain is felt most conspicuously in home life. The desire to restrain on the part of the parent, the growing resentment on the part of the children, the parents' complaint of irresponsiveness and ingratitude, the children's complaint that they are not understood and

that they are not allowed to do as they like or play the parts that they ought in life.

'This conflict of ideas and opinions, getting more bitter day by day, is the symptom of fractional distress.'

What all were agreed upon was that the twentieth century would be fascinating beyond all others. No one recalled that the toast 'may you live in interesting times' was a Chinese curse.

Everything, but everything was happening : from motor cars travelling at 43 miles an hour to Mr Marconi transmitting wireless signals from Poole to the Isle of Wight. Anything was possible and some remarkable prophecies were made in the fourteen years prior to World War I. Mr H. G. Wells wrote :

'We stand to-day towards radio-activity exactly as our ancestor stood towards fire before he had learnt to make it. He knew it then only as a strange thing utterly beyond his control, a flare on the crest of the volcano, a red destruction that poured through the forest. So it is that we know radio-activity today. This – this is the dawn of a new day in human living. . . .

'The energy we need for our very existence and with which Nature supplies us still so grudgingly, is in reality locked up in inconceivable quantities all about us. We cannot pick that lock at present, but we will. . . .

'Then that perpetual struggle for existence, that perpetual struggle to live on the bare surplus of Nature's energies will cease to be the lot of Man. Man will step from the pinnacle of this civilisation to the beginning of the next.'

Unfortunately he overdid the specific and forecast that by 1953 all the coalmines would be closed and the steel works shut down.

Sir Aston Webb, a famous architect, in January 1914, looked forward a hundred years. He took as his theme a return to London and a guided tour of the capital :

'I asked why everything looked so bright and clean, and my companion said that was because they had done away with the smoke, and only used smokeless fuel materials now.

'In a bird's-eye view I obtained of London, I noticed that, besides the railway tracks out of London, there were great arterial roads stretching out in all ways. They were 120 feet wide, and there were two divisions – one for slow moving traffic and one for swift traffic. The tramways had been done away with, and the people of the day had wireless telegraphy, wireless telephones, and wireless electric light.

'There was a belt of green round London, a sylvan glade, formed out of various town-planning schemes. My companion told me that all these things were arranged now by a Ministry of Art who had such matters referred to them.'

Sir Aston needed only half a century to have these dreams fulfilled : clean air, motorways, the green belt and a Minister for Arts.

Still more remarkable was a contribution made by Colonel J. D. Fullerton to a debate at the Royal United Services Institution on Thursday, 15 November, 1906. The *Daily Express*, with remarkable prescience, gave it front page treatment :

'There is no doubt that in the next great war flying machines will be regularly employed.

'As regards purely aerial warfare, the first object of each side will be by means of their air force to obtain command of the air. For this purpose, both sides will maintain high-speed flying machines armed with light guns.

'The aerial battles will practically settle the first period of the campaign, the victor gaining the command of the air, and all the advantages that will ensue therefrom.

'Against an enemy's sea forces the flying machines will be used chiefly for reconnoitring purposes, but it is probable that efforts will be made, by firing specially designed projectiles more or less vertically downwards on the decks of ships, seriously to damage the engines, boilers, etc., of the floating vessels.

'No doubt the flying machines will have considerable difficulty in carrying out this duty, but light high-speed machines painted so as to resemble the sky as much as possible will be able to do a great deal of damage.

'The location and destruction of submarines will possibly also be an important function of the aerial ships as their position high in the air will enable them to trace the course of vessels some thirty or forty feet below the water.'

Barely five years after the Wright Brothers' tentative lift, here was a British Colonel forecasting not merely aviation in World War I but in *World War II*. What was his reward? He was retired from the active

list in 1906. The War Office recommended in 1909 that the £2,000
a year being spent on aviation research be abandoned as an economy.
Colonel Fullerton died in 1927. His memorable address was not
recorded for reference.

Flying was still a joyous hobby when Blériot flew the English Channel
(the newspapers made the obvious noises that 'Britain is no longer an
island') and it was made a profitable one too when sponsors offered
£10,000 – the equivalent of £120,000 in the seventies – to the winners
of races from London to Paris or London to Manchester. The latter
race in April 1910 gave rise to the first night flight in England. Graham
White, the British competitor, had fallen behind his French rival,
Louis Paulhan. To make up the time, he decided to fly north through
the darkness. The *Express* man reported :

I was one of a little party of White's friends who, by the glare of
motor lamps, watched him as he started out on his mad night ride
from the field half a mile from Roade, where his aeroplane came
down last night.

It wanted more than an hour to dawn but Mr Paulhan had more
than an hour's start on the road, so Mr White's last chance lay in
catching up his rival before he could again start.

A line of dark motor-cars with dazzling lights stood in the shadows
of a hedge, and in the blackness of the field beyond there was the
aeroplane. So dark was it that even the white planes of the flying
machine could not be seen except when Mr Graham White flashed
the light of a lantern full on it.

His mother and sister begged him not to go, but he only smiled.

'I shall be safe,' he said simply. 'It is my last chance. Such a pity
to miss it.'

'Hood the motor car lamps,' came the order, and the glares were
hooded, for the lights dazzled the aviator. Another quick command,
and the motor engines were shut off and there was a sudden silence.

The same thought was in every mind but Mr Graham White's.
It was a race with death we were watching. 'Good old England!'
cried a cheering voice, and then 'Good old White!' was the cry and
three cheers rang round the shrouded field.

'Let's go!' rang out the voice of the aviator, and the Gnome
revolving motor loudly cracked. A few seconds later a misty ghostly
shape was soaring overhead, barely visible even a few feet up.

The motor-cars which were to follow the race darted off as the
aeroplane sped towards the lights of Roade Station which shone out

green and red against the heavy clouds.

The chase ran mile by mile through the darkness, and fear rode in each car. Twenty-three miles on was Rugby and as the first pursuing car rode up the hill policemen cried: 'He passed overhead at 3.28 flying strong.'

When I reached Polesworth I found the aeroplane in the hollow of a sloping field. Mr Graham White had been beaten by the wind. For fifteen minutes he battled with the air, and three times he was turned round completely. Therefore he was obliged to come down.

He descended all along by the railway line. His friends were miles behind and all he could do was to hold down the aeroplane.

Three-quarters of an hour he waited, holding the aeroplane down, and then the news spread, and at five in the morning hundreds of people flocked from Lichfield by car and dogcart and bicycle.

They gave him cheer upon cheer. He decided to start again, and willing hands dragged the aeroplane to the top of the field. There might still be a chance of wresting the glory and the prize from the Frenchman.

He never got away, for as he was on the point of starting the engine his mother and sister arrived on the field.

'Paulhan's won, dear,' gasped Mrs White. 'Then there's no hurry,' he said.

Graham White didn't even make Manchester. He took off again but having travelled little more than seven miles the canvas on the tail of his biplane became detached owing to the effects of rain. The flapping of the partly detached canvas so greatly impeded his progress that he had to come down. His machine was dismantled and returned to London by train.

On hearing of Mr Paulhan's victory Wilbur Wright declared, 'There is now no reason why a trans-Atlantic flight should not succeed.' Nine years later two Britons, Alcock and Brown, fulfilled that prophecy.

Graham White, however, did more for aviation by taking politicians aloft and convincing them of the need for aerial defence than he would ever have achieved by flying to Manchester.

With Churchill as First Lord, the Admiralty had been more alive than the War Office to the new dimension of the air. On 11 January, 1912, the *Express* recorded this important advance:

A dramatic step in connection with the development of aviation in the British Navy was taken yesterday when Lieutenant C. R. Samson

successfully accomplished a flight in a Short biplane from the deck
of the battleship *Africa* at Sheerness.

A specially designed launching stage had been constructed on the
Africa in the form of a wooden platform some 100 feet long, stretching from the fore bridge to the bows, with parallel rails reaching from
end to end and projecting a few feet out to sea.

Lieutenant Samson flew first from Eastchurch to the Isle of Grain.
There he was met by a working party of bluejackets who placed
his aeroplane on a lighter, on which it was towed out to the *Africa*,
anchored in mid-stream. It was hauled on board and placed on the
rails of the platform.

The aviator, after a preliminary inspection of the engine and plane
controls, took his place in the machine. He was wearing a white
sweater and an aviator's helmet.

A moment or two after, with his engine running at full speed,
he gave the word to let go, and the dozen or more bluejackets who
were clinging to the tail released their hold. The biplane shot down
the rails and with the grace of a bird floated out over the water.

Numerous pinnaces and tugs were scattered over the river, ready
to render help in case of accident, but the aeroplane rose steadily
without the slightest dipping and sailed away over the destroyer
Cherwell, lying some 100 yards nearer the eastern shore.

Then the aviator circled round and returned and circled round
the masts of the *Africa*, afterwards heading towards Eastchurch,
where he landed safely.

This was the first experiment of the kind ever made in connection
with a British warship.

Bulking larger by far in newspaper reports than the esoteric sport of
flying was motoring. In a leading article during the Boer War in
October 1900 the *Express* commented:

We are nowhere near a horseless age – as yet. None the less, we are
within measurable distance of an extended use of autocars for the
purposes of war. The fact that nigh a hundred thousand horses
have perished in the South African campaign is enough to make one
pause and ponder seriously over any possible escape from so appalling
a waste of substance.

The petrol car can be here, there and everywhere, so long as there
is a road to travel by, and can bridge distances with a swallow-like
flight.

Not everyone was prepared to rejoice at the onward march of the motor car. A little item in the same year headed 'An Equestrian Wedding' told how:

The Essex village of Downham has just registered a practical protest against the introduction of the motor-car into wedding ceremonies by celebrating an alliance the parties to which with their attendant knights and ladies rode on horseback to and from the church. The contracting parties were Mr A. W. Moore, a local tradesman, and Miss Agnes Thorn, a farmer's daughter. The bride wore a grey riding habit and her bridesmaids blue ones.

Young Mr Moore and Miss Thorn were making a sentimental demonstration; their livelihoods were not at risk. The chugging of the internal combustion engine, however, presaged the end of the horse-drawn cabs and far-sighted cabbies knew it.

'The London cab industry is like a consumptive patient that is gradually dying,' said Mr Sam Michaels, president of the Cab Drivers' Union, to a gathering of anxious cabmen at Clerkenwell.

'We are suffering from the scientific application of machinery to our trade. The electric tramcar is here; tomorrow the electric omnibus arrives; and after that the electrification of the District Railway.

'We were the lords of the road once; now, when the motor-cars whizz past us, we feel ashamed of ourselves, and sneak up a side turning so that the fare shall not see how slowly he is going.'

Mr Michaels urged cabmen to accept the motor-cab as inevitable, and to take every opportunity of learning to drive.

Mr Brett, a well-known cabman, took the side of the horse-drawn vehicle against the president, but was badly defeated. His chief point was that 'the vibration and the nauseous smell would tell upon the system.'

Cabmen did learn the new trade and by 1910 the horse cab had almost vanished from the streets of London and other cities. A disquieting feature was drunken driving by the taximen. Reporters recorded a day's toll at the courts in July 1911:

At Marlborough-street, Arthur Howe, aged thirty-nine, taxicab driver, was sent to prison for twenty-one days for being intoxicated while driving.

At Acton, Henry Martin, aged forty, of Riverview-grove, Chiswick, was sentenced to one month's imprisonment for being intoxicated while driving a motor-car.

At Bow-street, John Batter, taxicab driver, was remanded in custody on the charge of being intoxicated while driving, and with causing bodily harm to Louis Delvenue.

Drunken driving was bad enough. To the eyes of many non-motorists speeding or 'scorching' as it was then called was worse :

Canon Greenwell, of Durham, who on Wednesday warmly denounced scorching motorists, was asked by an *Express* representative yesterday whether he wished to amplify the statement of his views or not.

'No,' was the reply. 'I do not think I can say anything more. I am not like the Marquis of Queensberry in saying that these people should be shot, but at the same time I think it would do good if some of them were shot.

'I should like to see them horsewhipped and brought to wreck and ruin,' he added.

Authority was resolutely on the side of the pedestrian. After the abolition of the red flag law (requiring a man to walk in front of a horseless carriage) the police took it upon themselves to curb the motoring enthusiasts. A Mr Leycester Barwell of Ascot who was fined £3 for speeding observed : 'I emphatically state that it is impossible for any motorist to go through a police trap at, say, seventeen or eighteen miles an hour without being summoned for driving at twenty-seven or twenty-eight miles an hour.'

He raised a petition against police persecution for, as he pointed out, he only did his 18 miles an hour on 'a safe straight road with no one in sight.' In towns the speed limit was sterner yet.

The tradespeople of Godalming are alarmed by the threat of many of the residents in the neighbourhood to deal as little as possible in the town while the ten-mile speed limit for motor-cars is enforced as strictly as it is at present by the police.

A resident near the police trap explained that the police regard the business as a kind of sport.

Their favourite day is Sunday, and you will always find a host of children there enjoying the game as much as the police, who sometimes hide in the top window of a house ready to pounce on an unsuspecting victim.

If the police treated motorists as fair game, the Automobile Association treated the police as a foe to be beaten. From October 1905 came this report :

The campaign organised by the newly formed Automobile Association against 'police traps' began in earnest yesterday, when a large party of well-known motorists and their guests travelled down in eight cars to Guildford to test the methods adopted by the association.

The result of the day's run was another complete rout of the police, and it was evident that when the association is generally supported every road in the country will be so patrolled that 'police traps' will become a thing of the past.

At Cobham breathless association 'scouts' and 'patrols' had scented a police trap, and the members and guests cheered two cold and disgusted policemen who were seen moving their trap further up the road. The scouts, however, dogged the unfortunate 'force' who retired in confusion.

Between Ripley and Guildford the futility of the police trap was well demonstrated. Ripley village itself was quite unprotected. The police had chosen a safe piece of road without turnings or dangers of any kind to lay their trap.

One astute policeman, thinly disguised as a working man, made an attempt to get rid of one of the AA scouts by telling him he was wanted by a gentleman down the road.

This manoeuvre of the police is to be defeated by giving button badges to all members of the Association and scouts will in future be instructed to take their orders only from those wearing such badges. Among those who watched the 'sport' yesterday with keen interest were Colonel Bosworth, the chairman of the Association.

Such skirmishing was simply incidental to the inexorable drive of the automobile. Increasingly it was borne in on public opinion that not only a new means of transport, but a whole new industry had emerged. There was anguished muttering that Britain's industrial rivals were running away with the domestic market. A headline in 1902 pronounced :

CAR MARKET
IN FOREIGN HANDS

Ten years later manufacturers and traders met at the Ritz to consider the peril of 'excessive importation of cheap American motor cars'. One reader wrote to say that on a car journey from London to Carlisle two of the three cars he saw were cheap American models. The British, of course, were still building horseless carriages for the gentry, as witness this account from the 1912 Motor Show at Olympia :

> Luxurious interiors are of the utmost importance in these days, as the motoring woman is becoming an expert in the art of being comfortable, and all sorts of new refinements will be seen in this direction at Olympia.
> Soft footstools shaped like great cushions will be a popular novelty, and Venetian blinds made of polished wood is another new idea. They enable the occupants of the car to see out without being seen.

Ordinary motoring, with venetian blinds and footstools, was dear enough : a pneumatic tyre cost £12 (about £150 today) and a tyre's average life was three months.

Setting the pace for motoring as the rich man's sport was the debonair eccentric American millionaire, Gordon Bennett, proprietor of the *New York Tribune*, who had financed Stanley's search for Livingstone. Exiled from New York society after a scandal – and a threatened horsewhipping – Bennett came to live in Europe and founded the Paris-Vienna race, first in a long line of car rallies. In England Bennett gave his name to those who wanted a polite substitute for 'Gor Blimey'. It became 'Gordon Bennett' and in America the phrase was 'Oh my hat and Gordon Bennett' – Bennett having introduced a dashing form of headgear. It was his flair for the unusual, the exciting, the challenging which kept motors and motoring before the people, although only one in 1,000 could afford a car.

The Bennett era ended in 1914 when Henry Ford, paying the unprecedented wage of $5 an hour, introduced the Model T and mass standardised production ('they can have any colour, so long as it's black'). From that moment onwards those who built cars could afford to buy cars. The 'last word in luxury' was on its way to becoming an essential part of Western life.

*

Scientific advance was now pushing forward very rapidly indeed as can be gauged from the exhibits at the September 1911 electricity exhibition at Olympia :

> The nearest approach to perpetual motion yet discovered is shown on one stand. It is the 'earth-driven electric clock', the invention of Mr P. A. Bentley, a Burton-on-Trent watch and clock maker.
>
> The electric clock is driven by a power drawn direct from the earth, and once it is fixed it keeps going until its works wear out. It never requires winding.
>
> Among the electric devices at the exhibition are :
>
> Egg-boilers   Massage machines
> Vacuum cleaners   Knife polishers
> Hair-drying machines   Boot-cleaning stands
> Wasps' nest destroyers

In that same month :

> An innovation which may turn out to be epoch-making – football by night – was attempted at the Richmond Athletic Ground last night, and the experiment was attended with a satisfacory degree of success. The object was to give men who are engaged throughout the day an opportunity to practise on week-nights.
>
> Six acetylene lights were used. Two of these were hung some ten feet from the ground, but the other four were simply placed on trestles at less than half that height.
>
> Enough members of the Richmond Football Club turned out to make up the better part of two Rugby teams, and engaged in an informal practice game. It was a weird and novel sight – the men's faces shining white in the powerful glare, and outside the square of light and above it nothing but pitch-black darkness.
>
> It was agreed that for practice in passing and scrum work the innovation had admirable possibilities. The lights, however, were not high enough, for whenever the ball rose above a certain height it vanished into the upper blackness and became invisible.

The *Electrical Times* later listed further improvements including a 'complete electric cooking outfit consisting of a kettle, saucepan, frying

pan, and hot plate for 17s 6d : a breakfast cooker to stand on the table
that will grill a chop or toast bread.'

Eight months later came 'the talkies', or rather a faltering step
towards them :

Professor W. Stirling demonstrated before a distinguished audience
at the Royal Institution last night a perfect system of speaking
cinematograph films, which will have a far-reaching effect not only
in the world of entertainment but on our whole social life.

For many years inventors have been working to produce a syn-
chronised effect of gramophone and cinematograph, and two years
ago a demonstration of the 'Chronophone' – as it is called – was
given, which was not quite perfect.

Since then the inventors, Monsieur Leon Gaumont and his staff,
have overcome the difficulties that presented themselves, with the
result that living pictures, where the action is in dumb show, will in
a short time be as out of date as a boneshaker bicycle.

The Duke of Northumberland was in the chair, and after a few
explanatory remarks, the Royal Institution was the scene of a new
entertainment – the cinematograph music-hall.

The possibilities of the invention are obvious. At election times, for
instance, the great leaders can be seen and heard simultaneously in
every constituency. Records of famous people will go down to pos-
terity as they appeared and talked. Every town will be able to have
its chronophone opera house.

Carried away with the exuberance of their own inventiveness some
scientists, including Thomas Edison, saw the most glittering prospects
as being realisable. These are some of the things that didn't come :
On 31 January, 1905 :

We are in a position to give today further details of the remarkable
claims made by the Industrial and Engineering Trust Ltd to the
effect that they are able to obtain unlimited gold from sea-water at
a cost of under £10 for every £100 worth of gold extracted.

The syndicate in question is perhaps one of the strongest ever
formed in the City, including Mr Albert Sandeman, ex-governor of
the Bank of England.

Sir William Ramsay, one of the most eminent of British scientists,
has been retained by the syndicate to work solely for them in connection with the process of extracting gold from sea-water.

On 21 October, 1907:

Mr Thomas A. Edison announces that he has perfected the electric storage battery upon which he has been working for years.

Vehicles of all kinds will be able to adopt electricity as motive power by using the Edison accumulator which will only have to be re-charged at long intervals.

Mr Edison now claims to have overcome all obstacles and that motor-cars will soon be so cheap as to be within the reach of every man who can now afford to own a horse.

'I have at last succeeded in placing the electric storage battery on an economical basis,' said Mr Edison yesterday.

Mr Edison didn't stop at his own discoveries. He had visions of a whole spectrum of advances:

24 January, 1911:

Cloth, buttons, thread, tissue-paper, and pasteboard will be fed into one end of a machine and suits of clothing, packed in boxes, will come out of the other.

Nickel will be used instead of paper for books. A sheet of nickel one twenty-thousandth of an inch thick is cheaper, tougher, and more flexible than an ordinary sheet of book paper. It also will absorb printer's ink. A nickel book two inches thick would contain 40,000 pages. It would weigh only a pound, and the cost of the nickel pages would be 5s.

The most interesting of Mr Edison's predictions is that the old dream of transmutation of metals is certain to come true sooner or later, and a way will be found to manufacture gold.

The probability that the way to manufacture gold will be discovered sooner or later causes Mr Edison to believe the present financial system of the world will be changed. The time is coming, he thinks, when nobody will accept gold in payment for work, and no nation will issue gold as money, because any one will be able to manufacture it.

An *Express* exclusive on 24 January, 1911 proclaimed:

The air train has arrived! It is the most marvellous invention of the age. There is no locomotive on the air train. It needs such antiquated things no more than it needs rails. Electricity is the driving power, but it is electricity harnessed and trained to perform the apparently impossible and give a negative to nature. Electric coils hold the car in a state of suspension in the air and the magnets pull it along at terrific speed.

The Bachelet Levitated Railway is the title given to this new discovery and it takes its name from its inventor.

The inventor himself seems hardly to realise the vast possibilities of his work. Perhaps it is because he has lost some of the enthusiasm of youth, for Emile Bachelet is an old man who has spent almost a lifetime in bringing this wonder child of his to perfection.

But the saddest of all the things that never were was contained in a reflective, philosophical editorial to welcome the New Year of 1909:

The aeroplane is destined to restore calm to the feverish activity of today. When men fly they will cease to be mean and petty; they will put away little things. For the flying man is akin to the angels.

The historian of the future will say of the birth of this New Year, as Carlyle said of the birth of the French Revolution: 'The doubtful hour, with pain and blind struggle, brings forth its certainty never to be abolished.' We may look confidently to the aeroplane to put an end to war on earth for ever.

Whatever the present may say about the past, no one can deny the Edwardians the fresh taste of innocence.

*

Nowhere was wide-eyed trusting wonder better expressed than over the *Titanic*, the mightiest passenger ship in the world, the last word in luxury travel, the sea-borne miracle of the twentieth century – the unsinkable.

When she was launched in Belfast in May 1911, the *Express* Correspondent, Frank T. Buller (specially commissioned, for it was very unusual in those days to give reporters by-lines) wrote with eerily prophetic insight: 'Thus 20,000 tons of cunningly reveted steel [the *Titanic* weighed 46,000 all up] goes sliding steadfastly, surely down between the girders of the great gantry *as a glacier* glides to the sea, like some movement of fate.'

Almost a year later the newly completed vessel slipped her anchor and eased out of Southampton Water on her maiden voyage to America. Right at the start she seemed to be dogged with ill-luck :

A serious disaster was narrowly averted and a dramatic proof of the much-debated theory of 'suction' was given at the departure on her maiden voyage of the marvellous White Star liner *Titanic* – the largest steamer in the world.

As the *Titanic* passed from her berth to the open stretch of Southampton Water the gigantic new liner 'sucked' the water between her and the quay to such a degree that the strain broke the strong hawsers with which the liner *New York* was moored to the quayside, and for some time a collision between the two vessels looked likely.

Happily the prompt action of the men in command and the quick use of a couple of steam tugs prevented a collision, and the mighty *Titanic* at last steamed away down Southampton Water like a proud Queen of the Seas an hour late but not at all worried.

It is not very long since the *Majestic* was regarded as one of the world's wonders. This morning we looked down and laughed a kindly laugh at her and the two American line (*) boats moored beside her. They seemed such small affairs, with their 10,000 or 11,000 tons, compared with the *Titanic*'s 46,000.

Having looked down on the world from the *Titanic*'s boat deck, I went on the quay and looked up at the projecting heads of the passengers. It was like standing by the wall of St Paul's Cathedral and craning your neck to get a glimpse of the Apostles on the roof.

On the morning of Monday, 15 April, 1912, the news was received in New York that the *Titanic* had struck an iceberg and sunk. The first stop press announcement in the UK stated :

New York, Monday 15 April.
The *Titanic* sank at 2.20 this morning.
No lives were lost – Reuter.

The second, on the same page immediately below the first said :

*American ships were, however, rather more solicitous of passenger comfort and convenience. Some British lines still insisted on a general lights out and individuals could only switch on cabin lights by getting a doctor's permission via the steward.

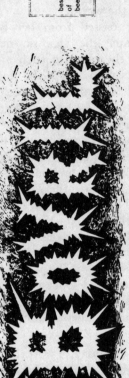

MANY LIVES LOST

New York, Monday, 15 April.
The White Star officials now admit
that many lives have been lost – Reuter.

Few events have caused such total disbelief as the sinking of the *Titanic*.
It was impossible. Things like that didn't happen any more. Some
people began to ask if it were perhaps divine judgement on a rich,
uncaring society that believed itself immune to disaster. Others, more
prosaic, pointed to the needless speed as the *Titanic* attempted to win
the Blue Riband for the fastest crossing of the Atlantic, that desire for
prestige and profit had sent 1,513 people to a needless death.

Three days after the disaster, the *Express* published two stanzas by
an anonymous poet and an exchange in Parliament that summed up
the current attitudes :

> They listened to wondrous music, in rooms
>   that were planned for kings;
> Beautiful notes from beautiful throats,
>   sung as a songbird sings :
> They revelled in baths of marble, like the
>   baths of ancient Rome,
> Twas a wondrous trip on a wondrous ship,
>   The ship that never came home.
>
> Music and baths and splendour, but where
>   are the noble men,
> Saying good-byes with glistening eyes – that
>   never shall glisten again?
> They called it a floating palace, and they
>   found it a funeral urn;
> Crowded by a fate with a hero freight,
>   The ship that can never return.

Colonel Yate, MP, asked the Postmaster General if the false wireless
messages – initially saying that the *Titanic* had been taken in tow, then
that there were no casualties – might have been prompted by the wish
to reduce the premiums for reinsurance. The Postmaster General referred the Colonel to the Board of Trade.

The Board itself was deeply embarrassed by Press disclosures that lifeboats, not only on the *Titanic* but many other famous British liners
were grossly insufficient. The *Olympic*, the *Titanic*'s sister ship, for

instance could provide lifeboat accommodation for only one-third of passengers and crew.

Harrowing scenes of distraught relatives and friends desperate to discover the fate of their loved ones were described in the press on 16 April:

> By the time the White Star office in New York opened this morning the lower Broadway front of the Shipping Trust's building was blocked with people, many weeping and hysterical, and inquiring for more news than that contained in the slow arriving list of survivors on the *Carpathia*.
>
> Mrs Benjamin Guggenheim, the wife of the 'smelter king' became hysterical when informed that her husband's name had not yet been received as saved. She offered all her wealth to charter a steamship to return to the scene of the wreck and continue the search.
>
> Mr Cornell, a prominent magistrate, was about to inquire at the desk about his wife when the woman in front of him – Mrs Weir – was told that there was no news of her husband, and she fainted in his arms. She was carried to her motor-car.
>
> Every effort was made at the New York theatres to keep the news of the disaster from the audience. Several spectators in one theatre who secured early information and were discussing it were requested to leave.

Dismay, wrath and bewilderment spread among the relatives. Why had the ship sailed on despite warnings of ice floes? Why had so many hours elapsed before radio calls from the doomed ship were answered? Why were so few of the steerage class passengers saved? What really went on after the pitifully few boats were lowered?

A Court of Inquiry was established under Lord Mersey. It sat in the Scottish Hall, Buckingham Gate, during May and June and took evidence from crew, expert witnesses and survivors. The Attorney-General, Sir Rufus Isaacs, made it plain that uninterrupted speed on the shortest route to America was the main cause of the disaster:

> 'The *Titanic* was warned of the ice fields towards which she was steaming but, beyond orders being given to the look-out to keep a sharp watch for ice, nothing was done.
>
> 'No reduction of speed was made. She travelled on through the afternoon and through the night at the speed of twenty-one knots until she struck the iceberg.'

Then came graphic descriptions of what happened from members of the crew. Seaman Joseph Scarrott:

'Three bells sounded (the look-out man's warning) about 11.30 p.m. I rushed on deck to see what was causing the ship to tremble.

'I saw ice on the starboard side of the deck,' he said. 'I looked over the rail and saw the iceberg we struck. It was then about abeam [amidships].

'Then the ship answered her helm, and swung clear of the iceberg which was about as high as the boat deck.'

'What was it like?' asked the examining barrister, Mr Aspinall, KC.

'It looked like the Rock of Gibraltar.'

The order came to get the boats ready. Scarrott helped to clear four of the boats for lowering, and then went to the boat which was his proper station – No 14. His boat was filled with women and children.

'Some men – foreigners – tried to rush the boat before the women and children,' he continued. 'They could not understand the orders I gave them, and I had to use a little persuasion with the boat's tiller.

'One man jumped in twice,' added Scarrott, 'and I had to throw him out the third time.

'Mr Lowe, the fifth officer, came and asked me how many there were in the boat. I told him as far as I could count, fifty-four women, and four children, one of them a baby in arms. Then there was myself, two firemen and three stewards.

'I told him of the bit of trouble about the rushing business,' continued Scarrott, 'and saying "All Right" he pulled his revolver and fired two shots between the boat and the ship's side as a warning to men not to jump into it. He fired into the water.'

Scarrott said in reply to questions that the people in the boats behaved 'exceptionally well'. There was a fresh supply of drinking water in his boat, but no lamp.

First and second-class passengers, he said, would have a better chance of getting into the boats because they had access to the deck from which the boats were lowered. (In later evidence a steward, John Hart, testified that a large number of third-class passengers refused to put on lifebelts or enter the boats. They believed, to the end, that they were safer on the *Titanic*.)

Scarrott added that before the *Titanic* left Southampton he did not see the boats overhauled for the purpose of ascertaining whether they had in them the articles required by the Board of Trade regulations.

An equally casual approach affected medical examinations. The look-out, a man named Lee, at the time of the fatal impact recalled that 'the doctors did not pay particular attention to my eyes. There was an inspection at Southampton but the doctor simply came along and made a casual examination.'

Able Seaman Poindestre testified to panic when the bulkhead between the flooded forecastle and the third-class cabins gave way :

'Did the passengers behave well?' he was asked, and he replied, 'They did not where I was.'

'What were they doing? 'They were trying to rush boats Nos 12 and 14.'

'Did you have to keep them back?' 'Yes, I and Mr Lightoller and the other two sailors did to the best of our ability. They could not lower the boats as they ought to have done because the men passengers were on the boat-falls crowding round and they could not get them clear.'

Charles Hendrickson, a fireman, had a sinister story to tell :

'An officer, who was lowering the emergency boat, which is smaller than the others, called out for any of the seamen. There were none about. So he told several firemen who were near, including myself, to get in.

'We saw the *Titanic* sink but our boat did not go back to pick up anybody. I proposed going back but they would not listen to me – none of the passengers or anybody else. We were about a hundred or two hundred yards away.'

'Am I to understand,' Lord Mersey asked, 'that when you were picked up by the *Carpathia* [the rescue ship] there were only twelve people in your boat?'

'Yes,' answered Hendrickson.

Of these twelve, how many belonged to the crew? Seven. There were five passengers, two seamen and four others. The passengers were two women and three men.

Who was it that objected?

'The passengers,' said Hendrickson.

'You say they were only five,' Lord Mersey said. 'Did the men object?'

'No. They said nothing,' was the answer.

'Did the women object? – Yes.

'You had room in your boat for a dozen more. What were the names of the passengers? –I heard the name of one of the passengers.

'What was that? –Duff Gordon.

'Did you hear the names of the others? –I think his wife was there, Lady Duff-Gordon.

'Did his wife object? –Yes, she was scared to go back in case of being swamped.

'Was there, so far as you know, any danger of the boat being swamped if you had gone back? –It would certainly be dangerous.

'Did you hear people crying for help? –Yes.

'In the presence of these cries from the drowning were you the only one to propose to go back to the rescue? –I never heard anyone else.

'When Lady Duff-Gordon objected did her husband reprove her? –He upheld her.

'He did not try to get her courage up to go back? –No.

'Tell me what each person said when you proposed to go back,' Lord Mersey asked.

'Duff-Gordon and his wife said it was dangerous, and that we should be swamped. I did not hear anybody else say it.

'Am I to understand then,' the President said, 'that because two of the passengers said it would be dangerous, you all kept your mouths shut and made no attempt to rescue any one?'

'That is right, sir.'

'Was any money given to you by any of the passengers when you got on the *Carpathia*? –Yes.

'What did you receive? –An order for £5.

'Who from? –Duff Gordon.

'What did other members of the crew get? –The same.'

Lord Mersey, in his low deliberate voice, put a question to him slowly: 'Did you know,' he asked, 'at the time that you would receive the £5?'

'No,' answered the fireman. 'Are you sure? –Yes.

'It came as a pleasant surprise? –Oh, yes! Of course.'

Mr Hendrickson claimed that the promise of money was made only when they were in sight of the *Carpathia* and not as an inducement to go straight there without attempting to rescue any other passengers.

How it was on another boat was described by Mrs Esther Hart who with her husband, Ben, and her daughter, Eva, were among the passengers for Canada.

'I knew that there was a cry of "She's sinking!" I heard hoarse shouts of "Women and children first", and then from boat to boat we were hurried, only to be told "already full". Four boats we tried and at the fifth there was room. Eva was thrown in first, and I followed her.

'Just then a man who had previously tried to get in succeeded in doing so, but was ordered out and the officer fired his revolver into the air to let every one see it was loaded, and shouted out: "Stand back, I say! Stand back! The next man who puts his foot in this boat I will shoot down like a dog."

'Ben [Mr Hart] who had been doing what he could to help the women and children said quietly, "I'm not going in, but for God's sake look after my wife and child." And little Eva called out to the officer with the revolver, "Don't shoot my daddy! You shan't shoot my daddy."

'That was the last I saw of my poor lost dear – no farewell kiss, no fond word – but in a moment he had gone and we were hanging over the sea – fifty or sixty feet above it, and then there were two or three horrible jerks as the boat was lowered from the davits and we were in the water, so crowded that we could scarcely move.

'The duty that the officer allotted to me was to bale the water out of the boat. While sitting here I had the impression that there was somebody near me who ought not to be there. So when I could get my elbows free I put my hand down under the seat and touched a human form.

'It was a poor wretch of a man who had smuggled himself into the boat and had sat there during all that awful time, under the seat, in about six inches of water. When we got him out he was so stiff he could scarcely move.'

The climax of the inquiry came with the appearance in the witness box of Mr Bruce Ismay, Managing Director of White Star.

He was charged with the terrible offence of saving his own life, with being privy to the driving of the *Titanic* at high speed into the ice region, and with being managing director of a company whose ship did not carry enough lifeboats to accommodate all on board.

Mr Ismay stood the hours of questioning and the glaring of

hundreds of pairs of eyes with a smile of cheerfulness. He smiled when he stepped into the witness-box, he smiled all the time he was there, and he smiled when he stepped out.

Perhaps the bitterest moment was when he was asked about his own escape, and he admitted that he knew that hundreds of persons who were still on the ship must go down with her when she sank.

His hands moved about uneasily. But still he smiled grimly.

'You, as managing director of the company were interested in the speed of the vessel? –Yes.

'Your intention was to get to the maximum speed before you reached New York? – The intention was, if the weather was suitable on Monday or Tuesday, to drive her for a few hours at full speed.

'There was no slowing down of the vessel after that ice report was read? –Not that I know of.

'You knew, of course, that the proximity of icebergs was a danger? –There is always more or less danger with ice.

'Had you no curiosity to know whether or not you would be travelling in the region in which ice was reported? –I had not. I knew we were in the region of ice.

'Did not the Marconi message convey to you that it was desirable to ascertain whether the latitude and longitude designated in that Marconigram would be the track you would have to pass?'

Mr Ismay replied that the captain was responsible for the navigation of the ship.

'Did you have any conversation with Captain Smith about the ice between the time of his giving you the wireless message and the impact with the iceberg? – The only conversation I had with Captain Smith was in the smoke-room on that night. As he walked out of the smoke-room he asked me if I had a Marconi message. I said, "Yes, I have," and I gave it to him.

'You had not been on the bridge?' asked the President.

'I had never been on the bridge during the whole trip,' was the reply.

'Is it your statement,' asked the Attorney-General, 'that from first to last on that Sunday you never had any conversation with Captain Smith about ice?'

'Absolutely,' was the reply.

'Or any other person? –Or any other person.'

The undoubted implication of the Attorney-General's questions was that Bruce Ismay had brought the power of rank in the White Star Line to warp the Captain's judgement and force him to go hell-for-leather to New York regardless of the iceberg menace.

From the representative of the men's unions came the cruellest questions heard during the proceedings:

Mr Ismay stated, in reply to a question by Mr Clem Edwards that he put the Marconigram warning to the *Titanic* of the proximity of ice in his pocket in a fit of absent-mindedness, and kept it there for five hours.

'If you had not held the view that the *Titanic* was unsinkable, would you have insisted on provision being made for a larger number of lifeboats? —No, I think not. She had all the Board of Trade required – in fact, largely in excess of the Board of Trade requirements.

'Did you get into a boat when the *Titanic* was sinking? —I did.

'Did you know there were some hundreds of people in that ship? —Yes.

'And that they must go down with it?' Mr Ismay nodded.

'Do you agree that, apart from the captain, you, as the responsible managing director, owed your life to every other person in that ship?' The President said he did not think that was a question which should be put to Mr Ismay.

'According to your statement, Mr Ismay, you entered this boat last of all? —Yes.

'So that if a witness says you entered the boat earlier and helped the women and children in that would not be true? – It would not.

'You say you took an active part in giving directions for women and children to be placed in the boat? —I did so far as I could.

'If you took this active part, why did you not continue and send others to see if there were any other passengers available for this last boat? —I was standing by the last boat watching everybody in and as the boat was being lowered away I got in.

'That does not quite answer the question. You had taken a responsible part, according to the evidence, in the filling of the boats? —I had not. I had helped women and children into the boats.

'Is it not a fact that you were calling out "Women and children first?" —Yes.

'If you took an active part at that stage, why did you not continue the active part and give instructions or go yourself to the other decks to see if there were other people you could find a place

in your boat? –I presumed that there were people down below who
were sending them up.

The President suggested that Mr Edwards' point was that, according
to Mr Ismay's position, it was his duty to remain in the ship until she
went down.

'Yes,' replied Mr Edwards. 'Frankly that is so. I don't flinch from
it a little bit. I want to ask Mr Ismay why, inasmuch as he took
upon himself to give certain directions at a certain time, he did not
discharge the responsibility ever after in regard to the passengers.'
'The boat was actually being lowered,' said Mr Ismay. 'There
were no more passengers who could have been got into that boat.'

Bruce Ismay was held blameless by the committee which commented :
he assisted many passengers and had he not jumped into the last boat
on the starboard side he would merely have added one more life to
the number of those lost. Guilt for the disaster was placed firmly on
the *Titanic*'s excessive speed :

'It is a proposition really beyond controversy,' said Sir Rufus Isaacs,
'that had the speed of the *Titanic* been materially reduced the
Titanic would not have been lost, or if she had been lost no lives
would have been lost.
'What is established beyond doubt,' said the Attorney-General, 'is
that if this vessel, instead of going twenty-two knots an hour, had
proceeded at a moderate speed of say, eight or ten knots, although
it might have been that she would not have avoided collision with
the iceberg, yet she would not have sunk, or if she had sunk she
would have been kept afloat for a sufficient time for the *Carpathia*
to have reached her and saved all the passengers.'

Heavy censure also fell on the liner *California* which was in view of
the *Titanic* when the collision with the iceberg took place; saw the
distress flares sent from the *Titanic*'s deck yet did nothing about it.
Whether – as has been suggested – the lookout crew of the *California*
were drunk or whether they took the flares to be celebratory fireworks
no one will ever know because no one on the *California* was telling.
Mystery and confusion, and a sense of horror still surround the
sinking of the *Titanic*. Did Ismay push Captain Smith to go for the
record and was Smith saddled with the blame because he was dead

whilst Ismay – and his powerful friends – were very much alive? (Bruce Ismay survived until 1937.) Were the third-class passengers given third class treatment while the privileged were helped to safety? Social writers have said the *Titanic* was a microcosm of all that was wrong with pre-1914 life. So the courage of wealthy, high-born British and American men has been obscured by the few cases of cowardice and selfishness. Whether the *Titanic* went down with the band playing 'Nearer My God to Thee' or a ragtime melody is neither here nor there. A lot of people met their end bravely. A code of conduct *did* exist. It existed in one of the endless little echoes of the catastrophe; one reported from Lille more than a year after the sinking in June 1913:

> A tragedy which was the outcome of the loss of the *Titanic* occurred at Hennin-Lietard, near Lille, yesterday.
>
> Among the *Titanic*'s passengers reported lost was Mme Brenys, whose husband after some months' mourning, married again.
>
> A few days ago, Monsieur Brenys learned that his first wife had escaped drowning, that she had just returned from America, and that she was trying to find him.
>
> He was so horrified at the prospect of a charge of bigamy and of the humiliation of his second 'wife' that he determined to kill himself and her. Yesterday afternoon he shot his second wife dead, and fired two bullets at himself. As death did not ensue he tried to hang himself, but the neighbours, who had heard the revolver shots, cut him down, and he is now in hospital, with a policeman guarding his bed.

Monsieur Brenys faced a murder charge but he was fortunate in this at least: the French did not exact the same degree of punishment for this kind of crime as did the English. In this, as in so many other ways, the two nations were far apart.

CHAPTER EIGHT

Nearest - Not Dearest

France, Britain's nearest but far from dearest neighbour, was regarded by press and public in the UK as the land of exaggerated gallantry, scandalous behaviour and political buffoonery as though the country's affairs were being conducted by Offenbach. In British eyes French merits – more and more pronounced as the century wore on – were that they were bitterly opposed to Germany ('My enemy's enemy is my friend') and that they were less and less a menace to Britain, either in colonisation or trade.

Coverage of French news concentrated on the bizarre, such as this telegram from Constantinople :

> Three French officers, one of them escorting a lady, were at the 'Concordia' a music hall in Pera. At the end of the performance the Frenchmen left the lady for an instant to get her cloak, etc., when a Turkish officer insulted the lady grossly.
>
> One of the Frenchmen promptly ran up and slapped the Turk's face. The latter drew his sword, but the Frenchman drew a revolver and shot his adversary dead.

Nowhere was duelling so closely identified with honour as in France. Ladies were sometimes – but far from always – the cause of the feud and social class was no barrier to indulging in the noble art of maiming by sword, pistol or whip.

The last was the chosen weapon of two Parisian cabbies. The *Express* of 4 April, 1910 recounted :

> Two cabdrivers, Jean Thibault and Pierre Roux, who occupied the same stand in the Boulevard des Batignelles and had been on excellent terms, quarrelled last week on making the hapless discovery that they were in love with the same washerwoman.
>
> Neither of them had proposed to Marie Hamard, the all-uncon-

scious object of their affections, and they decided to fight the matter out to settle who had a better claim before either of them approached the object of their affection.

A combat took place in a quiet street. It was a duel on totally novel lines. There were no seconds and the weapons were whips, with which the combatants mercilessly laced each other.

They were exhausted and bathed in blood when a policeman arrived on the scene and took them to the police station. Yesterday morning they were dismissed with a caution, and happily their enmity has been again turned to friendship for the washerwoman on hearing of their story, hastened to the cab-stand, where she expressed her regret at having caused the trouble and added that she had already been engaged for some time to a plumber.

A less bloody encounter had occurred shortly before when two sixty-year-old Senators decided that they could only resolve a political difference in a committee by recourse to the duelling ground. It was a colourful affair. Monsieur Lacroix, an ex-Minister for the Colonies, proceeded to the Parc des Princes in a motor car, leading a procession of vehicles containing thirty journalists and photographers. Swords were the chosen weapons. The newspaper account continued :

Monsieur Lacroix wore the usual unstarched shirt but his opponent set a new fashion in duelling costumes by appearing in an armless flannel singlet, trousers and white gloves. Monsieur Lintilbac was badly pressed by Monsieur Lacroix and after a minute and a half he was wounded in the wrist.

The surgeons decided that the wound was too serious to allow Monsieur Lintilbac to proceed, so the duellists proceeded to the Senate, where their friends congratulated them.

A much more outlandish contest involved the former Finance Minister, Joseph Caillaux, whose wife was at the time, May 1914, accused of murder. Caillaux alleged that he had been slandered by his opponent in a by-election. He challenged Monsieur d'Allières to a duel, and did so with a fair amount of confidence for, as the *Express* correspondent recorded :

From inquiries I have made I learn that if the duel is allowed, Monsieur Caillaux, having the choice of weapons as the offended party, will choose pistols. He declares that he will exact severe conditions. Monsieur Caillaux is one of the best shots in France. Both he and Monsieur d'Allières belong to a class in which the art of swordmanship and shooting is part of their social equipment.

Monsieur Caillaux's prowess as a crack shot is known. 'He can hit a five-franc piece thrown up in the air at a distance of seventy feet,' I was told by a friend of his to-night.

If the duel takes place, it will be the most sensational political duel in France.

The duel did take place, and the setting was as dramatic as could be imagined :

The assistance of Monsieur Rouzier-Dourcières was sought. He is the famous director of duels – a figure of the France of 1840 – slouch-hatted, with flowing moustaches and imperial, and a deadly swordsman.

Let us now set the scene for the last act in this encounter where an outraged ex-Minister seeks to establish his honour. In the open space of the velodrome of the Parc des Princes, where the cinder track for bicycle races circles the unkempt grass, the cinematographer was adjusting his tripod and the photographers were busy with focus and lens.

A little group emerged. First there was Monsieur d'Allières, immaculately dressed in a shiny silk hat – a tall, handsome, distinguished-looking man. His seconds followed him – the Count de Ludre and the Duke de la Rochefoucauld. Monsieur d'Allierès had also brought his doctor, Dr Lebreux, as a guarantee of good faith.

A few moments later another group came on the ground, Monsieur Ceccaldi carrying the case of pistols, tied with a string, under his arm; General Dalstein, thin and wiry, with the trim grey moustaches of a military man. In the middle Monsieur Caillaux walked, silk-hatted, frock-coated, his watch chain glinting in the sun, a little pearl set deeply in his necktie.

Monsieur Dourcières solemnly inspected the ground. The seconds, with a great deal of gesticulation, discussed the final details. The dreadful moment came for the draw for places, and Monsieur Caillaux drew the first choice. He chose a position facing south. Twenty-five paces away stood Monsieur d'Allières.

Courage, mon brave.' They were photographed. Monsieur Ceccaldi loaded the pistols with grim care. He was photographed. He gave the weapons to General Dalstein, who directed the duel, and

General Dalstein handed one to Monsieur Caillaux – it was photo-graphed.

Another to Monsieur d'Allières. It was also photographed.

'*Etes-vous prêts, messieurs?*' asked General Dalstein. They stood with their pistols hanging at their side. That dread moment came when the whirring of the cinematograph caused the duellists to look frightfully cross with each other.

'*Allez, messieurs!*' General Dalstein said. The pistols were raised. 'Feu!'

Bang!

Monsieur d'Allières fired on the ground.

Bang!

Monsieur Caillaux fired in the air.

One of Frances's leading duellists of the Edwardian era was Count Ismael de Lesseps, son of the builder of the Suez Canal, who, when not actually fighting himself (he had three contests with Count Just de Poligny in May 1910) acted as a second for his friends. The excessive chivalry and absurd conventions that led to some of these duels is perfectly illustrated by the case of the smoking compartment.

Monsieur Payer, a Paris manufacturer, and the Marquis de Campollano fought a duel, allegedly over the Marquis smoking in the presence of a well-known dancer, La Belle Otero, a fact which enraged Monsieur Payer. Accounts to this effect appeared in the French Press prompting the Marquis's second, Count de Lesseps to write a per-emptory correction to the duelling expert of the *Petit Journal,* the same Rouzier-Dourcieres who had umpired the Caillaux duel. Most news-papers in Europe carried the Count's epistle :

'Sir, I count on your good faith, and the care you are known to have for the truth, to set straight the facts which you set forth in your newspaper on Sunday. It would appear from your article on the duel that the Marquis de Campollano, to whom I am related, and who typifies Castilian bravery, is not, however, imbued with those tradi-tions of courtesy on which the Spanish people justly pride them-selves.

'Therefore, I ask you to correct a few errors in regard to the genesis of the affair you reported. If the Marquis de Campollana had jumped into a railway carriage and had lit a cigar under the nose of La Belle Otero he certainly would have violated the elementary rules of good-breeding and civility. But things did not pass thus.

'The Marquis de Campollano, lieutenant in the Cavalry of the King's Guard, was proceeding on duty from Paris to Madrid. Lunching in the wagon-restaurant of the Sud-express, facing the corridor, and back to back with some other passengers, he lit a cigarette. The train had already crossed the frontier and was on Spanish territory.

'A gentleman got up, and, going to Campollano, asked him in peremptory language not to smoke. The Marquis de Campollano pointed out that in Spain it was a usual custom to smoke in a restaurant. La Belle Otero, whom the Marquis had not noticed, then intervened, and declared "In any case it annoys me."

'The Marquis de Campollano at once threw away his cigarette and made excuses. Then, turning to Monsieur Payer, he said: "There are two ways of making a remark – courteous or discourteous. You employed the discourteous manner and I ask for reparation." He offered his card, but Monsieur Payer threw it on the ground. Blows were about to be exchanged, but the lunchers intervened. Monsieur Payer in his turn offered his card.'

A contest duly took place and by common accord between the seconds the fight was stopped after both combatants had been wounded in their sword arms.

La Belle Otero, a notorious courtesan, was the daughter of a Spanish gipsy and a Greek army officer, and knew all about duelling. Her father was killed in a duel and her mother promptly married the victor. She herself enraged so many of her colleagues on the stage that she did fight a duel and until her death at 97 bore a scar beside her left breast. La Belle's fiery temper was said to be a trait that attracted some of the most fascinating men of the time, including Edward VII and Kaiser Wilhelm.

One of still more violent temper was Madame Paissant, wife of a Paris clothing manufacturer. Out for dinner with her husband one night in July 1914 she objected to him looking at other women. For some reason or other they were both armed and fought a wild West duel in the garden. They both took shelter behind trees and shrubs, firing the while until Madame Paissant proved, once again, that the female of the species is more deadly than the male by putting a bullet clear through her husband's heart. She was acquitted on a plea of crime passionnelle.

It was, not surprisingly, a woman who provided France, and Europe, with a court case that ranks as one of the most dramatic of La Belle Epoque.

'Imagine Their Majesties sitting on two golden thrones under a 20-foot purple-and-gold canopy supported by 12 slender bronze columns and surmounted by a dazzling dome . . . such splendours few rulers of the earth have enjoyed.' The Nizam of Hyderabad pays homage to his King Emperor at the Delhi Durbar.

Fully protected against the sun . . . King George V and companions taking lunch during a Royal shoot in Nepal, 1912.

The type of tramcar hi-jacked by the Russian anarchists. '"You have got to drive the tram," said a man with a foreign accent pressing the warm muzzle of a recently-fired revolver against Conductor Wyatt's cheek.'

'The long history of London contains no incident so sensational as the desperate battle in Sidney Street between two Russian anarchists and a force of about 1,000 soldiers and policemen.' Mr Winston Churchill, the Home Secretary, urges on the forces of law and order.

It concerned Thérèse Humbert, whose extraordinary fraud provided the factual basis for the story 'The Million Pound Note'. Fletcher Robinson, special correspondent in Paris, sketches in the background :

Four persons take their stand in the dock of the Seine Assize Court. They are Madame Humbert, Frédéric Humbert, her husband, and Romaine and Emile Daurignac, her brothers.

The Daurignacs were born in the southern province of Gascony. They were of peasant parentage, the children of a strange old man, who proclaimed himself a sorcerer to his neighbours, and eked out a shabby-genteel existence on his little vineyard.

Thérèse Daurignac – the Madame Humbert of the future – was from her birth a notable liar and schemer. At thirteen she was accused of forging her father's name. Five years later she had obtained fashionable gowns from the tradesmen of Toulouse by declaring her approaching marriage with a rich man who never existed.

In her youth, as in her middle age, her expression was innocent, vacuous, stupid. She seemed indeed to strangers the very person who would be the victim of successful fraud. She lisped, increasing thereby her appearance of simplicity. Even her conversation was commonplace. She might have been a typical shopkeeper's wife – one of those good women who sit and pant behind the cashier's desk in so many French shops, with bunches of keys jangling at their ample waists.

Yet it was by her marriage to Frédéric Humbert that Thérèse obtained the strongest card she ever played. His father was one of the life senators, and climbed to the lofty office of Minister of Justice. It was her relation of this illustrious citizen that brought Madame Humbert into the best political society in France.

It was curious to notice that Thérèse managed to deceive the Humberts on her marriage to Frédéric by representing that she was bringing a dowry of £12,000, of which she did not possess a penny.

Emile and Romaine, her brothers, lived with her in Paris.

With such birth and breeding, husband and relations, did Madame Humbert invade Paris in 1879. Callous and impudent, but incredibly greedy for gold, she set to work to gather the money for which she longed.

The story she invented ran thus :

As she was getting into a train at Nice she saw a stranger in an apoplectic fit. She sprang into the carriage as the train was in motion and tenderly nursed the invalid. The stranger was a certain American, Robert Crawford by name. Shortly afterwards Robert Crawford died, leaving the lady who had assisted him every dollar he possessed in the world. It was then discovered that this legacy amounted to the extraordinary sum of four millions sterling. But people fought shy· of this tale, refusing to lend money to a lady who should not have been a borrower if in possession of £160,000 a year (£2,000,000 at present values). And so a pair of brothers, Robert and Henry Crawford, nephews of Robert Crawford the first, were promptly called into existence.

These phantom gentlemen produced, according to Thérèse, a second will made at the same time and place as the former, by which she was only left £10,000 a year. Yet these noble nephews were almost as generous as their uncle. They were multi-millionaires themselves; they respected the memory of their uncle, and they proposed that one of them should marry Marie Daurignac, Thérèse's sister.

If this could be arranged they would compromise over the will, giving Thérèse a large share. In the meanwhile the four millions sterling in securities was to be locked up in a safe in Madame Humbert's possession until the marriage was accomplished.

These securities were not to be mortgaged or exchanged, and if Monsieur and Madame Humbert failed in a single clause of the agreement they would get nothing more than the £10,000 a year left to Madame Humbert.

You will observe how admirable was the scheme which Thérèse had invented. She had the money there safe enough; but she could not touch it, or mortgage it, or exchange it. And thus began the story of the mystery millions in the great safe upon which she borrowed fortune after fortune for a quarter of a century, promising to pay huge interest when the matter was decided, and she and the Crawfords had divided the spoil.

In a little room in her town house stood the famous safe, patent to the world. And from its possession there came immediate wealth to Madame Humbert. She conducted her borrowing in a style of Eastern finance. From Monsieur Schotzmans, of Lille, she got £280,000; from Monsieur Girard she got £248,000; from Monsieur Lefèvre, £168,000; from Monsieur Gatheau £160,000; from Monsieur Paul Bernard £120,000; from Monsieur Brugnère £104,000, and so on through the list of bankers, brokers, jewellers, and the mighty ones of Jewish finance. With these great sums she bought herself the magnificent 'Castle of the Living Waters' – des Vives Eaux – with its splendid rooms, its flowing river, its pleasure craft and gardens. Her town house she filled with world-famous pictures, with marble staircases, with silver and gold plate, and every luxury that money can buy.

Her opera box, obtained by political intrigue, was rented at £1,200 a year. She had possessions in Tunis and in the Argentine. Some of these she paid for, some she did not.

Her debtors were dazzled with the scintillations that radiated from this remarkable safe as from a necklace of diamonds. Time after time the unfortunate banker or merchant who had lent her money found himself on the brink of ruin, beggared of all his possessions, and chose death as the easiest way to end his broken existence. Not that they doubted her; but they could wait no longer for the end of the lawsuits that still closed the safe. Girard put a bullet in his brain. Bernard asphyxiated himself with prussic acid, Schotzmans was found assassinated in a train, and others sought their deaths in various manners. But Thérèse Humbert still went on her way unmoved by the trail of blood she left behind her.

As time went by, and youth was no longer a bar to the marriage between her sister Marie and one of the Crawfords, Madame Humbert started her phantom litigation. The phantom nephews began to fight her over the phantom money in the safe. Their non-appearance was explained by eccentricity; and these creatures of her brain continued, by letters she concocted, to instruct their lawyers to proceed in one way or another for year after year.

The best lawyers in Paris were engaged on both sides. Sometimes the Crawfords demanded that Madame Humbert should procure a marriage between one of them and her sister Marie, who was supposed to object to the union from religious motives. Sometimes, Madame Humbert was appealing for liberty to open the safe, sometimes to keep it closed; sometimes the Crawfords suggested a settlement and a division of the property; sometimes they refused it.

And all the while Thérèse Humbert was exclaiming to the world about the persecution which the Crawfords inflicted upon her, and was telling her creditors that in another month or so the cases would be decided, the safe would be opened and her debts, with the vast interest she had promised paid.

But the net began to close round, and after twenty-five years of success the end was at hand. The editor of the *Matin* took the matter up, and in 1902 a new creditor began an action against her, in which he denied the existence of the Crawfords, and demanded the opening of the safe. To this her counsel, ignorant of the real state of affairs, agreed.

Parisians will never forget the morning on which the safe was opened. A great crowd thronged the doors, and round the safe where the locksmiths were at work gathered the dupes, still hopeful that the opening of the doors would show them the wealth that would restore their fortunes.

The door crashed open, and at once there rose from every lip a cry: 'There is nothing there!' One creditor tore his hair; another fell in epilepsy on the floor; another hung on the door of the safe staring inside with insane insistence.

The Humberts, too, had gone – disappeared, leaving no trace – and months were to pass by before their lurking place in Spain was discovered, and they were brought back to Paris to meet the trial.

Madame Humbert's defence was almost breathtaking as her pretence:

As the lady stood in the dock, holding a paper in her right hand, dead silence fell upon the court.

She began her extraordinary narrative in that peculiar low pitched, doleful tone of voice to which she has so accustomed us during the last ten days. 'I have said that I would speak,' she said. 'I wanted an honest and independent jury. I am confident in the result. I have always been honest, otherwise I could not bear to live. But I am strong, for I have always done my duty. I have never deceived anybody.'

In this style Madame Humbert went on, making disjointed and somewhat rambling statements.

She explained that she had been in the habit of lending money to a banker, Monsieur Bernhardt, who committed suicide a few years ago. One day she was induced to advance him a very large sum. The Crawfords got to hear of it, and accused her of having broken the trust by touching the Crawford money.

'We refuse to leave it in your keeping any longer,' they said, and she allowed them to take charge of it whenever they considered there was a danger of the safe being sequestrated by the law, or by the creditors – or when she went on a journey.

When she received notice that the safe was about to be opened by order of a judge, the millions were in the keeping of the

Crawfords. She went to the nephew, and asked for the money to be put back in the safe, but he refused. 'The judge would impound the money,' he said. 'Then give me enough to pay off all my creditors and I will abandon the rest to you,' Madame pleaded in desperation. The obdurate man refused. 'No; it is no use, my uncle would never agree to it.'

'I will have you arrested for illegally detaining the fortune,' Madame had threatened. 'We do not care; you cannot do anything to us. Our name is not Crawford at all,' answered the young man.

All this was told by Madame Humbert with an infinite number of digressions into side issues. The people in court had laughed outright at several points in the story.

Now Madame Humbert became dramatic; she spoke quickly and in an impressive tone and everybody opened his mouth and strained his ears as the great woman came to her 'terrible secret.'

'Gentlemen, when Crawford told me that that was not the name of his father and of his uncle, I asked him for the real name, the real origin of the fortune, and then it was that I learnt a painful and horrible thing – I was told the real name.' Here Madame Humbert paused, as though struggling with her sentiments, and people began to fear that the 'dreadful secret' would not be disclosed.

Turning towards her counsel, Maitre Labori, she asked him, with melodramatic voice, 'Shall I speak? Shall I say the name?' The eminent barrister gravely nodded, and Madame turned towards the jury again and went on: 'Well, gentlemen of the jury, when Mr Crawford told me that I could be told nothing about the origin of the fortune, and that Crawford was not his real name, I asked, "Then what is your real name?"'

'He answered, "Our name is Regnier. We are but the agents." Who is the real Regnier? I had innocently asked, and the man replied, "Regnier, the traitor." Thus it was that I learnt the real name of the Crawfords. I did not tell my husband. Ah, I swear on the head of my daughter that it is now for the first time that my husband hears this accursed name.'

Alas for Madame's dramatic disclosures, Regnier (who had spied for Prussia in the Franco-Prussian War of 1870) had died in very modest circumstances in 1885. The whole episode, like the rest of her testimony, was pure invention.

Madame Humbert was found guilty of fraud and was sentenced on 22 August, 1903, to five years' solitary confinement. Her husband received the same punishment; her brother Romanie was jailed for three years, Emile for two.

This practically forgotten case illustrates as few other tales the materialism of the age; an urge for wealth so strong that it crushed common sense and caused presumably sceptical bankers altogether to lose their bearings, their reason and their lives.

The French seemed to have an exceptional penchant for being duped. Charles de Ville Wells, 'The man who broke the bank at Monte Carlo,' established a bank in Paris in 1912 which offered to pay interest at 1 per cent *a day* to depositors. Six hundred thousand people invested in his enterprise. He paid interest for a period of six months and then decamped with more than 1,000,000 francs. He was arrested, sentenced to five years in jail and died, impoverished, in 1922.

Such credulity could almost evoke affection. France by the end of the Edwardian era was, at worst, an eccentric neighbour. Far different was the attitude to dark, brooding, baleful Russia which was viewed with deep distrust and distaste : a view heartily reciprocated by many Russians.

CHAPTER NINE

Autocracy and Terror

In 1900 Britain enjoyed a unique reputation – she was loathed by every country in Europe. German newspapers which ventured to give a balanced account of the Boer War were threatened with subscription cancellations at best or physical violence against plants and employees at worst. Russia was behindhand only in that her press was far more rigorously controlled and less widely read than the German. By and large the Russian aristocracy detested moneygrubbing, governessy puritan self-righteous England (it was a firmly-held belief that we had gone into Transvaal and the Orange Free State in search of gold and diamonds and not to protect innocent lives and British interests).

A despatch from Russia, datelined 30 December, 1900, put it succinctly :

> Some idea of the intensely hostile feeling which animates the Russians against the British may be gathered from the following letter, which is forwarded by our St Petersburg correspondent.
>
> The letter was written to an Englishman who had advertised for lodgings with a Russian family with the object of acquiring the language and ran :
>
> Any Russian family which received you, an English dog, in its midst, would be no better than cattle. Let such Russians perish like dogs in the street, without shelter or food. They are unworthy of pity, because you do not pity others, but only fill your bellies at the expense of the lives of unfortunate people, perishing from hunger and misfortune.
>
> May the devil take you! You spies and rascals who have come to St. Petersburg to carry out your devilish machinations.
>
> The first Englishman I meet I shall knock his teeth down his throat. Away you devourers; away, you devil's pack. May you and your land perish!

Apart from the war in South Africa, the Russian ruling class suspected –
rightly – that British liberal opinion was strongly opposed to the
autocracy symbolised by Czar Nicholas II.

The submerged status of the Jews in Russia was of particular interest
to England as refugees from the pogroms were coming in increasing
numbers to England. Sometimes the Russians, especially the Ukrainians,
just went mad and murdered Jews because they were better off or
were money lenders or simply because they had 'killed Christ'.

A German eye-witness of the Kischineff massacres says he saw a mob
enter a Jewish house. They bound the husband and wife, and compelled them to look on while a baby, aged one, was blinded with red-
hot irons, the eyes being literally burnt out. Next the husband was
compelled to see the ruffians assault his wife and then mutilate her
body.

The mob seized the old and feeble woman, bared her back and
knouted her till her body was one mass of wounds. Then they frac-
tured her skull with a sword. The woman is alive in the hospital
suffering agonies. Before her own maltreatment she saw her grand-
daughter, aged six, cruelly butchered.

An old man now in hospital praying for death had seen his wife
and children slaughtered before his eyes.

Another man had both his legs slowly sawn off. A child had its
teeth wrenched out. Both are in hospital, lying side by side.

A German named Arthur Stein, the proprietor of a shop in Kischineff, was killed.

Two Jewesses who were pursued by the mob fled into his shop.
Stein gave them shelter and barred and bolted shutters and doors.
The mob broke in and killed Stein and dragged off the women.

These massacres were usually prompted by rumour and fuelled by
vodka. But behind the ignorant rage of the peasants lay the calculated
campaign strategy of elements of the ruling caste. The Orthodox
Church regarded the Jews as carriers of social and political revolution
(the Russian Socialism had a high Jewish content). Certain members of
the Church, in concert with some landowners and representatives of the
official class formed the Black Hundred organisation and its political
front 'The Union of the Russian People' to hunt down Jews, suspected
of traitorous, anti-national activities.

At other times the Government took a hand as reported by the
Express of 1 July, 1902 :

It is reported from St Petersburg that another anti-Semitic measure has been taken by the Russian Government, the Russian Minister of the Interior having issued a decree enacting that Jews may not stay at any seaside place in Russia. Jews who have already arrived at the seaside have been visited by the police and ordered to leave within twenty-four hours. Russian Jews who want sea air must in future go abroad.

Two highly significant articles appeared in the *Express* of 1905-1906 at the time when revolutionary outbreaks had shaken the Czar's control and reinforced the resolve of the ultra-royalists to give nothing away to the revolutionaries. The first, shortly before Christmas 1905 described the delights of the Russian imperial kitchen :

One of the greatest dangers against which a Russian monarch has to contend is that poison may be surreptitiously inserted in his food by some revolutionary member of the kitchen staff. An interesting account of the organisation of the Czar's kitchens and the extraordinary precautions which are taken to prevent any tampering with the food of the Imperial Family is given by Mr Victor Hirtzler, who served two years in the kitchen of the Winter Palace at St Petersburg, and is now chef of the largest hotel in San Francisco.

The head chef of the palace holds a very important position in the Russian world. He has control of every imperial kitchen in Russia, and every two months makes his rounds of the different departments of his kingdom. His rank is that of a general in the Russian army, and he commands every person serving in any capacity under him in the different cuisines. His salary amounts to over £10,000 a year, more than that of the President of the United States.

Every morning a major of the army, selected by the Emperor himself and always in the kitchen is called into the royal presence and given the menu for the day by the Czar himself. The Czarina never orders a meal.

The major goes to the kitchen and gives the menu to the chef, who posts it in a conspicuous place. Every under-chef reads, selects the dish that comes in his department and proceeds to cook. . . . (The one main meal, a family affair with the children, takes place in the early evening.)

At a quarter to five everything is dished up in the kitchen as it is to be served in the Czar's presence. The major on duty comes and partakes of every dish that is on the menu. Then the food is placed in an elevator having a closed shaft, the major also enters the car with the food, is locked in, and the lift goes directly to the dining-room into the presence of the Czar.

Here again the major eats under the strictest surveillance of his royal master, and, nothing happening to him, the royal family sits down to dinner. No dish that is served on the table of the Czar is ever permitted to go to the dining-room except through the elevator-shaft. It never enters a corridor, so that the only possibility of poison being mixed with the food lies in the hand of the major, who would be the first to die after tasting without harming the Czar.

The dining room in which the regular meals of the family are served is a remarkable chamber. It is built entirely of cast-iron and sealed between meals like a great bank vault. It is not very large, but is perfectly bombproof.

The Czar is a gourmet. After several appetisers he always begins with bortsch, a typically Russian soup, and then goes on to hot and cold meats, four or five entrées of all nationalities, hot and cold poultry, hot and cold vegetables, hot and cold puddings, ices and cold cakes, wine and hot tea or vodka. The Czar eats through the whole menu, and never misses a course. He is fondest of cold soups, and frequently has several kinds served at a meal.

Hundreds of men are employed in the imperial kitchens and wine cellars and it is certain that the daily expenses of the 'Little Father's' meals would feed many of his subjects for a month. It is a quaint situation – an army of cooks to prepare food for one man, one woman, and some little children.

A remarkable and contrasting despatch was filed some two months later by one of the few named correspondents of the *Express* of the time, John Foster Fraser. He reported on the 'outback' of Russia, from Samara, Astrakan, 3,000 miles from St Petersburg, as the Government's policy of repression following the revolt of 1905 took effect :

The electric-light in the great station of Samara spurts vividly, crackles to dimness, and then radiates and glows as though the whole earth would be made effulgent.

Hundreds of *moudjiks,* their wives, children, and all their belongings crowd the platform. Bundles have been pitched in heaps, and there they themselves have fallen and dropped to sleep in awkward attitudes – savage men, bearded and animal of visage and clad in sheepskins, with sheepskin capes and thonged sheepskin about their legs; women with faces moony and characterless save for the resignation of their class; children with pinched features dead asleep and unheeding of the jangle of trains and the hubbub of travellers.

This is the highway to Siberia, the junction for barbarous Tashkent. And when the *moudjik* travels he does not bother about the time-table. Besides, wiser than he are worried by Russian time-tables, for whereas every town has its own time, the railways all over the Empire keep Petersburg time so that at Samara a train timed to leave at eleven at night is really intended to leave at one in the morning, and no Russian complains if it does not get away till 2.30.

Rolling about, singing and drunken, are Cossack soldiers. They are in the grimiest of uniforms; their top-boots are grey with usage. The men are dirty and unshaven. As they heave forward, their arms round one another's necks, kissing one another with vodka-coloured lips, chewing one another's beards in the customary manner of Muscovite affection born of intoxication, they tread on the *moudjiks* who grunt and turn on them the eyes of cattle – wondering why they are treated so, but making no complaint. Degradation and bestiality mark the scene.

There is a train going through the night towards the wild Trans-Caspian provinces. Most of the carriages are fourth-class, wooden trucks, filthy, foul-smelling, and each one is lit with a single candle. The *moujdiks* waken and seize their belongings. There is wild disorder and uproar as they fight for places on the train.

Cossacks are going down the line. In Eastern Samara province there is famine following the drought. People are likely to cry for bread, and they must be stopped from such seditious conduct by the terrorism of Cossacks.

The Cossacks press into the cars. 'Out of it!' and they seize the poor cattle-like peasants and pitch them to the doorway. A protest is met with a whack from a Cossack whip which has a piece of lead in the last of it. A family is escaping, but a leering brute catches a girl and would have her remain. In the candlelight I can see her face ashen as she shrinks and shrieks. The man laughs hoarsely, sinks to the floor and sleeps. . . .

Two days later I am in a village far removed from the railway. It is a woe-begone, bankrupt, wallowing place. The inn is disgusting. But though the glass given to me be foggy with filth, though the table be sticky with unwashedness, the bedroom – ugh – well, everything is to match – there is one evidence of Western civilisation – a gramophone.

Peasants sprawl their arms on the table, lower their heads and guzzle tea – too lazy to raise the glass. They insist on the gramophone, and that it play the 'Marseillaise,' the adopted air of the Russian revolutionaries, and therefore sternly prohibited in Russia.

Enter a *strajnik* – one of the rural police created recently to deal with country disturbances. He comes from a distant part, is badly paid, raggedly dressed in a left-off uniform, and has a sword by his side. He is a hobbledehoy fellow, with sandy face and sandy whiskers, a scowl, and a get-out-of-my-way walk. He has been planted here to see the *moudjiks* behave themselves and to knout them if they don't.

He is worse than useless. He is by himself and if he started to terrorise the peasantry, which is his duty, they, with the courage of numbers, would arrange for his body to be found stark and dead on the steppe. He is cold-shouldered. It is a crime among the peasants, punishable with house-burning, to house a *strajnik;* to give him food is to be placed under suspicion that the giver is in the pay of the Government.

'You'd like to hear that again,' says a stalwart fellow with a tawny beard and in a blue shirt. The *strajnik* scowls.

'The "Marseillaise" again,' commands some one. The handle is wound and the French anthem, throaty in tone, is screeched out with a rasp as though a nail had got into the works.

The *strajnik* widens his feet, sticks his hands into his pockets, and produce the inevitable *paparos* (cigarettes). 'You know that air is forbidden,' he grunts with the same breath that he blows out the first mouthful of smoke.

'Then why don't you stop it?' asks a little broad-shouldered man with hair all awry. 'Why don't you thrash it for revolutionary talk? Why don't you arrest it and send it to Siberia?'

'Why are you against the people? Why do you side with the Government?'

'The Government pay me.'

'Hear him! The Government pay him!' sniggers an old fellow with no teeth and with two wisps of long grey hair trailing from beneath his skin cap and down the side of his parched yellow cheeks.

'Ho! The Government pay him! And who pays the Government? I pay the Government – and I find the money to buy that sword to thrash me with.'

He chuckles at the thought of an uncommonly good clincher. As he lowers his chin to sip tea he eyes the policeman with merriment. The others chortle at the senile and ragged humorist, whose garments are rent patches.

'I wear the Government's uniform, and I do the work for the Government,' says the *strajnik,* half blustering and half apologetically.

'And when those trousers drop off you, will you be on the side of the people, eh?' asks the best-fed man in the dingy room.

The policeman gives no reply, but busies himself with lighting another *paparos.* He scowls darkly. But the *moujdiks* have him at their mercy. They ask him where he stole his horse; was it true that he had become a *strajnik* to save being sent to prison for stealing melons from an old woman?

He tries to answer back. He is one among eight. In the talk they rise and surround him. The chaff turns to savage abuse, and all jabber and shriek at the top of their voices.

The scene, in a muddy, starving hamlet east of the Volga, is an epitome of what is happening all over the realm of the Czar.

'Drink to the devil with the Government!' bawls the little man, who is lame but hobbles to the table, spills tea into a glass, and forces it into the hands of the *strajnik.* 'Drink!'

For an instant we are on the edge of tragedy. Then, like a rip of a paper-bag, the laughter breaks loose. They have been having fun with the affrighted *strajnik.* His sandy face is very yellow.

So, with black hunger in the land, oppression and terrorism everywhere, the poor *moujdiks* turn aside hatred with a laugh. . . .

This is Sunday night, on Russia's great lake, the Caspian Sea. On the ill-lit pier can be seen five soldiers, with bayonets fixed, having in custody two middle-aged men, stunt-whiskered, wearing prison shirts and trousers but owning neither caps nor shoes.

Politicals – banished to a far Trans-Caspian province for life. They are being taken by sea, shipped on board in the dark. They attract less attention and public sympathy than if conveyed by train. Besides, they are less likely to escape.

The people were battened back while the exiles are brought on board the *Grand Duke Alexis.*

The third-class section of the boat is a dark cabin, with wooden shelves. Into one corner are the prisoners put, and then caged in with netting such as is used in England to restrict the depredations of fowls.

Two soldiers with fixed bayonets keep watch outside the cage. When I pushed by head into the den last night I was promised a touch of steel if I didn't move out at once. The difficulty was overcome in the usual way. You can do a lot with a rouble in Russia.

Till they reach their unknown destination on the other side of the Caspian the Government is feeding the 'politicals' – allowing each twelve ounces of black bread a day – that, and nothing more.

But they have fared much better. Dried fish, slabs of water melon, chunks of cheese, bunches of cigarettes have been heaped upon them. It is kind of the sympathetic peasantry, but painfully like throwing buns to the animals at the Zoo. The men lie in their cages and smile and nod their thanks.

A man and a woman go through the ship making a collection to buy the prisoners tea and sugar. No one is too poor to find at least a couple of kopecks. Sometimes it is half a rouble. Only one person refuses, a big flabby woman in the first-class who bursts into vixenish abuse of all sympathisers with the blackguards who ought to be shot.

Terrorism was the principal weapon of the Russian revolutionaries. Most European newspapers of the first decade of the century abounded with stories of attempts on the lives of Royalty, landowners, generals and officials, like this one in 1907 :

The girl terrorist who assassinated Monsieur Maximowsky, chief of the prison administration of the Department of justice yesterday, and who confessed that she was a member of a flying column has been summarily sentenced to death by hanging.

When the police searched the murderess they made a startling discovery.

In one of the pockets of her dress was a cord, which appeared to be connected with some object beneath her corset. They asked what it was.

'Pull, and you will solve the mystery,' the girl replied smilingly.

They cut the cord, and on carefully disrobing the girl found thirteen pounds of high explosives in a wrapper of rubber next her skin.

The police believe that the girl had hoped to be taken to the Department of Public Safety, which would have been blown to atoms.

Another victim of the political assassin was the Grand Duke Sergius. His obituary, penned by Mr Fraser, could on no account be termed obsequious :

Sergius (uncle of the Czar) was, in fact absolutely mediaeval. It would, indeed, not be unjust to describe him as a morose, ill-tempered, sinister ruffian, and there is no question that the great majority of his nephew's subjects will regard his death not so much as an assassination as the execution of a relentless enemy of the common weal.

In appearance Sergius was a bearded, long-faced man, with a jaw of iron, hard-set teeth, cruel eyes, without a smile. He was the personification of Absolutism.

Absolutism's gentler face was that of the poor little Czarevitch, the Czar's son and heir. The child suffered from haemophilia. The slightest knock or cut could set up internal bleeding. Any abrasion could be fatal. The shadow of death over her son's life brought the Empress to the verge of mental breakdown and the monk Gregory Rasputin's extraordinary ability to stop the bleeding when orthodox medical methods had failed gave this strange man a terrible influence at Court.

How much depended on the Czarevitch's life may be gauged from this report in 1912 on one of his illnesses :

The commander of the Imperial Yacht *Standart,* Rear-Admiral Chagin, committed suicide this morning at his own residence by shooting himself.

The circumstances of the Admiral's suicide are so deliberate as to suggest harikari. He did not sleep during the night, but wrote letters to his relatives and left on the table a signed note saying : 'I ask that none shall be accused of my death.'

No motive is suggested for the suicide, except a report to the effect that it was directly connected with the illness of the Czarevitch. It is said that the accident from the consequences of which His Imperial Highness is suffering occurred not at Spala but on board the *Standart.*

During the past few days it has been affirmed that the Czarevitch was thrown from his pony, but it is equally positively asserted that he injured himself in his bath while imitating the diving of sailors. A third version says that he fell from the top of a cupboard while playing.

The public are clamouring for definite news, but in vain. The only information is contained in the laconic medical bulletins. It is therefore hardly to be wondered at that the latest story that the injury sustained by the Czarevitch was the result of a fall while he was clambering out on the spars of the *Standart* is meeting with widespread belief.

According to this account, Rear-Admiral Chagin committed suicide because he considered himself officially responsible. In fact, it was later announced that Admiral Chagin had committed suicide owing to a love affair, after having vainly awaited the arrival of a lady. The latter cut her throat with a razor when, too late, she arrived, and found that Admiral Chagin was dead.

What is significant about this story – and subsequent ones concerning leading Russian figures demanding to know the real state of the Czarevitch's health – is that in the twentieth century so much reliance was put on the life of the heir to the throne.

Nicholas II, Czar of All the Russias, had, in theory, the absolute powers of a Tudor monarch. In reality he had not enough authority to run his own household. The Russia of the early 1900s which was presented to the British people was that of an incompetent tyranny softened by personal tragedy. The incompetence was there right enough; so was the tragedy. But of personal tyranny exercised by the Czar and his family there was little evidence. Real tyranny, of the kind flaunted by Ivan the Terrible, Peter the Great, Nicholas I, lay in the future. Stalin was in the frame and mould of Russian autocracy. Nicholas II was a bewildered soul who came at the tail end of a 300-year-old dynasty whose blood had thinned to vanishing point. Yet it is as the autocrat that history leaves him.

On Monday, 22 July, 1918, the Czar's epitaph was pronounced by the Bolsheviks:

'At the first session of the Central Executive Committee elected by the Fifth Congress of the Councils a message was made public received by direct wire from the Ural Regional Council concerning the shooting of the ex-Czar, Nicholas Romanoff. Recently Ekaterinburg, the capital of the Red Ural, was seriously threatened by the approach of the Czecho-Slovak bands. At the same time a counter-revolutionary conspiracy was discovered, having for the object the wresting of the tyrant from the hands of the Council's authority by armed force.

'In view of this fact the Presidium of the Ural Regional Council decided to shoot the ex-Czar, Nicholas Romanoff. This decision was carried out on 16 July. The wife and son of Romanoff have been sent to a place of security.*

'It had been recently decided to bring the ex-Czar before a tribunal to be tried for his crimes against the people, and only later occurrences led to delay in adopting this course.'

*The Czar's son, wife and his daughters were all murdered at the same time and in the same cellar at Ekaterinburg.

CHAPTER X

White Man's World

If newspaper reports of duels, scandals, and political corruption coloured the public's view of France; if Prussian discipline and an obsession with honour caused Germany to be regarded with chill apprehension, and if a combination of incompetent tyranny, boorishness and terrorism brought Russia into disrepute, the attitude of the Press and its readers to race was yet more simplistic.

Before Adolf Hitler, race had a quite different connotation. It was generally applied to a nation: 'The genius of the French race for cooking.' Most nations were frankly jingoistic and none more so than the British who had much to be jingoistic about. One quarter of the earth was coloured Imperial Red and the seven seas were British lakes.

Newspapers reflected reality in a matter-of-fact fashion, and there was a relaxed, if patronising, attitude to coloured people as this Edward VII Coronation story testifies:

As a man is not a hero to his own valet, so a dusky potentate is not a potentate to his coachman. This story is being told of what happened at one of the big outdoor functions this week:

A coachman wearing the royal livery went up to another of the fraternity, and was overheard to inquire:

'I say, Harthur, 'ave you seen my bloomin' nigger?'

'No, James,' was the reply. 'Ave you lost 'im?'

"Eavens only knows, but I 'aven't seen 'im for 'alf-an-hour.'

The conversation was conducted with entire gravity, and the first coachman went off solemnly to look further afield for the dusky guest of the Empire.

The superiority of the British race was accepted without question, though the note was too shrill for comfort in this claim by a Professor Armstrong addressing the Public Schools Science Masters' Conference six months before World War I broke out :

'It takes ten Germans to do the work of two Englishmen in scientific research.'

Mr C. R. Ashford, headmaster of Dartmouth, said that the genius of the Englishman was more to give orders than to do mere routine work.

The effortless supremacy of western man over the lesser breeds fascinated Edwardian England (it also fascinated Adolf Hitler, whose favourite film *Lives of a Bengal Lancer* depicted a handful of Britons ruling thousands of turbulent tribesmen). Typical of the accounts about the outposts of Empire which enthralled readers at home is this one of February 1911 :

Ibadan, Oyo, Ife, and Illa – what do these names mean in England ? Who has heard of Ibadan, the town of 200,000 people, a Manchester of Southern Nigeria ? Out in those unknown places we have a British Resident, Captain C. H. Elgee, who is the virtual ruler of a province containing 12,000 square miles, with a population of upwards of three-quarters of a million souls; and we have his word for it that a great future awaits the people under his charge. Captain Elgee returns to Africa this week after a short leave in England.

It is one of the marvels of the British tradition that one man, with an assistant, should rule such a vast tract of the world in the name of Britain, while at home we know little or nothing, either of the man or his work.

Our administration of the country is not expensive. Apart from the military, whose services are not necessary, the total expenditure of a year in this area, according to a recent report, was under £2,000. The Government is conducted through hereditary chiefs, whose authority has been strengthened and developed – native councils backed by law, have been at work for the good of the people. But only a few of the chiefs, so far, can read or write.

The task of administration in such a land, where there is one white man to ten thousand natives, and when the natives are steeped in superstition, is stupendous – but our administrator has succeeded in obtaining an annual revenue of about a million and a half, covering his expenses so well that not a penny is drawn from the British taxpayer's pocket. We have our Resident's word for it that there is not a single disloyal chief in the whole of Nigeria.

Should differences arise between the natives and the white people, a council of the chiefs is called, and these meetings are the safety valve of all discontent and conspiracy. The great difference in the classes of the natives adds much to the difficulties of fair administration. They range from a splendid aristocracy to cannibals who would eat one with relish.

On the lower classes, paganism has a strong hold – one shrine may be seen built up of enemies' skulls, and skulls are sometimes in use as drinking bowls. As showing the unsophisticated character of some of the natives, Captain Elgee has this story:

'A certain native was invited to dinner at the house of a European lady, but at an early hour, before dinner, was noticed to be preparing to depart. The lady remonstrated: the native declared, "I never take dinner," and was backing hurriedly for the door when there was a sudden bang, a bottle of champagne, which he had secreted about him, having burst. Covered with confusion and champagne he made his retreat in good earnest, shedding as he went, from his garments, a large number of delicacies which had been destined for the dinner-table.'

He calculates that while as not long ago fewer than a hundred people in the country could read and write, fully twenty thousand can now do so. We have brought peace to the country, and now follows wisdom. So the seeds of civilization are being sown.

Here was the white man's burden extolled as noble duty marching with prudence, modesty and thrift; a very gallery of Victorian virtues.

An equally paternalistic attitude was adopted towards people with mixed blood. There were nearly 2,000,000 of them in the India of the 1900s; offspring of British soldiers and native women, or more likely descendants of Eurasians whose breeding was deliberately encouraged by the East India Company to provide acclimatised, ready-made clerks, junior administrators and the like. They had their place, such as running the railways, but should know it and keep it, as the Viceroy, Lord Curzon, explained to the press on New Year's Day 1901:

He told them at Bangalore that the first step towards securing the favour of Government was a candid recognition of the weakness of their position and the faults of their character, as well as of their strength and virtues.

Their dreams of a self-contained and self-supporting community was over-sanguine in character and incapable of realisation, and he declared that he could not create special opportunities for them or constitute a special preserve into which none but Eurasians might enter.

The Simla correspondent of the *Express* added his own bilious comment that 'The Eurasian, partly by reason of his own shiftlessness, but more as a result of the low estimate in which, as a half-caste, he is held by the white community, is rapidly drifting into a condition of misery and hopelessness.

Badly treated natives in any part of the Empire were not neglected. The *Express* and other national newspapers carried a horrifying account of the miseries experienced by the aborginals of Western Australia in 1905:

Briefly put, the case stands thus: the white settlers are continually killing off the black man's staple food – the kangaroo. The aborigines are faced by two alternatives – starvation or killing the white man's cattle.

No other provision having been made for them by the white settlers who have dispossessed them, the blacks, ignorant of the fact that they are committing any offence, kill the white man's cattle to avoid starvation.

Then the white man's armed and mounted police 'Round them up', put them in chains and carry them off to prison, taking with them, also in chains, scores of women and girls as 'witnesses'. These girls are subjected to treatment so infamous that it can only be hinted at.

Shameful evidence as to the cruel indignities to which these girls are subjected at the hands of the police and stockmen has been brought to light by Dr Roth, the Commissioner appointed by the Commonwealth Government to investigate the scandal. He shows beyond all doubt that young black girls are put in chains, stripped, flogged if they prove awkward, and forced to submit to indignities which should subject the perpetrators to ten or twenty years' penal servitude.

Armed and mounted police, accompanied by armed native trackers, hunt the blacks charged with cattle killing, arresting, without a warrant, as many as thirty at one time. The women are never arrested for cattle-killing, but they are compelled to go and give evidence against their husbands.

Young women, as Dr Roth shows, are almost always chosen for this purpose, and at night they are chained to the trees, and so left at the mercy of police, stockmen, and native trackers.

On the other hand, natives who got out of hand could not expect – and did not get – a friendly press. The *Express* approvingly recorded the action of an outraged Rhodesian settler in May 1911 :

A prominent resident of Bulawayo, Mr Sam Lewis, went to the local office, had ten native boys paraded, and picked out one who, he alleged, had made overtures to his girls.

Mr. Lewis calmly marched the native to vacant ground behind the building, and shot him dead. He then surrendered himself, and was charged with murder, but was released on £3,000 bail.

Public subscriptions were tendered for his bail while he was in court, but were not required.

Public feeling in Bulawayo seems almost entirely in Mr Lewis' favour, and a difficulty is expected in getting any jury to convict him.

When Lord Gladstone, the Governor General of British South Africa, reprieved a native who had been sentenced to death for ravaging a white woman, the local Cape Town correspondent wrote : 'There is only one penalty which the blacks fear for these crimes and that is death.' Mr Madeley, a Labour MP wanted capital punishment for attempted rape. But politicians and pressmen alike agreed that 'the general sentiment in Southern Africa is against lynching'.

Very different was sentiment in America towards that form of law enforcement. Hardly a month went by between 1900 and 1914 without mention in the press of a lynching in the USA.

From Watkinsville, Georgia, 30 June, 1905:

Seven negroes were lynched yesterday by a mob. They had committed various offences, including murder, robbery and assault, and were in general bad characters.

The mob quietly surrounded the prison, and overpowered the keeper. Taking his keys, they opened the cells, and marched the prisoners to a vacant plot of land in the heart of the town. There they bound their hands behind them, and placed them against a fence.

Then, at the word of command, the mob fired at the prisoners with rifles, shot-guns, and pistols. The prisoners fell, and the mob made off.

It is not likely that any legal action will be taken against the executioners. As a matter of fact, the public are delighted at the quick riddance of the prisoners, as it will relieve the county of the expense of prosecution.

From Hemphill, Texas, 23 June, 1908:

Nine negroes were lynched on Sunday evening, and a race war is in full progress.

The trouble began at a recent negro dance, where a white man was killed. Two negroes were arrested. A little later another white was killed at a negro dance, and six negroes were arrested. Then the fury of the whites was let loose.

One hundred and fifty armed whites marched to the gaol at Hemphill and broke down the doors. They dragged out six shrieking negroes and hanged them on oak trees near the gaol.

A general exodus of the terrified negro population began, while armed whites patrolled the roads. Some mounted whites encountered a party of blacks and a running battle ensued, during which three blacks were killed, another was wounded, and two whites were wounded.

The dead negroes were riddled with bullets; they were believed to be implicated in the murder of the second white.

From Cairo, Illinois, 22 November, 1909:

A few days ago the eighteen-year-old daughter of a respectable mechanic was waylaid by two negroes named Will James and Ben Alexander while on her way home from work. She fought desperately, but was finally overpowered, and after being treated in a shameful manner, was literally beaten to death.

The two negroes had been seen loitering in the vicinity of the scene of the murder, and when it became known that they had disappeared from their usual haunts the residents of Cairo promptly concluded that they were the guilty persons, and the entire town joined in the police hunt for the fugitives.

Bloodhounds were used to track the men to their hiding place in a forest ten miles from Cairo. Hundreds of prominent business men left their work in order to assist in the chase. After three days and nights of incessant effort the negro James was found hiding in some bushes.

Yesterday morning, a meeting of the townspeople was held, and it was decided in view of the terror which prevailed among the white women, to rush the gaol and summarily execute James.

The mob battered down the front door of the prison, overpowered the principal warder, took his keys, and dragged the negro, who was already half dead with fright, from his cell.

James was finally hanged to a telegraph pole, but the rope broke after he had been suspended for half a minute. The mob thereupon riddled his body with bullets, and dragged the corpse to the square in front of the town hall, where it was burned on a pile of wood. The funeral pyre was lighted by a woman.

Before James' body was reduced to ashes one of the leaders of the mob cut off the head and stuck it on a pole, which was planted in the ground. A placard was placed on the pole which read as follows : 'This is the fate of all negroes who molest white women.'

From Piercill, Oklahoma, Friday, 25 August, 1911:

Another negro was burned alive at the stake by a mob. He had attacked a white woman, the wife of a farmer, during the absence of her husband, and had then set the house on fire, almost burning her to death. He escaped, but was caught by three other negroes who were taking him to gaol when they encountered a search party, who seized the criminal and marched him to the centre of the town.

The sheriff tried to interfere, but the mob locked him in his own gaol, and then proceeded with the preparations for lynching the negro. Faggots were piled high on the roadway, the excited whites running to and fro to gather the timbers. The crowd cheered loudly as the pyre grew.

The negro, who was compelled to watch the preparations for his death, howled and begged for mercy, but no one paid attention. Oil was poured on the pile of wood, and then the negro was bound to a telegraph pole in the centre and a match was applied.

Flames shot all around him, and three thousand spectators cheered lustily, but through it all the negro's piercing shrieks of agony could be heard.

The news spread rapidly, and people had driven up in carts and motor-cars to be present at the lynching. There were at least 500 women in the crowd and many children. They stood on the seats of the cars to obtain a better view of the burning. They showed no evidence of pity, but cheered loudly when the pyre blazed.

The principal actors in the tragedy did not trouble to wear masks, as is generally done at lynchings to prevent identification.

Headed simply 'The Usual Result' a despatch from Lucedale, Alabama, on 21 October, 1906, tersely stated :

A mob stormed the gaol at Lucedale, Alabama, this morning where a negro was imprisoned on a charge of having attacked a young white girl.

After some resistance on the part of the gaol authorities the mob captured the negro – with the usual result.

An anthropologist, William Archer, wrote a book *Through Afro-America* which was widely reviewed in 1910 and attempted to rationalise this homicidal frenzy. Today Mr Archer would find himself in a court of law in either the USA or Britain. Then his views were conventional. His was the temper of the times : as well rail against the past's wholly different moral climate as denounce Boadicea for failing to use tanks against the Romans :

'Does any one really believe that the genius of Caesar and Napoleon, of Milton and Goethe had nothing to do with their facial angle, and could have found an equally convenient habitation behind thick lips and woolly skulls?

'The negro himself takes his stand on no such paradox. Whoever may doubt the superiority of the white race, it is not he; and it is a racial, not merely a social or economic, superiority to which he does instinctive homage. It does not enter his head to champion his own racial ideal, to set up an African Venus in rivalry to the Hellenic, and claim a new Judgment of Paris between them.

'If wishing could change the Ethiopian's skin, there would never be a negro in America. The black race, out of its poverty, spends thousands of dollars annually on "anti-kink" lotions, vainly supposed to straighten the African wool. The brown belle tones her complexion with pearl powder; and many a black mother takes pride in the brown skin of her offspring, though it proclaims their illegitimacy.

'There can be little beyond sheer animalism in the relations between a white man and a black woman; and such parentage cannot be reckoned the most desirable. . . .

'A white nation can scarcely be expected to renounce its racial integrity on the chance of breeding an occasional Alexander Dumas. . . ..

'I do not understand how any white man ˙who has ever visited the South can fail to be dismayed at the thought of absorbing into the veins of his race the blood of the African myriads who swarm ˙on every hand.

'Negroes may have been lynched or shot down, not only for crimes they themselves did not commit, but for crimes that were never committed at all. But there are quite enough authentic cases of crime – denied by nobody – to justify the horror of the South.'

Mr Archer recommended establishing a separate state for negroes in the USA. Strangely he dedicated his handbook for racialism to the English Socialist, H. G. Wells.

The attitude in America generally and in the South particularly towards the black man was summed up in two incidents, one superficial, the other tragic.

On 19 October, 1901, the *Express* reproduced this heading from the *New York Herald*:

> DINED WITH A NEGRO :
> PRESIDENT ROOSEVELT
> SEVERELY CRITICISED.

And from 12 September, 1912:

Mrs Jack Johnson, the white wife of the negro heavy-weight champion pugilist, committed suicide last night at Chicago during an attack of nervous depression caused by her regret at having married a black man.

Mrs. Johnson came of an old New York family. She was formerly married to Mr Clarence Duryea, a wealthy racing man, who held a high social position in the country. Later he secured a divorce.

Several years ago she married Johnson and lived with him in the cafe which he opened in Chicago. She had several attacks of nervous depression recently because all her relatives and white friends refused to have anything to do with her, while the negroes with whom her husband associated regarded her contemptuously as an outcast from the white race.

Yesterday Mrs Johnson called her two negro maids into her bedroom and, with an arm round the neck of each of them, she prayed fervently for forgiveness. Then, turning to the negresses, she said : 'God forgive a poor woman who is lonely. I am tired of being an outcast, but I deserve all my misery for marrying a negro. Even the negroes do not respect me; they hate me. I intend to end it all.'

She dismissed the maids and shot herself in the head, dying four hours later without recovering consciousness.

*

Stories from America in these early days of the twentieth century were always larger than life and, of course, not all had racial overtones. When in 1912 Woodrow Wilson defeated President Taft, the facet of the election that the correspondents of the UK popular press found so fascinating was that 'one person in every 47 who voted for Mr Wilson has applied for a position in his administration'. This was the spoils system by which the winning party took a large number of Federal jobs, notably in the Post Office where 8,841 Republican postmasters were obliged to vacate office for the hungry, triumphant Democrats. In all 131,530 registered Democrats applied for 10,384 posts.

Wild West violence kept cropping up in the British press. As good an example as any is the report from Hillsville, Virginia, on the aptly timed Ides of March 1912 :

A battle with revolvers took place in the courthouse in Hillsville, Virginia, this morning, after the conviction of Lloyd Allen, the leader of a notorious gang of mountaineer bandits, with the following result :

KILLED

The presiding judge
The public prosecutor
The sheriff
One juror

WOUNDED

The prisoner
Nine jurymen
Clerk of the court
Three spectators

Lloyd Allen escaped, but is reported to have been shot by the pursuing posse.

The scene of this unprecedented outlawry which wiped out the entire judicial corps of the court is a remote town in the Blue Ridge Mountains, where the Allen gang of bandits have terrorised the county for many years.

They hold despotic sway with rifle and revolver over southwestern Virginia and the north-western part of North Carolina, and the inhabitants obeyed them implicitly.

Allen was arrested with several companions and charged with larceny a few weeks ago. While out on bail himself, he headed a band of his own men, who rescued their companion from gaol. They escaped to the mountains. Allen refused to 'jump' his bail and go with them, defiantly asserting that no jury would dare to convict him.

At the conclusion of the trial today a number of Allen's bandits, including two of his brothers, were in court. Allen, who was in the dock, heard the verdict of guilty.

Judge Massie, one of the judicial leaders in Virginia, said 'I pronounce the sentence of one year's imprisonment.' Immediately the words were spoken a revolver was fired, and the judge fell dead. One of Allen's brothers had fired the bullet from the front of the courtroom.

He then rushed to the dock and handed the prisoner a second revolver. Both opened fire. Half a dozen members of Allen's gang who were in court brought their revolvers into action, firing at everybody.

All the jury were armed, and they joined with court officials in returning the fire. The battle raged with the utmost confusion for several minutes before reinforcements to Allen's gang arrived on horseback.

Another traditional feature of American life, the United States Marines, were also mentioned fairly frequently in their traditional role of providing the President with his 'big stick'. From New York on 2 December, 1909, it was reported:

ARMED FORCE TO

PUNISH A

NAUGHTY REPUBLIC

The American Government is preparing to make a strong military and naval demonstration to restore order in Nicaragua, and assure reparation for the recent torture and execution of two Americans who were courtmartialled by President Zelaya.

An American squadron has been ordered to assemble at Corinto, Nicaragua, with a strong force of marines ready for landing if the occasion requires.

Nicaragua caved in and finally allowed the Americans to run her foreign affairs and finances. In 1913 the *Express* explained that virtual US control of Nicaragua was dictated by the necessity for ensuring the safety of the Panama Canal. Nicaragua was to become 'an American protectorate resembling that exercised in practice over Cuba.'

On 20 April, 1914, President Woodrow Wilson declared 'peaceful war' against Mexico for the insult that General Huerta 'a person calling himself the President of Mexico had offered the US flag'. Wilson asked Congress – and was granted – authorisation to use the armed forces of the United States to avenge the insult.

Briefly, the 'insult' concerned the arrest of the paymaster and two sailors of the USS *Dolphin* which was loading supplies at the Mexican port of Tampico. Within half-an-hour of the arrest the military commander of Tampico ordered their release and offered his apologies for the blunder of over-zealous juniors.

President Wilson then announced :

'Admiral Mayo regarded the arrest as so serious that he was not satisfied with the apologies offered, but demanded that the flag of the United States should be saluted with special ceremony by the military commander of the port.

'I have felt it my duty to sustain Admiral Mayo in the whole of his demands, and to insist that the flag of the United States be saluted.

'Such a salute General Huerta has refused and I come to ask your approval and support for the course I propose to pursue.

'The present situation, however, need not necessarily eventuate in war. The United States has enforced its demands on many occasions by blockading other countries, and has even bombarded and destroyed towns to enforce its demands without ever formally declaring war.'*

That was the way of the world in the earlier part of the century.

Shortly before President Wilson embarked on the chastisement of

---

*Much the same argument was used by the Japanese at Pearl Harbor.

the Mexicans, the British Government gave Haiti twenty-four hours to pay £12,000 compensation to two Britons whose property had been damaged in riots. The Haitians paid up as the silhouettes of British warships appeared on the horizon.

Haiti's vulnerability to sea power led to this reputed exchange (in a book *Where Black Rules White*) :

Haitian judge about to sentence a foreigner for a minor misdemeanour:
'Where's your country?'
Foreigner: 'Switzerland.'
Judge (to clerk): 'Has Switzerland a navy?'
Clerk: 'No'.
Judge to foreigner: 'You will go to prison for one year.'

Haiti was practically the only place where Black ruled. Elsewhere the Whites ruled : black, brown and yellow.

Bliss was it in that dawn to be alive
To be white was very heaven.

To be British as well as white was to have drawn first prize in the lottery of life. Yet by the end of the Edwardian era there was a malaise that manifested itself in many aspects of British society.

CHAPTER XI

Strife at Mine and Mill

What has come to be known as the strange death of Liberal England occurred during the years 1911/1912. Suddenly the great party that had governed Britain for fifty of the previous hundred years seemed to lose belief in the twin pillars of its philosophy : free trade and the blessings of competition. Having been converted to the need for State-sponsored welfare services and having – at Lloyd George's prompting – instituted a growing web of social services Mr Asquith and his Liberals were horrified to discover that industrial strife bubbled and boiled.

The country buckled under an unprecedented number of strikes. It was as though organised labour was saying : 'If this much – why not more?' and it was increasingly to the Labour Party that the workers looked for an improvement in their lot while the self-employed and the middle classes turned to the Tories. Labour offered collectivism in place of competition. The Conservatives offered protection in place of free trade. The Liberals felt they couldn't cope any more. They died from bewilderment.

But in the first years of the century it was so different. Then a natural deference still suffused appeals for amelioration of industrial conditions. There was a remarkable acceptance of hardship.

The annual abstract for labour statistics, covering the 7,000,000 employees of the 'working classes', recorded 2,000,000 in agriculture (against 300,000 out of 24 million today). Most farm labourers were presumably content with their lot for they were, as now, rarely involved in disputes. But then it didn't really pay to air grievances. At Santry, near Dublin, a man who had worked on a Miss Quinn's farm for twenty-six years asked for a half-day's holiday. Indeed he demanded it. He was instantly dismissed.

Then there was the case of Mrs Thorogood of Lambeth which was raised in the House of Commons. Mrs Thorogood, aged sixty-three, 'finished' trousers for a contractor. Her pay was less than one penny an hour. She took on this extra work at home after doing a full stint at a factory.

'I work at a factory at Tooley-street,' she told the Press, 'and it takes me an hour to get there. I have to leave home at seven o'clock in the morning to be at work in time, and I don't leave till 6.30 at night – sometimes 7.30.

'The walk is a bit of a strain upon me now I'm getting old, and my boots aren't the best to go out in this damp weather.'

She exhibited a pair of boots she was wearing. At least, they were boots once, but nearly the whole of the uppers had disappeared, and the soles were of painful thinness.

The poor old woman was also ill-clad, although it was evident that she tried to make as neat a show as possible. An old blouse and ragged skirt comprised practically the whole of her clothing.

'What do I have for dinner?' she went on in reply to a question. 'Anything I can get for a penny. Sometimes a bit of bread and some water. I always have a cup of tea at tea-time, though,' she said, her face brightening.

Sweated labour was fairly widespread in the early 1900s. Fewer than twenty per cent of employees were organised in unions and those that were weren't all that successful. In the years between 1900 and 1904 unions won only seventeen per cent of disputes in which they were involved; the employers triumphed three times as frequently.

These were the days of minimal factory legislation; safety at work was neglected, as much by the men as by the masters. For instance, in 1904, 1,000 people died in workshops; more than 1,200 lost their lives in the pits and more than 400 railway servants were killed on the line. Today the industrial death rate is one-fifth of what it was then.

The figure of 400 annual deaths of railway workers is staggering. The average for the 1970s was four. The report of one incident involving a railway employee in 1905 is fascinating for the language used. Present journalistic practice is to employ sexual terms liberally and to be fairly explicit in descriptions of bodily functions. Coyness, on the other hand, inhibits discussion of mental illness. It was very different in the past. Headed :

MAD SIGNALMAN
Deserts Post after Supposed
Divine Command

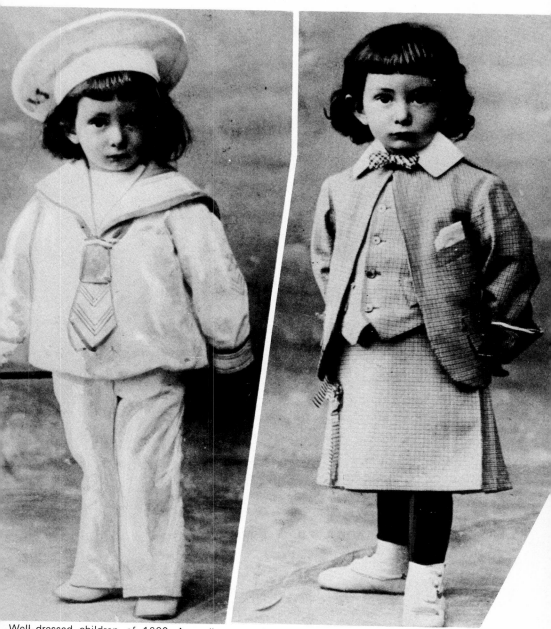

Well-dressed children of 1900. According to a Mrs Enid Campbell Dauncey some of their younger contemporaries were fed opium by their nannies to keep them quiet and good.

'These neurotic women clamour for a vote. What they need is a fire hose', wrote a male reader. Mrs Pankhurst being arrested outside Buckingham Palace.

a local correspondent wrote :

> Traffic on the Great Northern Railway between Leeds and Bradford was entirely suspended for an hour recently because of the vagaries of a mad signalman named Storey.
>
> The man went mad suddenly in his box, but fortunately set all the signals at 'danger' before deserting it. He locked the door at midday, walked down the line, and told a platelayer that God had commanded him, in a vision, to go out and preach the gospel to all the world.
>
> The labourer paid no attention to him thinking he was joking, and Storey went on till he came to another signal-box. There he repeated his story to the signalman, who promptly wired to the stationmaster at Laisterdyke.
>
> In the meantime, about a dozen trains had drawn up on the line near Laisterdyke, and the wildest rumours began to circulate among the passengers. A new man was put in Storey's place, and the line was quickly cleared.
>
> Storey was a man of exceptional attainments. His wife says that his mind became unbalanced by over-study on social and economic questions.
>
> He has been removed to the imbecile ward of the Bradford Workhouse.

If Mr Storey had not been committed to a hospital for the insane he would undoubtedly have been dismissed. There was no place for sentiment. When men went on strike they could hazard their homes as well as their livelihoods.

In Bethesda, Wales, Lord Penrhyn evicted cottagers for refusing to work his quarry in October 1901. The occupiers, or their fathers, had built their dwellings although they had been warned by Lord Penryn's father they could be evicted for opposing his will.

The town of Denaby in the West Riding of Yorkshire was owned by the coal masters. This is what happened when the colliers struck in 1902 over a five shillings a week allowance for the dust they inevitably collected when hewing out coal. The dispute lasted six months and the men could not pay their rents.

> Extraordinary were yesterday's scenes, when, as the sequel to the strike at the Denaby and Cadeby Colliers, a hundred of the 737 families of the Denaby and Cadeby strikers, under order of eject-

ment, were turned out of their homes, with all their household goods.

Trouble had been anticipated, for provision had been made to supply the 300 constables with cutlasses in case of emergency.

Happily the expected conflict did not take place, and the police, acting all through with consideration and tact, had to use no force to carry into execution the legally-authorised will of the masters.

From ten till one the work of wholesale eviction went grimly before the eyes of large and mournful-looking crowds, as the families, with all their bedding and belongings, were turned into the cold, wet streets.

The homes of some men who are agreed to return to work at the old rate of wages were left inviolate.

Though for the most part pathetic, the proceedings were not without humorous incidents, which were mainly furnished by the Irish element.

One son of Erin strutted up and down outside his house singing and dancing, while a woman in another street, after being evicted, sang lustily, 'I have no home, dear mother, now.'

Many of the people, however, were unable to take matters so lightly, and more than one woman fainted when the police entered, while others could scarcely stand because of their nervousness.

During the day Captain Russell, Chief of the West Riding Constabulary, and Colonel Yarborough, Chairman of the West Riding bench of magistrates, arrived in the village.

Three hundred more families remain to be rendered homeless, but the work goes sadly against the hearts of burly policemen.

Families evicted so far are being housed by friends or accommodated in mission-halls and chapels, but in these cases, as in those of homeless people who are to-day and to-morrow to be housed in marquees, the lack of sanitary arrangements and the herding of human beings like so many sardines in tins is sure to lead to trouble.

The men seem bent now on taking their evictions without causing trouble, and no riotous scenes were witnessed yesterday.

This is the result of the advice of their leaders, who express determination to fight fairly to the finish whatever the punishment involved.

When the colliers closed pits in Durham County – admittedly in breach of a court order – they were fined and when they refused to pay the fines, they were jailed for seven days.

This war, with the odds weighted heavily in favour of the employers, moved one coal master, Sir Arthur Markham, MP, the largest mine owner in Mansfield to denounce his own kind. He told thousands of miners that the owners constantly understated their profits and could well afford to pay more. Asked if he were prepared to tell his fellow-owners, he replied: 'If I went with that request it would be like holding a red rag to a bull. At a recent meeting of coal masters it was suggested that I ought to be crucified on the top of Westminster Tower and then thrown into the Thames.'

Discontent festered in the mining industry, breaking out in strikes in different districts – in those days the mineworkers' union was not a monolithic organisation but a federation of local unions – and reaching a violent climax in South Wales.

With their Celtic temperament and heavy dependence on export markets, swinging wildly from boom to slump as the vagaries of the market dictated, the Welsh were traditionally volatile. When the owners sought to cut miners' and railway men's earnings, as a result of reduced overseas demand for coal, the men struck – and a kind of madness gripped the valleys. Towns such as Tredegar, Brynmawr, Ebbw Vale, Bargoed, Giltach and Llanelli erupted. Llanelli was the worst of all. A distraught local reporter recorded the scene on 20 August, 1911. It has more in common with an uprising than with an industrial dispute:

The mob broke into the Great Western Railway Company's goods shed and obtained a large quantity of whisky and beer, which they drank.

Within a few minutes flames were seen to burst from the building, and the whole place was soon ablaze. At the same time a portion of the strikers turned their attention to trucks standing in a siding. These were looted and fired in the same manner as the goods shed.

In their haste to drink the looted liquor the crowd were not content to let it run out of the bunghole of the casks, but burst open the end and ladled it out with pails. Intoxicated boys staggered about in every street.

A woman entered a truck, and after taking off her clothes put on some of the soldiers' clothes. In these she exhibited herself to the crowd.

Two horses were burned to death.

Drunken and maddened rioters were dancing and shouting round the blazing trucks, when suddenly a terrific explosion occurred. One of the trucks contained either gunpowder or petrol, and this had blown up.

Portions of the blazing trucks and their contents were hurled into the air among the crowd, who made frantic efforts to escape in all directions. Four men, however, lost their lives. A woman was fatally injured, and others received minor injuries.

The fire brigade was soon on the scene, but were so hampered by the crowd that the flames were not extinguished until nine o'clock yesterday morning. While the fire was in progress the mob continued to loot wagons.

During the orgies young boys were seen staggering about with half consumed bottles of spirits in their possession.

In the meantime, looting was being carried on in the most un-blushing fashion in the town. Men, women, and children carried off hams, tins of biscuits, boxes of jam, casks of butter, chests of tea, and bags of sugar, without any attempt at concealment on their part or any interference on the part of any one.

One man was actually seen making off with a mangle, while another had a gramophone.

Eventually 500 men of the Essex Regiment arrived and a detach-ment having been told off to guard the power station, the main body, with fixed bayonets, marched through the town. The rioters fled before them, but on the soldiers taking up a position at one end of Market-street, looting at the other end was resumed, and pro-ceeded as briskly as ever.

The Worcestershire Regiment made a bayonet charge near the station, and several persons were injured.

The disturbances continued until three o'clock yesterday morning, only ceasing after definite intimation had been received that the strike had been settled. The Great Western Railway began the work of repairing the line.

The Home Office issued yesterday the following statement : 'Order has been restored at Llanelli. The military officers report the railway-men were not themselves responsible for the rioting.'

Intervention by outsiders, some from as far distant as the capital, was evidenced by this news item :

Leonard Worsell, a Londoner who was killed, had a premonition of death, for in a letter to his mother written on Friday he said : 'Don't trouble about me now. I expect death at any moment, and when-ever it comes I am ready.'

Three other members of the Worsell family died suddenly, and all had a premonition of death. In each case a heavily-framed picture in the parlour of their home dropped from its place on the wall. The picture fell once more on Friday.

Jewish shops received special attention, presumably because the rioters owed them money and the proprietors were not prepared to extend credit for an unlimited period.

Three months previously striking miners had demonstrated in Ton-y-pandy and the hooligan element added its own brand of licence. The police could not cope. The Deputy Chief Constable of Glamorganshire was injured in the fighting and his superior asked the Home Office for troops; two squadrons of cavalry and two companies of infantry. To this appeal, Winston Churchill, the Home Secretary, replied :

'You may give the miners the following message from me. Their best friends here are greatly distressed at the trouble which has broken out, and will do their best to help them to get fair treatment.

'Confiding in the good sense of the Cambrian Combine workmen, we are holding back the soldiers for the present and sending police instead.'

Rioting however resumed and Churchill felt constrained to release the troops to the Chief Constable.

Churchill was violently assailed for his timidity. The local correspondent reported that 'indignation has been aroused by the Home Secretary's wait-and-see policy. Had firm action been taken at once there would probably have been no serious rioting or pillage and many thousands of pounds worth of property would have been saved.'

Now in the public mind, or at least in the mind of Mr Churchill's rabid opponents on the Left, the events of Llanelli and Ton-y-pandy became inextricably confused and a black myth was created that was to dog Churchill for many a day.

It was said that Churchill had ordered the troops to gun down the miners of Ton-y-pandy. In fact Churchill *restrained* the troops. There were no fatalities at Ton-y-pandy. Those who died at *Llanelli* did so by their own actions. Yet the massacre of Ton-y-pandy took its place in the martyr's monument along with Peterloo fields and the Tolpuddle farmworkers. Churchill was forever after regarded by millions as 'the man who shot down the workers'. Antipathy to him was so strong that the Conservative leadership reckoned that as a Minister he would be a grave political liability. The spectre of Ton-y-pandy haunted Churchill and continues to haunt his memory. In some parts of the country his name is execrated – for a crime he never committed.

How much of Britain's poor economic performance is due to long memories and industrial mythology no one can say for certain. But the British labour movement constantly recalls strikes and unemployed marches as though they were battle honours, and by fighting the struggles of the past, keeps alive bitterness in the present.

Ton-y-pandy and Llanelli were the harbingers of a year of industrial strife unequalled – apart from the General Strike of 1926 – in British history.

Dr Harry Roberts who worked as an independent industrial conciliator gave his expert views :

A considerable number of the most efficient citizens who do work for England are seriously proposing to throw down their tools and cease to do that work until their conditions are altered. This intention is not confined to the men engaged in any one branch of industry; it is almost general.

We may dismiss at once the view of certain well-fed persons that working people are a set of lazy, discontented scoundrels who never know when they are well off. It is the bulk of the able-bodied people of England who are in a state of revolt. To put it down to their natural blackguardism is to insult our country.

Money is worth what money will buy, and during the past ten years the prices of food, clothing, and almost all other necessities have increased to such an extent that a pound to-day will buy no more, and is worth no more, than eighteen shillings in 1900. The price of bread has risen by 14 per cent, the price of bacon by 39 per cent, the price of sugar by one-quarter, the price of textile materials by 36 per cent, and prices are still increasing.

The workers have found themselves not only relatively but absolutely poorer than they were ten years ago; the purchasing power of their week's wages is fully 10 per cent lower than it was in 1900. To the upper and middle classes that rise in the price of commodities has been a matter of much less consequence; first, because their money incomes have been growing much more rapidly than prices; second, because there is in most cases a considerable margin of unnecessary expenditure, where retrenchment is possible without touching necessities or even reasonable comforts.

But the working people are in a very different position. Even in times of full employment it is certain that the income of quite one-quarter of working-class families in the United Kingdom is not enough to provide sufficient food, housing, and clothing to maintain the family even in a state of bare physical efficiency. One shilling deducted from the purchasing power of the weekly wage means, for millions of families, an appreciable step along the road to semi-starvation. It has been estimated that not less than eight millions of our people are living under conditions represented by a family income of under a pound a week. In the majority of instances this means not merely discomfort but real physical deterioration of the future English men and women who are now the children of such families.

In the mines, at the docks, in the textile mills and the Potteries, men's work stopped. So did wages:

Dean Ring, of St Mary and St Michael's, Commercial Road, London, has been working night and day among the destitute thousands in his dockers' district, and has succeeded in keeping many families alive who must otherwise have starved to death.

He has contracted blood-poisoning following weeks of exhausting toil in the slums of his district.

'It is impossible for the outside world to realise all the ghastly horror of this strike,' he said.

'The people are literally starving to death by thousands. They have pawned everything they possess in the world and have nothing to do but sit at home and starve.

'I could take you to homes where everything has been sold and the members of the family crouch on the floor and watch each other starve. They have nothing left to buy food with, no clothes to go out in, and no furniture and no fuel. What use would a fire be when there is nothing to cook?

'So they just sit on the floor in speechless despair, day and night, waiting for something to come and end it all.

'Few people know that there is really such a state as "speechless despair" but I can see it every day – agony which can find no words to express its depths.

'It was only the other day that I saw one wretched mother begging feverishly that a pawnbroker should give her twopence for two little glass vases. They were all she had left and she wanted to buy two cods' heads with the twopence to keep her children alive a little longer.

'The pawnshops are full of the miserable wreckage of the dockers' homes, and the pawnbrokers will take no more. So even those who have anything left to sell are in a dreadful plight.

'I am constantly giving bread to people who rend it to pieces like wolves, not having tasted food for forty-eight hours.'

The situation in the Potteries was no better :

Many in the Potteries are quiet, reserved folk, who, even if they earn small wages, live above the poverty line as a rule, and are the last to confess that now the strike has caught them unawares, they are all but penniless.

Many of them would almost as soon die of starvation as line up in the streets with the yet poorer or less thrifty who stand by the hour waiting their turn for bread and soup, but even the thrifty who have spent their 25s. a week on their homes and their children without being able to save are being discovered on all sides with bare cupboards, and sometimes bare boards, furniture and clocks and carpets and clothes having been sold or pawned for food.

'I was going along the street last night,' a man told me today, 'When I met a chap I know carrying a chair in each hand. "Where are you off to?' I asked him. "Going to sell these," he said, and then he broke out : "By God, they must have a bit to eat."'

Another man told me he met a neighbour with the parlour table on his head. He was looking for someone who would buy. That is the difficulty the folk have – no one will buy, and the pawnbrokers want no more.

There are 250,000 people in the Potteries, and almost all employment has ceased, and so the quiet families who keep themselves to themselves are starving alone and unknown until some good soul with a richer share of the world's wealth breaks in on them and gently works up to the question, 'How are you getting on?' Then with a shake of the head the wife of the starving man admits that they have 'nothing coming in'.

You press the question, 'What have you got in the cupboard?' At last pride gives way, there is a torrent of hot tears, and the foodless cupboard is opened.

You cannot invade homes like those; their sufferings are sacred. But some of the good women in Hanley, who go round finding these grim secrets out, have told me of the fortitude of those who 'clem' behind closed doors. They have found families who have had no food between their lips for twenty-four hours or more at a stretch.

Private charity fed the starving and it was, on the whole generous, tactful and kindly.

But if some proud folk bore their sufferings with tight lips others went on the rampage. By March 1912 with nearly half the trade unionists in the country on strike the Army was involved in quelling riots. Two men had been shot dead by troops in Liverpool, two others (see page 196) at Llanelli. On 2 March, the *Express* reported :

We understand that should troops be sent to the mining districts, the majority of them will be billeted on the civil population, under the billeting clause inserted in the Army Annual Act.

A meeting of the Generals commanding military districts took place on Monday last at the War Office, and preparations were begun that night by issuing orders for all troops to stand by and all leave to be stopped. It was decided to make every man available for strike duty, and convert the field artillery for the time being into infantry.

Each commander who has any troops under arms 'standing-by' has arranged with the railway companies for rolling-stock, and these have prepared a number of special trains, lying convenient for entraining the troops.

Although they have engaged skating rinks, schools and other buildings for conversion into barracks, it has been decided that accommodation would be inadequate and that billeting must be resorted to. The police are acting in co-operation with the military authorities, and in many cases have helped to compile records showing the housing accommodation of almost every dwelling in various towns and villages.

When troops are billeted on private houses the regiments are simply marched along the street, in double ranks, which halt at a given order outside the houses to be occupied, either singly or in twos, according to the accommodation known to exist. A knock is made on the door, and the soldier enters.

If the household should refuse to obey the dictates of the authorities he will become amenable to the civil law. He may protest that his house is small and his family large – the authorities will decide whether there is room for the soldiers or not.

He must allow the soldiers the use of fire and cooking utensils, and he or his servants may be asked to perform menial duties. The greater his means the greater number of soldiers he must house.

Payment will, of course, be made for food, and if his means are too slender to provide provisions he may be given a contract note by the paymaster.

To this 'provocation' the miners' 'friends' reacted by publishing seditious propaganda designed to suborn the soldiers from their duty :

At Aldershot a man giving his name as Frederick Crowsley, a railway fireman, was charged with inciting soldiers to commit treasonable practices.

Crowsley was arrested on Sunday by the military police at South Camp. It is alleged that he was distributing among the soldiers a leaflet containing the following incitement to mutiny :

'Men, Comrades, Brothers – you are in the Army. So are we. You are in the army of destruction, we in the industrial army of construction. We work in mine, mill, factory, forge, producing and transporting goods which make it possible for people to live.

'You are working men's sons.

'When we go on strike to better our lot, which is the lot also of your fathers, mothers, sisters and brothers, you are called upon by your officers to murder us.

'Don't do it ! You know it happens and always has happened. We stand out as long as we can. Then one of our and your irresponsible brothers, goaded by the sight of his and his loved ones' misery and hunger, commits a crime on property.

'Immediately you are ordered to murder us as you did at Mitchelstown, Featherstone, and Belfast.

Don't you know that when you are out of the colours and become a civvy again that you, like us, may be on strike, and you, like us, be murdered by other soldiers ?

'Boys, don't do it ! "Thou shalt not kill," says the Book. Don't forget that it does not say "Unless you have a uniform on." No, murder is murder, whether committed in the heat of anger on one who had wronged a loved one, or by pipe-clayed Tommies with rifles. Boys, don't do it ! Act the man, the brother, the human being.

'The idle and rich classes who own and order you about, own and order us about also. They and their friends own the land, and the means of life of Britain.

'You, like us, are of the slave class. When we rise you rise. When we fall even by your bullets, you fall also.

'Comrades, have we called in vain ? Think things over, and refuse any longer to murder your kindred.'

Tom Mayfield, in a revolutionary Socialist paper, *The Dawn,* went further:

> 'Strikes and lock-outs may still continue for years, and the worker pays his 6d. a week into his union. Why not save 3d. per week for a revolver? The time will surely come, if it is not already here, when you will need it. . . .
>
> 'Therefore, arm! Meet the soldiers and police on more equal terms. They proved themselves to be the enemy of the workers, and when the time comes, shoot low, not too low, but just low enough. . . .
>
> 'If blood has to be shed, I do not see why it should always be the workers' blood. Let us see how the master class like the operation of blood-letting. If it would take too long to get a shooter saving 3d. per week, let the unions get them for you. It would be money well spent, I am sure. Or join the Territorials; here you would get guns and instruction. . . .'

Such appeals to soldiers to join their industrial comrades or to strikers to shoot the soldiers had no effect whatever. The troops remained entirely unmoved by calls to put working class solidarity before their oath and the strikers did not attempt to arm themselves.

Radicals in the Liberal Party had for some time been departing from the stern, unbending Manchester School doctrine of laissez faire which frowned on all forms of regulation or state interference as intolerable infringements on personal liberty and damned obstacles on the way of profits to boot. One radical MP stated:

> *'Unemployment is the problem of the hour, and that problem is not confined to periods of trade depression and will not be solved by trade revival.
>
> 'The social machinery at the basis of our industrial life is deficient, ill-organised and incomplete. While large numbers of persons enjoy great wealth, while the mass of the artisan classes are abreast of and in advance of their fellows in other lands, there is a minority – considerable in numbers, whose condition is a disgrace to a scientific and professedly Christian civilisation, and constitutes a grave and increasing peril to the State.

*Unemployment, inflation . . . and there were other examples of the truth that nothing changes. Trade union bullying of non-union members was reported from Bury in 1912. The flood of foreign imports sparked off a 'Buy British' campaign in 1911. Poor productivity was attacked in an editorial on New Year's Day, 1901.

'It ought to be possible for some authority in some Government office – which I do not care – to view the whole situation in advance, and within certain limits, to exert a powerful influence over the general distribution of Government contracts.

'There is nothing economically unsound in increasing temporarily and artificially the demand for labour during a period of temporary and artificial contraction.

'When the extent of the depression is foreseen, the extent of the relief should also be determined. There ought, further, to be in permanent existence certain recognised industries of a useful but non-competitive character – like, we will say, afforestation – managed by public departments and capable of being expanded or contracted according to the needs of the labour market, just as easily as you can pull out the stops, or work the pedals of an organ.'

The radical MP was Winston Churchill speaking in October 1908. Fourteen months later he presided over the introduction of labour exchanges. The *Express* commented on those who queued for vacancies:

There are men of many types, and of all ages, from fifteen to fifty or more. Some had the brand of the unemployable on their faces while others looked strong and able and willing to work. The majority seemed just ordinary decent men of their various trades.

Many were labourers and carmen, but the labourers formed nothing like a majority. The diversity of trades was indeed surprising.

Two of the first jobs on offer in Shoreditch were for a 'piano regulator' and a 'picture gilder'.

As the labour scene darkened, Churchill and his ally, Chancellor Lloyd George, prompted and guided legislation through the Commons. Long-suffering shop assistants were given relief by an Act which limited their working week to sixty hours, exclusive of meals. A free trade Liberal querulously asked: 'How is it possible to restrict the hours of milk delivery to sixty a week?'

Anti-free trade Tories claimed that low wages, unemployment and consequent labour discontent were directly attributable to foreign competition undercutting the British working man: impose tariffs and all would be well.

The *Express,* tirelessly campaigning for tariff reform, instanced the tale of the little town of Glemsford in Suffolk as the quintessential victim of free trade :

Free Trade has rarely ruined a town so thoroughly as it has ruined Glemsford. Glemsford is still famous for the silk it used to make and its clatter of looms was once very loud. In later years there was a prosperous mat industry, too, but it had been crushed to death with the silk trade.

Glemsford is really a large village perched on the top of a hill. A few years ago there were 3,000 inhabitants, as prosperous and independent as any in the three counties.

Now there are less than 2,000, and I am assured that 200 workless men are waiting for something to turn up. More than forty families left the village together a month or two ago, when Kolle's mat factory closed its doors.

As I entered the village to-day three or four men walked close by me, at intervals touching their hats. The last one came right up and asked if I could spare him a glass of beer – or the money.

Mr Ezra Game, a member of the district council, noticed the man's salute and he said to me quietly: 'That's how they have to live, you know, now.'

Afraid to challenge the outer world, of which they know nothing, they touch their hats to strangers while they wait for a new industry to spring up. The more fortunate of these men are still receiving 7s 6d a week from a trade union fund; the others have not a penny.

Mr Game, who is a Liberal, and in most matters a Free Trader, admits that a duty of 15 per cent on imported silk would set the staple industry on its feet again.

Others, Winston Churchill among them, did not accept that either protection or free trade held the answers. In days to come that great argument would give way to another doctrinal struggle between nationalisation and private enterprise. A strong hint of what lay ahead was given by Lloyd George in May 1912 at the height of the year of strikes:

'We have had the labour unrest problem with us for at least a hundred years. The cause of the unrest is the feeling of the workmen that they are not getting a fair share of the general prosperity.

'I do not object to the nationalisation of railways. There is a good deal to be said for it from the point of view of traders and the country generally. There is a great deal of waste under the present competitive system but I am not sanguine enough to believe that nationalisation would put an end to labour troubles.'

No one would deny the Welsh Wizard's gift for prophecy. Yet it is hard to imagine that Lloyd George would have foreseen that the Welfare State he did so much to bring into being would be accompanied by a sharp rise, instead of a fall, in crime.

CHAPTER XII

Crime and Punishment

Any doubts about whether or not we have become a more lawless community as the century has advanced are removed by reference to the press files for 1900.

'Moral Birmingham' ran this heading for an item on Wednesday, 12 December, 1900: 'The calendar at Birmingham Assizes provided Mr Justice Lawrence with the opportunity of congratulating the city on its morality. There was not one charge under the Criminal Law Amendment Act.'

Ten years later the headline referred to the situation in the capital:

CRIME AS A DYING
INDUSTRY

Crime as a profession is declining. This the Londoner can learn from a perusal of a primly-bound panorama of London, issued yesterday under the title of *Report of the Commissioner of Police of the Metropolis for the year 1909.*

In the year 1870 there were 19,095 felonies relating to property when the population was 3,618,992 – and only a few more than half the felons were caught. Now the police catch 13,322 people for 17,983 felonies; and although the population has doubled the total amount secured 'by professionals' only advanced from £79,223 to £133,211, while the amount recovered advanced from £19,174 to £42,984.

The crime rate, which declined in London between 1870 and 1910, rose 1,400 per cent in the succeeding 65 years.

Not that the whole nation was a model of rectitude. Black news was given of Scotland's misdemeanours:

'The most notable fact of the statistics for 1899 is the immense increase of the criminal work of the country.' Thus opened the report

on Scotland's prisons and court for the past year, which was an
unenviable record.

No fewer than 176,524 persons were apprehended or cited, a figure
which has never before been reached by 10,000. Drunks and dis-
orderlies alone totalled 112,033.

South Queensferry holds the proud position for 1899 of being the
most drunken Scottish town, 1,424 in every 10,000 of its population
being charged.

An alarming precociousness was shown in the fact that there were
forty-two convicted house-breakers under twelve years of age and
ninety-two between twelve and sixteen years.

When the nationalities of the convicted are closely examined the
Scottish race are relieved of much of the discredit the foregoing
figure would appear to cast upon them, for they total but 52 per
cent, while the Irish make up 43 per cent, and the English 4 per cent.

These were the days when sentences were passed to deter and punish
and little thought was given to reform, rehabilitation or mitigation.

The *Daily Express* and other newspapers waxed indignant over the
'excessively light sentence' (seven years' penal servitude) passed by Mr
Justice Darling on the 'ruffian Beels' who killed a Mr Murray Spicer on
the night of celebrations following the South African peace treaty of
1902.

Mr Justice Darling's desire not to inflame a law-abiding populace
against the hooligan as a class has filled the aforesaid populace with
amazement. The judge was entirely right in saying that some might
think his sentence unduly light.

Lord Norton, a justice of the peace of very long standing, is
indignant at the growing leniency with which the street ruffian is
treated by some writers and administrators of the law.

'Stuff and nonsense!' he declared to a representative of the
Express. 'What is the good of flattering the vanity and pampering the
pride of these ruffians by sending them to gaol for short sentences.'

'Give them the proper treatment. Flog the brutes. It is the only
thing they are afraid of. It is the only thing that will cure them.'

And as to inflaming the public mind against them by inflicting
short sentences?

'If I had my way,' replied Lord Norton, 'something would be
inflamed, but it would not be the public mind!

'You remember the recent case where a young scoundrel, who

actually boasted that he was the champion of the hooligan gang, was convicted of a series of gross outrages and sentenced to only fourteen months' hard labour?

'I cannot do better than repeat what I wrote at the time:

'By recent wise and successful legislation this was just the case intended for severe corporal chastisement. This would have cured a vicious vanity, made a pestilent fool wise, and rid the country of much brutal annoyance. The so-called punishment inflicted adds to the violence gloried in, and imposes a charge on the public for housing, feeding, and clothing for fourteen months the uncured villain. At the close of his entertainment he will be stronger, keener, and greatly encouraged to resume his championship. With such stupidity on the bench we must learn wisdom from the hooligans.

'Really,' concluded his lordship, 'I have no patience with some of the writers of to-day, who want us to go cap-in-hand to the young hooligan and lead him by tender steps to the haven of reform. Upon my word, I am sometimes tempted to think they deserve a little touch of the cat themselves.'

Mr William Wheatley, the secretary of the Discharged Prisoners' Aid Society, was also a believer in the wholesome efficacy of the cat.

'When a case such as this is proved beyond a doubt,' he says, 'I cannot think that seven years' imprisonment is too much or requires any apology on the ground of its severity.

'When a scoundrel goes out into the street, and deliberately and without provocation inflicts a blow that kills a peaceable member of society – no, I can't think that seven years is too heavy a punishment. I doubt whether it is heavy enough to put down this class of crime.

'That which they give to others let them receive themselves. The lash is the only remedy. I have got into trouble for saying that before, but I know the breed, and I say it again.

'Don't call these brutes hooligans! They have become proud of the title, and boast of it. Call them what they are, ruffians and brutes, and deal with them accordingly.'

Flogging criminals – a practice that continued until the end of the Second World War – was much in vogue during the first decade of the century. A five-line item in April 1908 stated simply: Mr Justice A. T. Lawrence sentenced James King to twelve lashes with the cat and five years' penal servitude at Cardiff for robbery with violence. This is the fourteenth flogging ordered during the present assizes for this crime.

Considering that the Secretary of the Discharged Prisoners' Aid Society was in favour of the lash, it is not surprising that the newspapers gave vent to praising condign punishment, like this editorial from the *Express* of 5 July, 1902 :

The cynic might be pardoned a sneer and the philosopher a sigh when the one or the other reads that Mr d'Eyncourt, the magistrate, had to ask whether any one in authority over a youth understood the art and artifice of thorough and proper flogging. The flogging suggested for the youth was, let it be understood, a kind subterfuge on the part of the magistrate, for the culprit was too old for the law to command the safe and salutary method of purging an offence. Passing the father's hesitancy to step into the breach, and the brother's alacrity to act as the arm of the law, we may ask with the magistrate : How many persons understand the art of flogging properly. It might be summarised as an outward application of merciful justice, accurately directed force, and benevolent severity to the spot provided by an intelligent and anticipatory Nature for the purpose. Should any one feel qualms of conscience about preparing and mingling the prescription, an easy way out may be suggested. Why should not parents form a syndicate and depute the task of flogging to the incorruptible representative of law and order – the local policeman? A solatium of half-a-crown would surely make him eager to guide many a wayward foot in the path of prudence and probity. In this way the rod would neither remain in pickle nor the child spared his own subsequent undoing.

  In any case, Mr d'Eyncourt's hint, duly taken to heart and executed, might do infinite good. It would for the time being cause tingling sensations on the person of the young victim, but would lead to a corner of his heart being kept warm in the future. There are few things many of us recall with more sincere gratitude than the thorough flogging we so richly deserved and so thoroughly received. Modern parents should not allow the art of flogging to pass into the limbo of forgotten achievements. Many a man's career has been made by the birches at school, even if it was difficult to sit down under the insult. If we are going to be anything, let us be thorough, even when we punish personally or by proxy those for whose misdoings, major or minor, we are to some extent responsible.

When Parliament in November 1912 debated the use of the cat for procuring and for crimes against women and children, the *Express* rejoiced at the fierceness of some MPs and deplored the milky-watery views of others :

The ethics of flogging were the main subject of debate when the House, getting back to realities today, assembled to strengthen the Bill.

Mr George Greenwood (Liberal, Peterborough) moved the omission of the clause which provides that any procurer convicted of a second or subsequent offence should be liable in the discretion of the court to be once privately flogged. 'It's a return to the methods of barbarism,' cried Mr Greenwood, amid pitying smiles.

Mr Arthur Lynch (Nationalist, West Clare) who seconded, described the horror of flogging – which in the eyes of many members seemed a good argument for its infliction on vile brutes.

Mr Lynch told of a friend of his who saw a man flogged twenty-five years ago and said the memory of the sight was 'an invariable nightmare' to him now. His friend told him the man who did the flogging 'rejoiced in the work'.

'He was an artist in it,' said Mr Lynch. 'He laid on the lash with such vigour that at every stroke the victim's whole frame quivered, his eyes rolled, his muscles stood out as though they would burst through his skin, and his face turned livid. Even the hardened warders present, whose hearts had been inured, turned almost sick at the sight and were unable to face it.

Mr F. B. Mildmay (Unionist, Devon, Totnes) declared that flogging is a deterrent for men whose instincts are animal instincts.

Mr McKenna, the Home Secretary, replied saying : 'I am informed that in London there are a number of young men, almost entirely of foreign origin, who live on young women even to the extent of £15 or £20 a week. These men accumulate fortunes in the trade. The police ask that what hitherto has been a defence, namely that they have means of their own – shall no longer be a defence. This bill meets the point.

'The police say that after the first conviction, if there is power to flog, there will be nobody to flog. London has become a dumping ground for this trade by men whom the police believe will be intimidated by the fear of flogging.'

Colonel Lockwood (Unionist, Epping) said 'he would like to see flogging introduced in regard to all offences against women and children.'

'How many members here would take the "cat" in their hands and administer the flogging?' asked Mr Leif Jones.

'I would,' answered Colonel Lockwood.

Mr Will Crooks (Socialist, Woolwich) said : 'There's a lot of maudlin sentiment about all this. I'm glad these scoundrels have a skin that can be tanned.' (Cheers.) He said if they wanted anybody to do the flogging they could call on him.

The Hon Edward Wood (Unionist, Ripon), son of Lord Halifax, said : 'When I was at school I was whipped three times before breakfast on one occasion, and I'm none the worse for it. It had an extremely deterrent effect on me.'

The anti-flogging amendment was rejected by 297 to 44, a majority of 253 for flogging.

Then the House went further and put in an amendment to flog for the first offence.

Mr Austin Chamberlain, who summed up in his strong common-sense way, said : 'The infliction of physical pain on a few men would be as nothing to the infinite misery which would be prevented.'

The House of Lords cordially endorsed the lower chamber's decision. The Parliamentary report for 29 November, 1912, reads :

The House of Lords, which contained a number of bishops, gladly passed the second reading of the Bill without a division. There is excellent prospect now of the measure being passed into law.

The flogging provisions in the Bill were praised by the Lord Chancellor, the Lord Chief Justice, and the Primate. The following are the various views expressed on this particular clause of the Bill :

The Lord Chancellor : It would be an advantage if the power was given to inflicting corporal punishment for a first offence.

The Archbishop of Canterbury : I am willing to risk one innocent man being flogged in a generation.

The Lord Chief Justice : I do not think any one can doubt the influence of flogging as a deterrent.

Lord Willoughby de Broke : I certainly favour flogging for a first offence, and I am willing to run the risk of being flogged in mistake.

Lord Lansdowne : A punishment which may not unfairly be described as 'brutalising' is a proper punishment when we are dealing with men who are brutes.

Lords Crewe, Lytton and Russell dissented.

Mild-mannered Justice Darling was so impressed with Parliament's grim resolve that he took the first opportunity in January 1913 to sentence Timothy O'Connor, aged 40, to 18 months' hard labour and

30 strokes with the cat o'nine tails for procuring his wife for immoral purposes.

Procurers were not the only targets for those who sought to chastise wrongdoers. The Mormon Church had begun a campaign of conversion in the UK and this provoked an angry response from the Established Church:

The Rev G. Ernest Thorne told a rally of the anti-Mormon League at Caxton Hall that he would like to see an enactment making it penal for a Mormon elder to be found proselytising servant girls and young women.

'I should like to see the birch used on Mormon elders,' he stated amid applause.

The American way with miscreants was looked on with a considerable degree of approbation. Recording the fact of 'four executions in 39 minutes' in 1914, the *Express* recounted the details:

'Dago Frank', 'Whitey Lewis', 'Gyp the Blood', and 'Lefty Louis', the four gunmen who were convicted of the murder nearly two years ago, in front of a Broadway hotel, of Rosenthal, the gambler, were electrocuted this morning in Sing Sing Prison.

An hour and a half before his death, 'Dago Frank', whose real name was Frank Cirofici, yielded to the importunities of his mother and sister and Father Cashin, the prison chaplain, to purge his soul by confession. The two women and the priest had sat all night in front of his cell, but the condemned man remained obdurate until 4 a.m., when he consented to make a full confession.

Forty-eight witnesses were present during the executions – a number so unprecedentedly large that they had to be divided into four squads, one for each victim. All the prisoners had received slight doses of morphine before being led into the death chamber – just enough partly to daze them and prevent their collapse.

The first led in was 'Dago Frank', who appeared at 5.38 a.m. supported by Father Cashin. He appeared dazed, and muttered, 'God have mercy on my soul.'

He sat quietly in the death chair while the electrodes were being adjusted, mumbling under his breath. Then he was heard to say: 'Mother – Father, look out for my mother.'

The current was turned on, and he stiffened for a moment and then collapsed. Two more shocks were administered before the physicians pronounced him dead.

'Whitey Lewis' entered at 5.47 a.m. with Rabbi Goldstein. He also was dazed, but had less need for support than 'Dago Frank'. He was obviously trying to say something but could not utter any words until the attendants were actually strapping him in the chair. Then, as the death mask was fixed in place, the water which streamed over his face from the wet sponge, which is part of the apparatus, seemed to startle him into consciousness.

'For the sake of justice, gentlemen,' he said, 'I would like to say that the people who testified on the witness stand that they saw me fire a shot were perjurers. I want to say they are perjurers.

'I swear to my God I fired no shot at Rosenthal. I did not want to go to court. Stannish testified.'

The electric shock interrupted his sentence, and then three others were sent through his body.

'Gyp the Blood' was brought in by Rabbi Goldstein at 5.56 a.m. and 'Lefty Louis' by Rabbi Kopstein at 6.07 a.m. Both were so dazed that their mumblings were indistinguishable, except their low repetitions after the Rabbis of the Jewish confessional : 'Hear, O Israel ! There is one God, only one.'

'Lefty Louis,' the last of the four, was pronounced dead at 8.17 a.m. The bodies were all claimed by relatives, to whom they will be surrendered after the post mortem.

Newspapers, however, did report sympathetically criticisms of excessive punishment and campaigned – in the case of the *Daily Express* vigorously – for the improvement of the lot of the convict. As late as 1910 sentences were being passed reminiscent of the eighteenth century Judge Braxfield who once told a reforming zealot who had pleaded that he had acted as Jesus Christ would have done 'Aye and ye ken what happened to him !' One such case of cruel justice was reported in the issue of 12 April 1910 :

The Hayward's Heath magistrates yesterday sent a boy of twelve – a first offender – to a reformatory for seven years for stealing a lump of coal valued at 5d as well as ordering the lad to receive six strokes with the birch rod.

The lad's explanation of the theft of the piece of coal was that he did not want to have to go next morning to buy some with his mother. So he went to the wharf in the evening and took the lump home.

The little offender's name is Charles Bulback. His father burst into tears on hearing the sentence imposed on the child, and told the magistrates that he thought they were a bit hard.

The magistrates laughed at the father's plea, and Mr R. J. Waugh said: 'You should look after your boy better.'

Although the boy had never been charged before the magistrates ordered the father to pay £1 9s 11d costs and to contribute to the lad's maintenance in the reformatory.

Merciful judges found themselves saddened by the mandatory sentences they were obliged to pass, as with this case in July 1911:

A painful scene occurred at the Old Bailey yesterday when Mrs Margaret Murphy, aged 38, a Shoreditch flower-seller, was sentenced to death for murdering her little daughter Gertrude. Her other children were waiting outside the court to hear the sentence, and when it was announced their distress was pitiable.

The woman's husband died recently, and the family were in very poor circumstances. Then she lost all her money in a business venture in Epsom, and this so distressed her that she poisoned her infant and attempted suicide.

Evidence was given that she was emotionally unbalanced by her misfortunes, and the jury strongly recommended her to mercy.

'Very few people outside can know how painful it is to have to decide in such a case,' said Mr Justice Darling. 'But we have a duty to perform to the State, and are not entitled to gratify our own feelings of sympathy.

'It is my duty to pronounce the only sentence which it is in my power to pronounce, but I will in every way support the recommendation to mercy, and I have not the slightest doubt that the recommendation will receive all the consideration to which it is entitled, and in my judgement most strongly entitled.

Confidence in the rightness of sending people to the gallows was somewhat shaken when the *Express* published this in October 1913:

The *Express* has received the following remarkable letter from Dr Albert Wilson, late president of the Royal Medical Society, Edinburgh:

'Having always been doubtful of the value of capital punishment, about four years ago I asked Berry, the ex-hangman, to come and see me. I found him an interesting man with a pleasing, kindly face, stout and hearty. He was previously a police constable, and always had the desire to be public executioner. He assisted Marwood on several occasions and described his method (the knot under the chin) as cruel and clumsy. Berry placed the slipknot under the left ear, and said his victims "looked beautiful".

'He told me that he gave up his office because the executions by him of two innocent persons got on his nerves.

'The first was a farm boy, aged about eighteen, accused of shooting a policeman, I think in Gloucester or Somerset. In the cell the lad kissed him and protested his innocence. Before the drop fell, he said, "Mr Berry, you will live to see that I am innocent".

'Some time after this he hanged the two Netherby Hall murderers. No one could sympathise with them. The first murderer while being pinioned asked Berry if he had hanged this youth, adding that his confederate, Jack Martin, shot the policeman in his presence. Jack Martin confirmed this.

'The next case was more painful, that of Mary Leffley, in Lincolnshire. Berry said he never got over it. The poor woman clung to the bedstead, protesting her innocence. The governor, the matron, and Berry forcibly dressed her. She was carried screaming to the gallows. The rope was put round her neck and she was thrown into the pit, making frantic efforts all the while to free herself. This was Berry's description, which may not coincide with the Home Office official report.

'Mary Leffley was accused of poisoning her husband with arsenic. There was no evidence that she ever possessed arsenic, but there was much popular indignation against her.

'Some years later a farmer, dying of cancer, confessed to the crime. He had a quarrel with John Leffley and when both Mary and John were out he entered their cottage and put arsenic in a milk pudding baking for John's dinner.'

Increasingly the Bench tempered justice with understanding. When a certain George Lawrence, 68, appeared before the London Sessions in May 1912 he admitted that he had spent fifty years in jail. He had, during the 1860s, 1880s and 1890s received three ten-year terms for stealing forks, a box and an overcoat, the total value of all the things he purloined amounted to £20. He was given 12 months' hard labour for stealing a plant. The old man expressed deep gratitude.

Moved by injustices caused by the rigidity of the law a group of

Parliamentarians suggested amendments that would prevent the death sentence being passed on accused whom it was never intended to execute – such as women who had committed infanticide. The reformers also suggested two degrees of murder : the first degree, carrying the capital penalty, for those who murdered with malice aforethought : the second carrying varying terms of imprisonment depending on the circumstances of the killing. Degrees of murder were finally introduced in to the UK penal code in 1956.

Equally in need of reform was the method of reporting suspects. The Press blithely ignored the concept of prejudicing the rights of the accused by such passages as :

So far no trace of the perpetrator of the revolting child murder in Liverpool has been found.

The man, John Bennett, on whom suspicion has fallen as being the destroyer of the little girl Evelyn Christopherson, is nowhere to be found, a fact which is held to strengthen the belief in his guilt.

The papers were apt to record the named criminal's cliche 'It's a fair cop' at the moment of arrest and before charges had been preferred. Sterner legal rules governing reporting did not become common practice until the 1920s.

But if the Press had a somewhat slap-happy approach to legal ethics the courts themselves were grievously at fault in accepting 'evidence' of guilt that ought not to have convicted a cat.

A classic case which changed the law and led to the establishment of the Court of Criminal Appeal in 1908 was that of Adolf Beck. This Scandinavian adventurer had come to England in the 1880s. His English accent was atrocious until the day of his death, saying 'yury' for 'jury', 'dat' for 'that'. Yet he was accused and convicted in 1895 of impersonating an English nobleman and robbing women both of their virtue and their valuables. Having been 'identified' by ten victims – but not by the twelve others whose evidence was suppressed – Beck was jailed for seven years.

Shortly after his release he was arrested for a second time. On this occasion justice was done and Beck commented : 'I pray that I may be the means of giving England a Criminal Court of Appeal, and if I am the means of bringing this about, I shall not regret my imprisonment.'

Five years after that generous observation Beck died. The *Express* published his obituary :

Adolf Beck, the victim of one of the most remarkable miscarriages of justice in modern times, died yesterday in the Middlesex Hospital from bronchitis and pneumonia.

It may be taken as an index of the state of poverty in which he died that yesterday afternoon his furniture, which had been seized for debt on Thursday, the day he was taken to hospital, was sold by auction.

The story of Beck's wrongful imprisonment stirred so much public comment and indignation five years ago that it earned him the name of the 'English Dreyfus'.

He was born in Norway, but spent a considerable part of his life in England on business connected with the mining industry. In 1895 he was arrested on a charge of defrauding women, and was sentenced at the Old Bailey in the following year to seven years' penal servitude.

He served five years and a half, protesting his innocence all the while, and was released; then, however, he was arrested again in 1904 on a similar charge. Again he was convicted; but, providentially for him, Mr Justice Grantham deferred his sentence, and while he was in custody awaiting his second committal to prison another man was arrested on a similar charge, and happened to pass in front of him.

The man was not his double; this was the strangest part of the case, for Beck had been identified by several women who claimed to be his victims; but the stranger walked like Beck, and had a small scar on his face, which several of the women said they remembered.

This almost miraculous chance meeting of the two men saved Beck a further term in prison and cleared his name. The haunting yet elusive likeness between the men induced Inspector Kane to begin exhaustive police inquiries, which proved beyond doubt that Beck had suffered for the crimes of another man.

He was granted a 'free pardon' which established his innocence; but his business had been ruined and in consideration of this he was offered a 'solatium' of £2,000 by the Treasury.

Public indignation and sympathy had been so aroused, however, by his case, that the solatium was on every hand pronounced insufficient, and he was finally awarded £5,000. Since receiving his award he lived in comparative seclusion, never regaining the health which he lost during his undeserved imprisonment.

A far graver instance of wrongful arrest, and one that so nearly led to lawless execution, was Oscar Slater's.

Mr Slater was not a nice man. It is doing his memory no injustice to say he tempted fate : but he did not deserve the fate that overcame him.

This is the story told by contemporaries of the man who was so obviously innocent of the crime with which he was charged, that undue influence on the police must be suspected. From the *Express* file of 22 December, 1908 :

A terrible murder was committed about 8 p.m. yesterday in a flat at Queen's terrace, Glasgow, one of the best residential quarters.

The victim was Miss Marion Gilchrist, eighty years old, a woman of considerable wealth, who lived with one servant.

The servant had only been absent from the flat for five to ten minutes, having gone to purchase an evening newspaper. Apparently the man who committed the murder had burglary as his object.

It is supposed that he must have gone up to the house and rung the bell, that the door was opened by Miss Gilchrist, and that he attacked her.

He then evidently carried her into the dining-room as she was found with her skull battered lying in front of the fire-place. Her head was covered with the hearth rug.

The man had forced open a box in Miss Gilchrist's bedroom, as a number of papers, rings and gold watches were found on the floor.

On 4 May, 1909, the *Express* wrote :

Crowds besieged the historic High Court of Justiciary in Edinburgh yesterday when the trial of Oscar Slater, a German, on a charge of murdering Miss Marion Gilchrist began.

The atrocious circumstances of the crime, the position of the victim, the dramatic arrest of Slater on board a liner, and many remarkable rumours concerning the motive of the murderer had aroused intense interest in Scotland.

The only clue the police had was that a stranger was seen coming out of the house after the murder had been committed. Slater was suspected, and was tracked to New York, where he was arrested on board a liner.

There are ninety-eight witnesses for the prosecution, and the case is expected to occupy four days. The Lord Advocate, Mr Ure, KC, MP, is the chief counsel for the Crown, and Slater is defended by Mr McClure.

Shortly after ten o'clock a trapdoor in the court was raised and

Slater emerged. He is a middle-aged man of light but athletic build. His complexion is dark, and his features heavy.

The most prominent of his features is his nose, which is very large and slightly bent, as if he had been injured. Because of this he has been referred to by some of the witnesses as 'the man with the twisted nose'.

While the jury were being empanelled he nervously bit his moustache, and it was evident throughout the day that he was suffering from the strain of his position.

The story of the discovery of the crime was told by Helen Lambie, a servant, who was the only companion of Miss Gilchrist. She said that on the night of 21 December she went on an errand, double-locking the door of the flat and closing the street door.

'When I returned I noticed that the street door was open, and I saw a wet footmark on the stairs,' she continued. 'I found Mr Adams, our neighbour, at the door. He told me that there was a noise in our flat, and that it seemed as if the ceiling would crack.

'As I unlocked the door I saw a man coming from the spare bedroom. He passed close to me, and I saw his face. When I went into the dining-room I saw Miss Gilchrist lying in front of the fire.'

Lambie positively identified Slater as the man she saw.

'While I was in the entrance of the New York court [Lambie had gone to New York to help in the extradition proceedings against Slater] I saw three men coming along a corridor,' she declared. 'I turned to the detective who was with me and said, "There is the man I saw in the lobby of Miss Gilchrist's house."'

'I only saw the side of his face.' 'I did see his fact a bit.' 'I was excited the first day I was in America', were some of her replies when counsel pressed the point that she had not seen the man's face.

'I recognised his walk,' she said. 'He shook forward a little bit.'

A number of witnesses swore they saw Slater loitering outside the flat on several days before the murder. Other witnesses thought Slater was the man they had seen near the flat, but were not certain.

Detective Piper said a girl named Mary Barrowman gave the police a description of a man she saw running out of Miss Gilchrist's house on the night of the crime.

What did Miss Barrowman identify him by? – By his nose, principally. She said it was a twisted nose – a little turned to the right side.

Mr McClure observed: 'Do you think it is fair, while conducting an identification, to put a man among a number of other men whom he does not in the least resemble?'

'That is not for me to say,' Piper stated.

In reply to further questions by Mr McClure, Piper admitted that when he searched Slater's luggage he found no garments which bore the slightest appearance of blood stains.

'Can you conceive of the man who executed the murder not having bloodstains on his clothing? counsel asked.

'I should fancy there would be a lot of stains,' the detective stated.

Mr Arthur Adams, who lived in a flat below that of Miss Gilchrist, told how, hearing a thud on the floor and three knocks, he ran upstairs.

'When the servant entered the flat a well-dressed man approached me,' he continued. 'He came up to me quite pleasantly and coolly, and I did not suspect him, but when he had passed me he went down the stairs like lightning, and banged the door. I identified Slater as the man, but the case is too serious for me to be confident that he was.'

Slater was again asked to stand up and show both sides of his face, when Mrs Laura Liddle stated that she saw a man loitering near Miss Gilchrist's house. Mrs Liddle stepped down from the witness-box and approached close to him.

'Yes,' she said after some hesitation. 'I do believe he is the man.'

Professor Glaister described in detail the terrible injuries that were inflicted on Miss Gilchrist.

'The murderer must have knelt on her chest and struck nearly forty violent blows with almost lightning rapidity,' he declared. 'In the hands of a strong man and violently wielded the hammer might have produced the injuries.'

The professor said that in his opinion the murderer's clothes would be blood-stained.

On Friday, 7 May, this report appeared:

There was a painful scene in the High Court of Justiciary, at Edinburgh, yesterday when Oscar Slater, the German with the twisted nose, was sentenced to death for the murder of Miss Marion Gilchrist.

When the foreman of the jury announced that the verdict was 'Guilty', Slater, who had shown remarkable coolness and self-possession throughout the trial, jumped from his seat, the slight flush that had tinged his cheeks giving place to a death-like pallor.

'My Lord,' he gasped, his arms spread wide, 'will you allow me to speak.'

'Silence,' the ushers cried loudly, and the judge, Lord Guthrie, commanded Slater to sit down.

Then followed a long period of intense silence while the verdict was being recorded.

Slater rocked to and fro, his mouth twitching. He cast his eyes to the roof, and from the roof to the floor. He seemed to collapse in his seat, but pulled himself up again.

'My Lord, my father and mother——' he began again, sobs choking his voice. In his terror he lapsed into his native tongue, declaring his innocence, and saying he had not been allowed to tell his own story to the jury.

'I think you should advise him to reserve anything he has to say for the Crown authorities,' the judge told Mr McClure, who defended.

Mr McClure walked towards the dock, but Slater waved him away with outstretched arms.

'My lord, I know nothing about the affair – absolutely nothing,' he sobbed. 'I never heard the name. I could not be connected with the affair. I know ——'.

He collapsed in his seat, and the sentence remained uncompleted.

Lord Gutherie sentenced him to be hanged at Glasgow on 27 May, and he was removed through the trapdoor in the floor.

In Scotland the verdict of the majority of the jurymen is accepted, and it is understood that nine of the jurymen voted for a verdict of 'Guilty', five for a verdict of 'Not proven', and one for an acquittal.

Under the law as it then stood the accused could not go into the witness box to be examined by his counsel so Slater* was denied what is now regarded as a basic right. Identification was minimal and Lambie, the maid, had said 'that's him', after having seen Slater under escort in New York. The diamond he'd pawned had never been Miss Gilchrist's. He had announced his intention of going to New York long before the murder. It was rather as if Scottish justice had decided that he would be 'Nane the waur o' a hingin' (none the worse for a hanging). But such justice was fortunately tempered by mercy. He was reprieved just before he was due to be 'launched into eternity', as the poetic phrase of the time had it. The Slater case was not over, however. For now entered Arthur Conan Doyle, creator of Sherlock Holmes. For years he campaigned to get it investigated. Finally in March 1914 the

*His case led to reform of the Scottish law in this respect.

Lloyd George at the age of 16.
really was good-looking which
to explain the extraordinary
ction for women.

George playing in the Parliamen-
olf handicap. Once, his round was inter-
d by rampaging suffragettes.

Nowhere was wide-eyed trusting wonder better expressed than over the *Titanic*, the mightiest ship in the world, the last word in luxury travel, the sea-borne miracle of the twentieth century – the unsinkable. An artist's impression.

Scottish Secretary of State, Mr McKinnon Wood, agreed to an inquiry.

Oscar Slater was not released then, nor at subsequent inquiries. He was finally pardoned – in 1928, having served nineteen years in jail. He received £6,000 compensation from the State, and died in 1948. Echoes of the scandal were heard as late as 1969, when the Glasgow magistrates re-examined the dismissal of Detective Trench from the Glasgow police force for passing on 'confidential information' to the solicitors acting for Slater in the 1914 enquiry. The magistrates – by a majority – decided that Trench should not be exonerated.

There are theories, including a sensational one, implicating a flawed young sprig of a famous, aristocratic Scottish family, who, it is said, encouraged the police to pursue Slater and put obstacles – through bribes – in the way of committees of inquiry.

That is speculation. What is certain is that Oscar Slater did not murder Miss Gilchrist and that this case, like Adolf Beck's, helped to change the law in favour of the accused. It was also Beck's and Slater's misfortune to be foreign, ugly and of known bad habits.

No such misfortunes or vices marred the bland features of Frederick Henry Seddon. He and his wife Margaret Ann Seddon were charged with poisoning by arsenic Miss Barrow, an eccentric wealthy spinster who lodged with them in 1912. Unlike Beck and Slater, Seddon was articulate; he delivered a 25-minute oration after being found guilty, but before the judge passed sentence. And he concluded by crying out, 'I swear before the Great Architect of the Universe I am innocent.' That was a Freemason's code phrase. Seddon was a Mason and he knew the judge, Mr Justice Bucknill, was one too. The judge was in tears as he ordered Seddon to be hanged.

To appreciate the awesome drama of sentencing at the time of the death penalty, there is no substitute for the words of the court reporter. From his account, published on 15 March, 1912 :

Suddenly there came a silence. It was five minutes past five. Hundreds of voices ceased magically in one moment. The jury men went back to their seats, one by one. They had an unforgettable look in their eyes. The eyes of those twelve men looked neither to right nor left. They were set straight ahead, inexpressibly grim and stern, seeing nothing of the grey wigged rows of barristers.

Something of what had passed in that hidden hour they had spent among themselves was stamped on the features of those twelve men. One guessed that those working muscles, those tight lips and narrowed eyes, as of men searching themselves inwardly, came with a message of death, if not for both, at least for one of the prisoners.

The stillness was suddenly shattered by three sharp knocks on the private door that is the judge's entrance. Those three loud knocks were like the death sentence itself knocking at the door of life. The door opened. Others were with the judge – the Sheriff and the Lord Mayor, grave and venerable in robes of fur and red – but the eyes of all were impelled now from the jury to the sturdy figure in scarlet and black and grey who passed under the hanging sword to his seat on the bench.

There was something in his hands besides his white kid gloves that seemed to bring with it a note of dreadful significance. It was a small square of black cloth – the black cap. Never, after listening to the summing up and looking at the faces of the jurymen was there any doubt among us that the judge would have to wear that piece of black cloth.

He tossed both cap and gloves on the table beside him with an odd gesture that seemed to be visualisation of a sigh. As he sat down, one saw him no longer as 'Mr Justice Bucknill' but as a figure remote from all, the personification of an abstract justice – not a man, but a symbol.

The man in black who hovered behind his chair in the dress of a chaplain became also a symbol.

Into the solemnity and the strained silence of the seconds that the clock told us were passing, there came the noise of footsteps echoing from the staircase that led into the dock.

Warderers and wardresses and the tall prison doctor – and side by side in the forefront of the dock they placed the husband and wife to listen to the verdict that gave life to the woman and doomed the man to death.

One word stabbed the silence : 'Guilty !' A tremor passed through Seddon, and then he was calm again. The clerk continued his questions : 'Do you find Margaret Ann Seddon—' 'Not guilty,' said the foreman interrupting him.

With a quick bold movement as though defying the judge and death Seddon threw out his arms and sprang to her side. He caught her to him and kissed her full on the lips.

That poignant moment was not interrupted. Warders and wardresses, judge and jury, lawyers and all the people in the court looked at the farewell of these two : one on the brink of death, the other free to go out into the world again.

Seddon stood away from his wife. She tottered and put her hands before her in a pitiful gesture, blinded by her tears, seeking her way out.

They led her downstairs, sobbing so terribly that, even when she was below the court, the sound of her cries were heard, long and heartbreaking, until they grew fainter and died away in distant corridors.

The touching parting between Mr and Mrs Seddon was somewhat tarnished eight months later. On 18 November this item appeared in the press:

A dramatic confession of how she saw her late husband poison Miss Barrow has been made by the widow of Frederick Henry Seddon, the insurance manager, who was hanged for murder.

The former Mrs. Seddon, who has recently remarried and is now Mrs Cameron said:

'I saw him give poison to Miss Barrow. Seddon was no husband, no father, no friend even.

'I declare that he deliberately, on the fatal night substituted for the doctor's medicine a mixture made up from water, from fly-papers and white precipitate powder and gave it to Miss Barrow. Soon afterwards she breathed her last.

'That I threatened to call the police at once, and he pointed his revolver at my head and told me if I informed on him he would blow my brains out.

'That I acted as I did and kept quiet about what I knew in the faint hope that if Seddon was acquitted, although justice would have been defeated, my children would be spared the terrible disgrace of being branded as the children of murderers.'

For atmosphere reporting in a murder trial, however, there is probably nothing to beat the Crippen case, again involving a poisoning and joint charge against a man and woman.

What has made the Crippen case so compelling that books about it appear over and over again is its enthralling human tragedy: the little 48-year-old American dentist living in miserable timidity with his large, overbearing wife Cora, whose music-hall pretensions (she luxuriated in the name of Belle Elmore) far outdistanced her talents, his sudden passion for a young typist, Ethel Le Neve; Cora's disappearance; the discovery of her mutilated body in the cellar of their house in Hilldrop Crescent; the lovers' flight to Canada disguised as father and son; their

unmasking by Captain Kendall, master of the liner *Montrose;* the
despatch of the implacable Inspector Dew to effect their arrest – no
script could surpass that. Songs and ballads about the principal characters were sung in the halls and in the streets. Dr Crippen was as well
known as Dr Frankenstein and better known than Dr Livingstone.

Hawley Harvey Crippen appeared at the Old Bailey on Tuesday,
9 October, 1910. He was not accompanied by Ethel Le Neve because
the Director of Public Prosecutions decided she should be tried separ-
ately as an accessory after the fact, should Crippen be found guilty.

Holt White, the specially commissioned scene-setter of this 'theatre
of the real', described the accused on the first day of the trial :

Crippen's calm is most obviously not merely studied but natural. He
is altogether an imperturbable man. The marvel of it is that when
one studies him his calm, however natural, is well nigh unaccount-
able.

Yet to all appearances Crippen is a very ordinary little man – a
short, slight, cheaply but well dressed man, such as one might meet
any day in any tube or omnibus. He has scarcely one distinguishing
feature. His head is small and round, and covered with fine textured
but wiry hair. He is a little bald on the forehead.

His brow is neither good nor bad. His eyes – of a watery, impene-
trable blue – are heavy lidded above and heavily pouched below.
They are shielded by formidable and powerfully lensed glasses, the
ends of which curl round his small ears.

It is his nose which makes one look at him. It is not big, but is
strikingly strong, broad boned at the bridge and fleshy about the
nostril. His tight shut mouth protrudes with the pressure of strong
prominent teeth. A shaggy bristly moustache gives him somewhat the
appearance of a walrus. His chin recedes, and yet his jaw is obstinate
and strong. The whole of Crippen's face suggests reflection and
endurance.

Reflection and endurance he must have to an extraordinary degree,
or it would have been impossible for him to withstand, without any
sign of concern, the measured but appalling attack which Mr Muir
(prosecuting counsel) launched on him.

This little, half-bald, bespectacled ordinary-looking little man
listened without flinching to allegations which were sickening in their
wealth of horrible detail.

Mr Muir's outline of the medical evidence he proposes to call was
the most terrible, but Crippen listened to the grave statements con-

cerning mutilation and poison without so much as the droop of his eyelid.

Throughout this section of Mr Muir's indictment Mr Pepper, the Home Office pathological expert, the actual living Sherlock Holmes of crime today, sat keen-eyed and watchful.

By a curious coincidence, just behind him sat Sir Arthur Conan Doyle, the originator of the relentless Sherlock Holmes of fiction. Sir Arthur's face was a pleasant note in a sombre scene. He sat, his chin resting in a great strong brown hand, and his eyes as he searched Crippen's face, smiled shrewdly and yet good humouredly.

Crippen's case was woefully weak. In brief, it was that his wife had gone to America to live with her lover. In fear of scandal, he had pretended she had died in the States. He freely admitted his love for Ethel Le Neve who had come to live with him at Hilldrop Crescent as soon as Mrs Crippen vanished. The body in the cellar was not that of his wife and he had not, as the prosecution alleged, bought the poison hyoscine to do away with Cora. His counsel, Mr Tobin KC, did not lack emotional zeal in the defence of his client.

It is no disgrace to Mr Tobin to say that as he opened his case, the most spontaneous tears welled to his eyes, and that plucking off his eye-glasses, he dashed them away with the back of his hand.

His cry to the jury throughout a really wonderful speech was: 'You Have To Know! You Have To Know!' He implored the jury not to let suspicion darken or warp their outlook. He taught them it was not their right to guess.

'You have to know,' he said over and over again.

To no avail. The prosecution's summing up was deadly. Mr Muir addressed the jury:

'Ask yourselves these questions: Where is Belle Elmore? Is your answer to be "She is dead?"

'Whose remains were those in the cellar? Is your answer to be "Belle Elmore's?"

'If they are not those of Belle Elmore what conceivable explanation is there? None has been offered.

'Who mutilated her body and put those remains there? Who but the occupier had the opportunity, the skill, the access to the pyjama jacket, of which pieces were found in the grave?

'How did she die? Is your answer to be "By hyoscine poisoning"? If not, how did that person die?

'If your answer is to be that she died of hyoscine poisoning, where did she get it, and who administered it? Crippen bought hyoscine on 19 January, and Belle Elmore disappeared from the world on 1 February.

Half an hour after the judge's summation, the jury returned.

Crippen is back in the dock, and all eyes are bent upon him. He sits in his chair erect but shrunken.

His clothes hang loose upon him and his face is the colour of mottled clay. His hands are tight clasped together. He is twiddling his thumbs at a terrible rate.

Crippen is back in the dock. His shoulders are bowed, but his obstinate little chin is thrust forward. He protrudes his face boldly but the short, strong neck, whose redness has seemed such a token of virility, is now white. His face is turned towards the judge, but his eyes glint sideways at the jury. They speculate; they dread; they appeal. Not one of the jury looks at him.

'Do you find the prisoner guilty or not guilty?' The question comes almost as a whisper from the clerk.

The foreman of the jury stands upright and protrudes his jaw. His face is pale, too. He is a man who is taking his courage in his hands.

But his voice is loud and clear.

'We find the prisoner guilty,' he says.

A week later Ethel Le Neve was acquitted. The judge summed up strongly in her favour and her counsel was the redoubtable F. E. Smith. He told an *Express* journalist many years afterwards that he could have saved Crippen from the gallows by pleading that the little Doctor had bought hyoscine to diminish his wife's excessive sexual appetites; that he had accidentally given her an overdose and buried the body in fear of discovery.

Crippen went to his death protesting his innocence.

Yet there seems to have been a compulsion among all but the most hardened to unburden themselves.

George Breeze, a miner from Durham, convicted of murdering Margaret Chisholm in 1904, broke into verse in a letter to the football team, Seaham White Stars, of which he had been a goalkeeper:

It is hard to die so young
Especially by Billington to be hung;
But when all is reckoned right
Life is just a miserable sight.

For in love I madly fell,
Which now in prison I must dwell.
Ere long my neck it will be bared
For the fate which I am quite prepared.

William Edge, a billiard-marker, compiled both prose and poetry before he was hanged at Stafford for murdering a child :

'My dear Liddie, – I am sorry to think this is my last letter to you, but never mind, I shall meet you in Heaven. I can see father and mother with arms open to receive me. What a pleasant world it will be. I hope to see my own child there and to let father and mother see him.

Fancy to think of last Christmas, and then to think of this. Kindly remember me to all friends.

Farewell dear sister, I must bid adieu
To those joys and pleasures I've tasted with you.
We've laboured together, united in heart.
But now we must close, and soon we must part.
Though absent in body, I am with you in prayer.
And I meet you in Heaven; there is no parting there.

From your loving brother, Will.

PS. Farewell till we meet in Heaven.

Yet the chilliest crime item that the *Daily Express* carried had nothing to do with domestic killers. It came from Bohemia in May 1912 and read :

Frau Marie Borick, aged seventy-three, the wife of a Bohemian brickmaker, was yesterday condemned to death for having murdered her husband with an axe the day after they had celebrated their golden wedding.

After committing the murder she prepared her son's dinner, and then informed him of what she had done, explaining that she had long intended to get rid of her husband, but had decided to wait until after the golden wedding, in the hope of getting some valuable presents.

CHAPTER XIII

A Matter of Honour

'Death before dishonour' had real meaning in the pre-1914 era : it was sometimes carried to its literal conclusion. On the day of Archduke Franz Ferdinand's assassination, which sparked off World War I, this item was despatched from New York :

> A duel, with both contestants clasping each other's left hand, was fought yesterday at Freeling, Virginia, by Anderson Estep and James Vanover, members of wealthy families and friends and neighbours from childhood.
>
> Vanover objected to Estep's attentions to his sister, and the challenge to fight the duel followed.
>
> The duellists climbed to the top of Cumberland Mountain, and then, clasping their left hands to make the result deadly, began firing at each other with revolvers held in the right hand. Vanover received two and Estep three bullets through the body and both are expected to die.

This was not, of course, a regular practice in America where the conception of 'honour' was, even among the socially lofty*, far more commensensical than in Europe.

Proud Spaniards would find nothing strange in reading in their newspapers on 12 October, 1904 of the sad fate that had overtaken the Marquis Pickman, who chose to insult a mere captain – who happened to be a better shot :

> The Marquis Pickman, who belonged to an old Andalusian aristocratic family, was shot dead in a duel yesterday near Seville.
>
> A quarrel of long standing had existed between the Marquis and

*How much more was instanced by an English baronet, Sir Cecil Moon, resident in Colorado, who was granted a divorce from his wife on the grounds of henpecking – and achieved £450 a year alimony.

Captain Pardes, of the Civil Guard, respecting the Marchioness Pickman, who is celebrated for her beauty and great wealth, and a few days ago the Marquis horsewhipped the captain in the foyer of the Cervantes Theatre.

The affair came before a court of honour, presided over by a general of the army, and it was decided that the only course open was for the parties to fight a duel.

The Marquis and captain met under the severest duelling conditions. Pistols were chosen, and the firing was at fifteen paces, with a proviso that, failing a hit, the duel should be continued with swords.

Two shots were fired without effect, but at the third shot the Marquis fell with a bullet through his heart, and died without uttering a word.

The Marquis, who was thirty-six years of age, was a well-known sportsman.

Italians brought a touch of the ridiculous to the deadly game when Senator Chiesa accused the beautiful, twice divorced Madame Siemens of being a German spy. Swords leapt from their scabbards in defence of Madame's honour. The Senator agreed to accept one challenge; that of General Prudente, Under-Secretary for War. Senator and General turned up near Rome's Porta San Paolo on the morning of 8 March, 1910, to find 'a crowd of several thousand people'.

The windows of the neighbouring houses were filled with spectators.

The seconds endeavoured to measure out the distance and arrange the other preliminaries, but they were so harassed by photographers and curious spectators that they abandoned the attempt in despair. General Prudente and Signor Chiesa thereupon agreed to fight in another part of the city, but the crowd followed, and scores of motorcars, cabs, and bicycles raced after the carriages containing the duellists and their friends.

Before the combatants had a chance of shooting at each other at the second meeting place the police intervened.

Officers and gentlemen were expected to be chivalrous – and to what length chivalry could be carried! From the *Express* of 26 June, 1914:

A British Army officer's determination to undergo penal servitude rather than defend himself at his wife's expense, although she was proved guilty, is told in a document which has just been sent to all members of Parliament by Sir Herbert Raphael, MP, who is trying to secure a rehearing of the case in order to vindicate the officer's honour.

It is the story of Lieutenant Cecil Aylmer Cameron, of the Royal Artillery, and his wife, who were both convicted in 1911 of fraudulently claiming £6,500 insurance on a pearl necklace which Mrs Cameron said had been stolen from her, but which she never even possessed.

Lieutenant Cameron, whose father won the VC in the Indian Mutiny, and whose grandfather fought in the Guards at Waterloo, refused to go into the witness-box at the trial to prove his non-complicity in the fraud for fear of making his wife's case worse. The result was that both were sentenced to three years' penal servitude. The husband served two years of his sentence, but the wife was released after a few weeks owing to a dangerous illness.

Mrs. Cameron, fearing that she was about to die, made a complete confession exonerating her husband. She showed that all along she had duped him, and that to the very last she had feared to confess her deception lest she should lose his love.

Some years previously a senior army officer had felt obliged to commit suicide to shield the honour of the Army. The shame of Major General Sir Hector Archibald MacDonald, KCB, DSO, ADC, was that he had allegedly committed homosexual acts in Ceylon. The man who was the idol of the Highland Regiments – he was himself a Highlander from Dingwall – could not face the court martial that was waiting for him in London. The King, Edward VII, did not want him to face it and, as is implied in the newspaper reports of the time (in the entire account neither the term homosexual nor the details of the charge are mentioned) the French papers had already damaged his reputation beyond repair by describing his crimes.

This is how the British people heard of the death of one of their heroes : the man who had saved the life of their greatest general, Lord Roberts, in Afghanistan; the one who had risen from the ranks – an almost unheard of feat; who had once written to the MacDonald Society; 'you may rest assured, dear clansmen, that it will be my duty to see that neither the army nor the clan shall suffer in name through me.' This is how Fighting Mac died on 25 March, 1903 :

General Sir Hector MacDonald committed suicide at the Hotel Regina in the Rue de Rivoli today.

This morning at nine o'clock, he came down from his bedroom at the hotel, and, making his way through the lounge on the ground floor, entered the reading-room.

The morning papers had more or less sensational accounts of the accusations that have been made against him, and one of them published his portrait in military uniform. There was no mistaking the man, and as he passed into the reading-room of the hotel he was curiously regarded by the clerks of the bureau.

This he seemed not to notice, but sat down and took up the morning's papers. Suddenly he was seen to start, and the paper he was reading fell from his hand. For a moment he remained as if turned to stone, and then, bending forward, picked up the paper from the floor.

He appeared to read the story through with great deliberation.

For a short time Sir Hector MacDonald remained deep in thought and then, slowly folding the newspapers, he rose from his seat and paced slowly up and down the room, his left hand the while stroking his moustache.

Then he seemed to have an inspiration. He stopped short, lit a cigar, and the highly nervous expression which his face wore disappeared. He quietly passed upstairs to his own room on the first floor.

At half-past one a chambermaid knocked at the General's bedroom door, and let herself in with her key to make the bed.

Immediately she rushed out screaming, and brought a valet to the scene. On the floor of the room, face downwards, lay the General.

He was dressed only in his shirt and trousers, his arms were outstretched, and an inch from his right hand lay the service revolver of the British Army.

Homosexuality, 'the love that dare not speak its name' appeared again, as a question of honour, in intensely dramatic form before the King's Bench in April 1913. The plaintiff was Lord Alfred Douglas, the object of Oscar Wilde's extravagant affection. The defendant was Arthur Ransome, author of *Oscar Wilde: A Critical Study* and later to become a world renowned writer of children's stories.

Lord Alfred claimed that Ransome had traduced his (Lord Alfred's) honour by suggesting that he had helped to ruin Wilde. Because the newspapers wouldn't mention homosexuality they could not go fully into the background of the case and only those readers who had a fair knowledge of the facts could follow fully the court proceedings.

Oscar Wilde had prosecuted the Marquis of Queensberry in 1895 for describing him as posing as a sodomite. Wilde lost the case and was himself promptly arrested and charged with indecent behaviour with young men. He was found guilty and sentenced to two years in Reading Gaol. There he wrote *De Profundis* (Out of the Depths) and Arthur Ransome used this as part of his critique of Wilde. Lord Alfred alleged that Ransome had inferentially libelled him (Lord Alfred's name did not actually appear) and to sustain their defence Ransome's lawyers were obliged to call for Wilde papers that had been lodged in the British Museum and were not due to see the light of day till 1960, if ever. The case hinged on the defence's submission that the papers proved Lord Alfred's guilt. In short, the libels were justified.

The case opened on 17 April, 1913 before Mr Justice Darling, a judge with some literary and political pretensions, and one who loved publicity. He was not to be disappointed. Dry legal quips and artistic analogies were greeted with knowledgeable laughter, and extensive coverage.

But at heart, this was a profoundly moving event, unique in character and now almost forgotten.

Blue foolscap prison paper was brought into the court – the hand written, unpublished* part of Oscar Wilde's *De Profundis*. Lord Alfred did not wish to sit and listen to it read out. Mr Justice Darling ordered him to do so. Lord Alfred was asked if he recognised Wilde's writing. Lord Alfred – still handsome at forty-three – exclaimed angrily: 'It is a letter written in prison by a man trying to save his own face by turning on me.'

So the passages were read by Mr Ransome's counsel, Mr J. H. Campbell, KC:

H.M. Prison, Reading.

'Our ill-fated and most lamentable friendship has ended in ruin and public infamy for me, yet the memory of our ancient affection is often with me, and the thought that loathing, bitterness, and contempt should for ever take that place in my heart once held by love is very sad to me.

'Ah, you had no motives in life; you had appetite merely. . . . Your defect was not that you thought so little about life, but that you knew so much. The morning dawn of boyhood, with its delicate, its clear pure light, its joy of innocence and expectations, you had left far behind.

*It has since been published in 1961.

'With very swift and running feet you had passed from romance to realism. The gutter and the things that live in it had begun to fascinate you. That was the origin of the trouble in which you sought my aid, and I, unwisely, according to the wisdom of the world, out of pity and kindness, gave it to you. . . .

'The real fool, such as the gods make or mar, is he who does not know himself. I was such a one too long. You have been such a one too long. Be so no more. Do not be afraid. The supreme vice is shallowness. Everything that is realised is right.

'I will begin by telling you I blame myself terribly, as I sit in this cell in convict clothes, a disgraced and ruined man. In the tortured and fitful nights of anguish, in the long monotonous days of pain, it is myself I blame.

'From the very first there was too wide a gap between us. You had been idle at your school : worse than idle at your university. You did not realize that an artist, and especially such an artist as I am – one that is to say, the quality of whose work depends on the intensification of personality – requires an intellectual atmosphere, quiet, peace and solitude.

'You admired my work when it was finished. You enjoyed the brilliant success of my first nights, and the brilliant banquets that followed them. You were proud, and quite naturally so, of being the intimate friend of an artist so distinguished but you could not understand the conditions required for the production of artistic work.

'I remember, for instance, in September 1893, to select merely one instance out of many, taking a set of chambers purely in order to work undisturbed.

In that week I wrote, complete in every detail as it was ultimately performed, the first act of *An Ideal Husband*.

'The second week you returned, and my work practically had to be given up. I arrived at St James's-place every morning at 11.30 in order to have the opportunity of thinking and writing.

'At twelve o'clock you drove up, stayed smoking cigarettes and chattering till 1.30, when I had to take you out to luncheon at the Cafe Royal or the Berkeley. Lunch, with its liqueurs, lasted usually till 3.30. For an hour you retired to White's. At tea time you appeared again, and stayed until it was time to dress for dinner. You dined with me either at the Savoy or at Tite-street. We did not separate, as a rule, until after midnight, as supper at Willis' had to wind up the entrancing day.

'While you were with me you were the absolute ruin of my art, and in allowing you to stand persistently between my art and myself I gave to myself shame and blame in the fullest degree. You could not know, you could not understand, you could not appreciate.

'Your interests were merely in your meals and moods. Your desires were merely for amusement, for ordinary, or less ordinary pleasures.

'My ordinary expenses with you for an ordinary day in London, for lunch, dinner, supper, amusement, hansoms, and the rest of it, ranged from £13 to £20. [£150-£250 at present values.]

'But most of all I blame myself for the entire ethical degradation I allowed you to bring on me. The basis of character is will power, but my will became absolutely subject to yours.

'Had I cared to show that the Crown witnesses, the most important, had been carefully coached by your father and his solicitor, not only in reticences merely but in assertions, in the absolute transference of deliberate, plotted, and rehearsed actions and doings of some one else on to me, I could have had each one of them dismissed from the box by the judge. I could have walked out of the court with my tongue in my cheek and my hands in my pockets, a free man.

'The strongest pressure was put on me to do so. I was earnestly advised, begged, entreated to do so by people whose sole interest was my welfare, and the welfare of my house. But I refused. I did not choose to do so.

'I have never regretted my decision for a single moment, even in the most bitter periods of my imprisonment. Such a course of action would have been beneath me. Sins of the flesh are nothing. They are maladies for physicians to cure, if they should be cured. Sins of the soul alone are shameful.'

Lord Alfred then went into the box to be cross-examined by Campbell, who quoted a letter written by Wilde to 'Dearest of all boys' rebuking him for 'letting your curved lips say hideous things to me . . . you are the divine thing I want.'

This and other echoes of the past (Wilde had died in 1900) provoked Lord Alfred to describe Wilde as 'a devil incarnate, a beastly man'.

The extraordinary relationship between the young Lord Alfred – who was in his early twenties before Wilde's ruin – and the forty-year old playwright was brought into the open by Mr Ransome's counsel, who also quoted from Wilde's unpublished reminiscences from Reading Gaol :

'Your tears, breaking out again and again all through the evening, falling over your cheeks like rain as we sat at dinner, first at Voisin's, at supper at Paillard's afterwards; the unfeigned joy you evinced at seeing me, holding my hand whenever you could, as though you were a gentle and penitent child, your contrition, so simple and sincere at the moment, made me consent to renew our friendship.

'Two days after we had returned to London your father saw you having lunch with me at the Cafe Royal, joined my table, had my wine, and that afternoon, through a letter addressed to you, began his first attack on me.

'Of course, I discerned in our relations not Destiny merely, but Doom — Doom that walks always swiftly because she goes to the shedding of blood. Through your father* you come of a race marriage with whom is horrible, friendship is fatal, that lays violent hands either on its own life or on the lives of others.

'It makes me feel sometimes as though you yourself had been merely a puppet, worked by some secret and unseen hand to bring terrible events to a terrible issue. But puppets themselves have passions. They will bring a new plot into what they are presenting, and twist the ordered skein of vicissitude to suit some whim or appetite of their own.

'I thought life was going to be a brilliant comedy, and that you were to be one of many graceful figures in it. I found it to be a revolting and repellent tragedy, and that the sinister occasion of the great catastrophe, sinister in its concentration of aim and intensity of a narrowed will power, was yourself; stripped of the illusion of joy and pleasure by which you, no less than I, had been deceived and led astray.

'The memory of your friendship is the shadow that walks with me here; that never seems to leave me; that wakes me up at night to tell me the same story over and over till its wearisome iteration makes all sleep abandon me till dawn; at dawn it begins again; it follows me into the prison yard and makes me talk to myself as I tramp round.

'The gods are strange. It is not our vices only that make instruments to scourge us. They bring us ruin through what in us is good, gentle, humane, loving. But for my pity and affection for you and yours, I would not now be weeping in this terrible place.

'But you, like myself, have had a terrible tragedy in your life, though one of an entirely opposite character to mine. Do you want

*The Marquis of Queensberry, author of the Queensberry Rules of boxing.

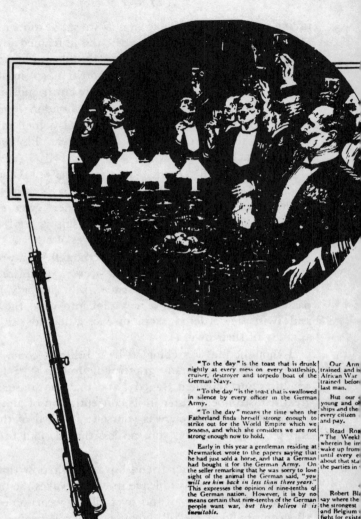

"To the day" is the toast that is drunk nightly at every mess on every battleship, cruiser, destroyer and torpedo boat of the German Navy.

"To the day" is the toast that is swallowed in silence by every officer in the German Army.

"To the day" means the time when the Fatherland finds herself strong enough to strike out for the World Empire which we possess, and which she considers we are not strong enough now to hold.

Early in this year a gentleman residing at Newmarket wrote to the papers saying that he had just sold a horse, and that a German had bought it for the German Army. On the seller remarking that he was sorry to lose sight of the animal the German said, "*you will see him back in less than three years.*" This expresses the opinion of nine-tenths of the German nation. However, it is by no means certain that nine-tenths of the German people want war, *but they believe it is inevitable.*

ARE WE READY FOR THE DAY?

Our first lines are far more ready than people think. Our Navy is sleepless and at present invincible, although fast being out-built.

Our Arm
trained and is
African War
trained before
last man.

But our
young and o
ships and the
every citizen
and pay.

Read Rol
"The Weekl
wherein he im
wake up from
until every ei
about that sta
the parties in

Robert Bla
say where the
the strongest
and Belgium
fight for existe

In spite of
ing predictio
despondent y

to learn what it was? It was this: In you, Hate was always stronger than Love.

'Your hatred of your father was of such a stature that it entirely outstripped and overthrew and overshadowed your love of me.

'The idea of your being the object of a terrible quarrel between your father and a man of my position seemed to delight you. . . . You scented the chance of a public scandal and flew to it; the prospect of a battle in which you would be safe delighted you.

'You knew what my art was to me – the real, great, primal note by which I revealed, first to myself, and then myself to the world; the real passion of my life: the love to which all other loves were as marsh water to red wine, or a glow worm of the marsh to the magic mirror of the moon. Don't you understand now that your lack of imagination was the one really fatal defect of your character? What you had to do was quite simple and clear: but hate had blinded you, and you saw nothing.'

Against this torrent of denunciation, every word of which indicated author Ransome's claim that Wilde considered himself destroyed by Lord Alfred Douglas above all, the plaintiff produced an astonishing rejoinder. He disposed of his implied degeneracy by informing the court that he had won the school steeplechase and the seven mile event at Winchester. Then he added:

'Wilde wrote the play *The Importance of Being Earnest* at Worthing while he was in the house.

'He read it to me as he wrote it, and he would ask "What do you think of this?" and I would reply, "I don't like it; I should put it this way," and so on. A lot of the dialogue is really mine. He got it from me as one literary man would from another discussing the matter with him.'

Where did he write *An Ideal Husband*? inquired Mr Hayes.

'Partly in Tite-street and partly in some rooms he had at St James's-place,' said Lord Alfred. 'At that time I was constantly with him, and spending hours in his company while he was writing it.'

'Did he recognise the assistance you gave him in his literary work?'

'I do not think he did,' said Lord Alfred. 'He was much too conceited to do that. He recognised it privately, but I did not want him to recognise it publicly.'

The burden of J. H. Campbell's defence of Arthur Ransome was that

Lord Alfred had indicted himself out of his own mouth and confirmed the very charges that Wilde (and Ransome) had made. 'Lord Alfred,' said Campbell, 'fled the country and Wilde shouldered the blame and took the punishment.'

The jury brought in the inevitable verdict : the libel of Lord Alfred was true. Arthur Ransome was upheld and went on to write many famous books. Lord Alfred went on to a life of litigation – suing and being sued. And the shade of Oscar Wilde? Perhaps it allowed itself a smile at the thought of Lord Alfred defending honour.

*

If honour was a paramount principle among the upper class, fear of being shamed was at the root of many other people's behaviour.

An item on 11 September, 1912 was headed :

FOREIGNERS AND

ENGLISH GIRLS

Thrashing and fine for

Street Insult

'In this country women are able to walk about without being molested by young blackguards,' declared Mr Fordham, the magistrate, at West London Police Court yesterday.

The case is one in which Ricardo Bacha, aged twenty-one, an Italian student, living at Westwick-gardens, Shepherd's Bush, was charged with attacking Miss Rita McGarry, of Granville-mansions, Shepherd's Bush.

Miss McGarry stated that she was walking along Goldhawk-road. As she passed Bacha, who was standing with other young men on the pavement he touched her under the chin.

'He did not say anything?' inquired the clerk.

'Oh, no,' replied Miss McGarry. 'I am afraid I was rude enough to call him a pig and I hurried on.'

Police Constable Riddell stated that Mr McGarry came up to him with his daughter and Bacha, whom he was holding, and made a complaint about Bacha's conduct.

'I believe that Bacha's leg was dressed at the police station by a doctor,' said Mr Ellis who defended.

'What was the matter with his leg?' asked the magistrate.

'That was part of the punishment he received from the young lady's father,' explained Mr Ellis.

Mr Ellis said Bacha pleaded guilty to the charge and wished to offer his sincere apologies to the young lady and her father, and to express his profound regret for his conduct.

'It was purely a piece of gratuitous impudence which he now greatly regrets,' added Mr Ellis. 'I wish to point out that he has already received considerable punishment at the hands of the angry father, and I ask you to remember that he is a foreigner.'

'Yes,' replied the magistrate, 'we have too many of these foreigners in this country. I am glad to think you are not an Englishman. It is a monstrous thing that you should come over here and insult English girls.

'As long as you are in this country you must behave decently, and keep your filthy tricks for the country you come from.

'I shall take into consideration the fact you are a foreigner, and a young fool as well as a blackguard, and also that you were very properly thrashed by the father of the girl. If the law allowed, I should order you to be flogged before you left this court as a lesson to you and a warning to others like you. You must pay a fine of 40s, with 7s 6d, the doctor's fee, and I hope you will tell all your friends what I say to you.'

The hapless Ricardo Bacha could at least take comfort from the fact that *any* foreigner was liable to get a bad press in England. The social chit-chat column of 5 May, 1900 remarked :

The suggestion that an alliance is in prospect between the Czarevitch and the Princess Margaret of Connaught is one of those easy predictions to which social prophets are prone.

The most that can be said is that it possesses many elements of attraction, both from a domestic and from a political point of view. The Grand Duke Michael speaks English with great fluency and he shares with his Imperial relatives that affection for things English *which spring from a recognition of their worth and superiority.*

A different aspect of pride – the anguish of failing to keep up standards – was shown again and again in varying contexts in press reports during the pre-1914 era.

Men and women could not bear to fall below what was expected of them and ideas of the unacceptable ranged from the truly tragic to what today would be regarded as almost flippant. Like Walter Ernest Comber, aged thirty, who in September 1912, was stated at an inquest to have committed suicide after being jilted because he had over-slept.

> Evidence was given that he overslept himself on several occasions. One day the girl to whom he was engaged called at his lodgings and found him in bed. She said that he ought to have been at work, and that she would not marry a lazy man.
>
> On 31 August he went to lodge with Mr Morgan at Pelham-road. 'He was very downcast and miserable,' said Mrs Morgan, 'and he told me he had been disappointed in love.'
>
> On Saturday last he closed the windows and door of his room, and pulled down the blinds. A little later he called Mrs Morgan and then informed her that he had taken poison because his girl friend had given him up.

More serious, but still far from being a doomsday situation was the overspending of Mr Alfred Pearce, 39, who committed suicide in November 1906 :

> Mr Pearce, who was a Stock Exchange clerk at a salary of £175 a year, lived in good style at Westville-road, Thames Ditton. He kept a small motor-car, and his general expenditure was on the scale of a man with a very much larger income.
>
> Mrs Gertrude Pearce said that before her husband went to business on Thursday morning last he asked her to go and stay with a friend in London, as he intended to go to Ripley for a few days. She did so, and the next day she was informed that her husband had been found dead in bed from opium poisoning.
>
> The coroner stated that a long letter written by Mr Pearce to his wife had been found and that it clearly indicated that the writer had committed suicide. The coroner read the following extracts from the letter :
>
> 'My darling wife, – I am sure this will be a terrible shock to you, and I only wish I could have prevented it; but I am sorry to say all the money we have is spent, and only the few pounds in my purse remain. I was afraid some time ago it could not go on for long.
>
> 'Of course we have lived in a very extravagant way for a couple like us with such a small income, and no doubt I was very foolish not to let you know that we were spending all we had. But somehow I could not bring myself to do it. I always liked to give you anything you wanted. No doubt that was stupidly extravagant.

'I fear I have been very selfish in not telling you the true position of affairs. But I don't mind telling you now that you are well rid of me. I suppose everyone would look on me as a downright coward, which no doubt I am.

'Get Price to sell the motor-car, which is still worth £50, and the silver and all that sort of thing. I should not have done you such a bad turn, but I hated to tell you my position.

'You are young and pretty. Do not go on the stage but marry a good man with an assured income, that will be kind to you. I do not mind the idea of your marrying again, because, thrown on the world as you will be, it will be the best thing for you. You have always been a dear, good wife to me. I must end now, darling, asking you to forgive me the pain and trouble I have given you, and to forget me.'

Stories such as these were repeated endlessly in the pages of the *Express* between 1900 and 1914. Much less common – but indicative of the lengths people would go to to protect their own and their loved ones' good names – was this story from the paper of 18 May, 1900 :

A remarkable story of man's wrong-doing and his wife's Spartan devotion in holding the door against the police while he saved himself by suicide was told at an Edmonton inquest.

Grave charges had been made against Mr Thomas Murlis, a schoolmaster of Gambia House, and the father of one of the boys, Mr Brown, who drove round to the boarding school late on Friday night. Murlis, in his dressing gown, opened the door, and was immediately knocked down by the indignant Brown.

He jumped to his feet and ran upstairs, followed by Brown and a detective. When they reached the bedroom, however, Mrs Murlis, pale and trembling, but defiant, was standing alone against the door.

'Where's your husband? panted the pursuers.

The wife pointed within, and muttered between clenched teeth – 'My God! you can't get him now. He's gone from you.'

From within came sounds of a man in fearful agony, groans, shrieks, and the rattling of his heels against the door in the tortures of death.

Outside the men stood paralysed with horror. The wife maintaining her Spartan attitude, fell on her knees and prayed : 'My Lord, dear Lord, end it soon.'

Gradually silence closed in on the horrible scene. Then the tension on the faithful woman's nerves relaxed, and she swayed and dropped in a swoon.

At last the men were stirred into action, and, bursting open the door, paused horror-struck at the sight. Murlis, lying on the floor, his face and mouth contorted with agony and seared with acid. They lifted him on to a bed and administered an emetic.

But it was too late. And, while a clergyman, hurriedly summoned, was praying by the bedside, the man's soul passed away from his earthly judges.

Turning defiantly on the detective and Mr Brown, the widow said: 'My Tom, you are safe from your enemies now.'

Mr Brown's recital of the story overcame the foreman of the jury, who fainted, and the inquest was adjourned.

Significantly the reporter allowed his own, and no doubt his readers' conventional views to intrude by writing 'he saved himself by suicide'.

*

A woman's honour had a precise monetary value when she took a faithless betrothed to court for breach of promise. Such actions provided the Press with a great deal of copy, much of it amusing, some of it piteous. Prurience there was in abundance – *in the courts*. No mention, however, was made in the public prints to abortion or sexual intercourse which bulked large in the proceedings.

Breach of promise threats provided women with a weapon at a time when they were woefully short of rights. If a man put a girl in the family way, or blighted her prospects by remaining engaged to her for a long time or enticed her by promise of marriage into spending money she could ill-afford on a 'bottom drawer' she could sue him. Recovery of damages was often a poor second, in these circumstances, to revenge. And, if the damages were puny, the loss of self-esteem attendant on the publicity outweighed the satisfaction of seeing the male miscreant in the dock.

Leading advocates, notably silver-tongued orators like Marshall Hall, made their reputations in breach of promise cases. Judges waxed fiercely indignant at caddish treatment of the gentle sex, as did Mr Justice Darling in April 1903:

'Mean, despicable, heartless' – these were some of the adjectives applied by Mr Justice Darling to Mr Frank Noakes, who was ordered to pay £1,000 to Miss Alice Collins for breach of promise of marriage.

Noakes, a man of thirty-three, held appointments successively at Stratford and Brixton with large firms of furniture dealers, and claimed to be earning £1,000 a year. He was a 'paying guest' at the house of Miss Collins' father at West Kensington and there made love to her.

In a letter he addressed her as 'My dear little baby,' and said :

As I told you the other day, there was not a happier man on the face of this earth, nor is there today, than the writer of this epistle.

Just as I told you then, I'll tell you again. Now I have always loved you, Daisy, dearie. I am no hand at this work, so must stop now; but I can only say you have my undivided love.

After Miss Collins had consented to marry him, he took advantage of her. Subsequently, finding the girl was about to become a mother, he refused to fulfil his promises, though she piteously implored him to marry her, and undertook that if he did she would never molest him nor ask him to contribute to her or her child's support.

Miss Collins who gave her age as twenty-six, stated Mr Noakes had asked her to allow a certain woman [an abortionist] to visit her.

'You don't happen to know her name and address?' asked the judge.

'No, my lord,' was the reply.

'Is she in court?'

'I don't think so.'

'I daresay she will be in the dock some day. We should all like to see her there,' remarked his lordship.

In summing up, the judge advised heavy damages, and severely criticised the lover's conduct. The proper and manly course to have taken, said his lordship, was to have married the girl, instead of which Noakes suggested her doing something that was a felony. It was lucky for him that the woman did not see her until 'too late' for the offence to have been attempted.

To make sure of a man without actually carrying his child (for that could be a passport to misery, not marriage) some women had a kind of bond drawn up :

Vouch of Honour:– I, Richard Ernest Lang, hereby promise to marry Mary Ann Gordon at whatever date shall be selected by either party. This means our engagement for ever.

Lang is a theatrical decorator and upholsterer, of Everton, and Miss Gordon is a barmaid of Ashton-under-Lyne.

Lang signed the above bond in April 1904 and yesterday, 15 December, 1905, it formed indisputable evidence against him in an action which the girl brought at Preston for breach of promise.

'Lang was so much infatuated,' said counsel, 'that he wrote to the girl by every post.'

Eventually Lang became engaged to another girl. The jury assessed the damages at £75.

On the same day an unfortunate watchmaker of Nottingham, Harry Wilson, who defended himself against the charge of breaking a promise to marry Mary Tunnicliffe foolishly admitted to having £40 in the savings bank :

'I never bought an engagement ring or anything of that sort,' said Wilson.

'You have talked about what we would do when married and that was good enough for me,' replied the girl. 'You gave me a brooch and a purse.'

Mary got the £40.

Joviality was apt to break out when plaintiff and defendant were both personable, reasonably well-off and merely indulging an expensive squabble :

> There was a young lady of Jay's
> Who rumour said never wore stays
> Yet her waist was so slim
> And her figure so trim
> That the Johnnies did nothing but gaze.

This limerick was contained in one of the many entertaining documents which convulsed Mr Justice Grantham's court on 3 April, 1908.

It was written by Mr Herbert Watermeyer to Miss Violet Carr, a 'girl from Jay's', and formed part of the evidence in a breach of promise case brought by Miss Carr.

Miss Carr, a tall, graceful, and pretty girl, is the daughter of a schoolmaster and the granddaughter of a barrister. When she met Mr Watermeyer, she was employed in the sale room of Jay's in Regent Street.

Mr Watermeyer is thirty-seven, of Boer extraction, and the nephew of Judge Watermeyer. He was educated at St Paul's School and Cambridge, and possesses considerable property in South Africa.

In 1903 they became engaged but Mr Watermeyer wished the engagement to be kept secret, as he thought an old aunt, who was eighty years of age, might object to a 'girl from Jay's'. Accordingly he gave her a bracelet instead of an engagement ring.

The couple had met in 1901. The case came before the courts in 1908 : an old-style variant of the seven-year itch. Miss Carr did her best to convince the jury that she had suffered from the abuse of her affections. In answer to counsel's caustic comment that she was hardly pining away, she replied, 'I am getting thinner.' Her efforts were unavailing. Jury found for the defendant.

Evidence at these breach of promise hearings enthralled the spectators, and not only the spectators. At Mr Justice Horridge's court in October 1912 the good judge himself cried out 'Speak up, do not let me lose anything' when counsel began reading the love letters of a City bank manager to a jilted actress.

Actresses were natural litigants. Their careers could be helped by publicity; they rejoiced in the limelight and usually had wealthy escorts who could be plucked of worthwhile sums.

Herr Heinrich Thyssen, son of the millionaire German industrialist, in November 1906 was sued by an American actress, Miss Marion Draughn.

Her pet name for Herr Thyssen was Tumti No 1 and his for her was Tumti No 2. Counsel's cross examination and the dialogue brings back the atmosphere of stage door johnnies and mashers :

The searching cross-examination of Tumti No 2, Miss Draughn, who has in moments of depression signed herself 'Tumti One and A Half,' and even 'Tumti Nought', was continued by Sir Edward Carson, and the witness was at times in tears.

'When did you first meet Mr Thyssen ?' he asked.

'While I was appearing in Daly's Theatre in October 1903,' Miss Draughn replied.

'What were you then earning ? – £5 a week. It was a stop-gap engagement. I had just finished a good engagement at the Garrick.

'You were not introduced to him ? – No, he introduced himself by flowers and notes and asked me to tea.

'Were you in the habit of picking up gentlemen in this way ? –

No, but it is quite a common thing in the theatrical world for men to invite girls to tea. I complained, however, of his conduct.

'Were you surprised? – Yes, I showed the note to other girls in the company, and said, 'How dare he write to me.'

Sir Edward Carson : 'The dreadful man! How dare he write!'

Miss Draughn with a smile told how she forgave his impertinence, and wrote to him, saying she would meet him at a ladies' club – the New Victoria – in Sackville Street.

'It is one of the oldest ladies' clubs in London, and I have been a member for years,' she explained. 'I met him at tea, I knew there would be no harm.'

'I am sorry the name of this club has been dragged in,' she added, 'but Mr Thyssen has persecuted me there, and the committee have written to me about this case.'

After the tea Herr Thyssen invited her to join him and a friend at the German Embassy for a 'little supper'. She agreed, and met him after the theatre.

'Did he drive you home in his private cab?' asked Sir Edward.

'Yes, it is quite the custom in the theatrical world,' was Miss Draughn's reply.

On the Saturday, Sunday and Monday following they met at Marlborough Tea Rooms in Bond-street.

'Did he afterwards visit you at your rooms? – Yes.

'Where did he first make overtures to you? – In my little sitting-room in Coulson-street.

'When did he first offer you marriage, as you say? – In about two weeks' time. He said he loved me better than anyone else in the world and that nothing should ever come between us.'

It was a pathetic scene, as described by Miss Draughn. Herr Thyssen went down on his knees, and with tears streaming from his eyes declared that he would always be true.

'Was anything said about money? – He told me I should have an allowance when I married him.

'Did he say he would give you £15 a week? – It came to that, but there was nothing said about £15 a week. He said he would be prepared to allow me £750 a year as his wife.'

The jury could not make up its mind so Herr Thyssen was spared further expense.

Rather different was the case of the Marquis of Northampton who in July 1913 created a record he may secretly have been glad to create :

The Marquis of Northampton, who succeeded to his title three weeks ago on the death of his father, agreed in the Law Courts to pay Miss Daisy Markham, the actress, £50,000 [£600,000 at today's values] instead of marrying her. No such sum has even been paid before as damages in an action for breach of promise of marriage.

Thirty years ago Miss Fortescue, the actress, won a verdict by consent for £10,000 against Viscount Garmoyle, afterwards Earl Cairns, and a similar sum was awarded to Miss Gladys Knowles when she sued Mr Leslie Duncan of the *Matrimonial News*. Those were the high water marks until yesterday.

There was no haggling in court. The young Marquis did not fight.

The Marquis is now twenty-eight; Miss Markham is twenty-seven. The Marquis looks just what he is – a wealthy young nobleman, who is also a lieutenant in the Royal Horse Guards : tall, handsome, soldierly, with a square, intellectual forehead and neatly trimmed brown hair.

Miss Daisy Markham, who in private life is Mrs Daisy Annie Moss, has the look of the theatre where she had won her own way by her talents, and has played leading parts in some of the best West End companies. She is a slim girlish figure, with a pale complexion and dark eyes, which seemed sad as she was in court gazing, as if in a dream, at the young Marquis, who sat not far from her with a wall of lawyers in between.

Sir Edward Carson, for Miss Markham, spoke quietly, but with feeling.

'I am glad, he said, 'to be able to state that I shall not have to open the case. It was an action brought by Mrs Moss, whose stage name is Miss Markham, for breach of promise against Earl Compton, as he was at the time the engagement was made, and the Marquis of Northampton as he now is.

'The parties met last year, and there was a promise, which I understand is not denied. The Marquis, at a subsequent stage of the proceedings – I think on the desire of his father – broke off the engagement.

'It is not necessary that I should weary your lordships nor would it do any good, if I went into any other part of the case. He broke off the engagement, though he was fond of the lady and in every way respected her, as is made apparent by the letter he wrote :

'Dearest Daisy, – I must just write you a line, as I am so wretchedly miserable. I want to assure you that I am trying to do the right thing, and though you will perhaps find it difficult I am going to ask you to believe that I always have and do at the present moment, love and respect you more than any one in this world, and that you are absolutely my ideal of perfect womanhood.

'But, Daisy, the ways of the world are hard and I want you to believe that what I am now doing I am doing from a sense of duty, genuinely believing it to be the best for both of us.

'Darling, I have known it all along. I have tried to smother my reason, to stifle my thought for your sake. But when my father talked to me on Friday he only faced me with the same thoughts that I told you of when I first loved you, and which I have ever since been trying to suppress.

'Daisy, you don't know how the so-called "ladies" would treat you, and I really couldn't bear to see you suffering it, and with your sweet, sensitive nature it would be torture to you.

'Oh, if only I could escape my position.

'Daisy, I want to beg your forgiveness for the way in which I have done it. I was so distracted between my feelings for you and my convictions of what was really best, that I am afraid I wavered, in a way most unfair to you.

'Well, darling, I really have nothing more to say. You will always be my ideal and you will always be my beautiful dream.'*

A happy exception, from the male point of view, to the usual outcome in breach of promise actions was occasioned by this verdict, in February 1908:

Mr Walter Lazarus Phillips who claimed damages for breach of promise against Mrs Flora Goodman – who is a grandmother and a woman of means – was awarded £50 damages.

Mr Justice Darling, in summing up, said that the case reminded him of a production of the Stage Society *Cupid and Commonsense.* Counsel might decide between them which was Cupid and which was Commonsense. 'A man has just as much right to sue for breach of promise as a woman,' he declared.

In spurning honour and going for cash, Mr Phillips was breaking the conventions of the time – and anticipating the future.

*The author telephoned the Marquis, who died in 1978 aged ninety-two, to ask why he consented to be sued by a married woman. His Lordship replied: 'I have no more to say on the subject. Honour is honour in 1977 as in 1913.'

The combative instinct which informed breach of promise actions was true to the British character in one sense; it was the legal equivalent to that substitute for war: sport – then, as now, more a religion than a relaxation.

CHAPTER XIV

Sport and Entertainment

By and large football was the sport of the working class; cricket was a shared enjoyment; Rugby Union was the preserve of the upper brackets being mainly a public school game, except in Wales and south-east Scotland; boxing and horse racing broke the class barrier.

Soccer in the early days of the century had as much drama, on and off the field, as today.

When Scotland met Ireland in an international match in Belfast in March 1902 spectators invaded the field. Police were called in but were totally unable to cope with the mob . . . spectators in the back rows stoned and threw mud at those in front. Eventually the crowd was forced back and the game commenced three-quarters of an hour late. Scotland won 5-1.

They were still at it in Belfast ten years later. On 10 September, 1912:

Belfast was the scene of a fierce faction battle on Saturday afternoon, in which about 100 persons suffered injuries, many of them serious.

Two local football clubs, supported respectively by Orangemen and Nationalists, were playing a match on the Belfast Celtic ground. During the half-time interval the crowd of spectators – some twenty thousand in all – turned their attention from football to politics. The Orangemen hoisted a Union Jack, the Nationalists a green and white flag, and within a few moments the two sections, like two great armies, were engaged in a free fight.

Stones were thrown in volleys, revolver shots were fired, and at one period of the riot so many men were laid out that the football ground resembled a battlefield. Ambulances were summoned, the injured were removed to hospital, while a large force of police was despatched to the scene. When they arrived the riot, which ended as suddenly and dramatically as it began, was over.

The Belfast Celtic Football and Athletic Company, which owns the ground, is a Roman Catholic and Nationalist organisation, and all its supporters are drawn from that section of the population. The Linfield club and its supporters are as distinctly Protestant and Unionist as the Celtic are the reverse.

Nor were venomous football mobs an Irish phenomenon. From the issue of 19 April, 1909:

Football madness reached its height at Hampden Park, Glasgow, on Saturday.

Sixty thousand Scottish sportsmen, enraged because the match between the Celtic and Rangers, for the final of the Scottish Cup, culminated, for the second time in a draw, mobbed the handful of police on the ground, and burned or broke up all the woodwork on which they could lay their hands. More than fifty persons were injured. The trouble arose at the end of the game. Like that of the preceding Saturday, it ended in a draw. The crowd, regarding this as an arrangement made between the authorities and the players in order to hold another match and secure another 'gate' – that for Saturday's match amounting to £1,710 – swarmed over the field, causing a riot such as had not been seen in connection with sport.

A number of men and lads, tearing up the barricades around the ground, piled them in heaps, with planks and wooden rails, and set them alight. All the time the police, who were charging through the crowds to get at the offenders, were pelted with bottles and stones.

The final effort of the mob was to wreck the pay-boxes at the entrance to the grounds, and then set them alight. Whisky was thrown on the woodwork to make it burn more fiercely. Firemen drove up and did their best to get at the flames, but the crowds slashed the hoses with knives.

Even the ambulance men hurrying across the ground carrying the injured were not only hindered by the hooligan crowd, but even assailed by volleys of stones.

It took the police three hours to clear the ground, One of the mounted men was thrown and trampled underfoot; an unmounted constable who slipped was kicked into insensibility, several of his ribs being broken; and all along the line policemen were seen with their faces streaming with blood.

When the mob had all been driven outside it was found that no fewer than thirty-eight policemen had been so seriously injured that

Nicholas II, Czar of All the Russians, had, in theory, the absolute power of a Tudor monarch. In reality he had not enough authority to run his own household. The Czar and Czarina on board their yacht, *Standart*.

On 20th April 1914 President Woodrow Wilson declared 'peaceful war' against Mexico. 'The United States', he said, 'has even bombarded towns to enforce its demands without ever formally declaring war.' An etching by Bernard Wall.

they had to be taken to the infirmary, while most of the little band of citizens who stood by them had been hurt.

The Cup was withheld and apparently as a consequence of this display the Legislature in faraway Little Rock, Arkansas, introduced a Bill making the game of football illegal and punishable by a heavy fine: doubtless setting back the cause of American soccer for many years.

Ireland . . . Catholic and Protestant . . . Celtic and Rangers: it could be inferred that these were special occasions spiced or poisoned with politics and religious bigotry, except that similar, though not as drastic, scenes were witnessed in England.

From a sports report of 29 January, 1909:

The Preston North End team, which played a drawn game with Sheffield Wednesday at Owlerton on Saturday, were violently treated at the conclusion of the match by a crowd of spectators who were dissatisfied with the result.

Councillor Houghton, who was in charge of the Preston team gave an *Express* representative the following account of what took place:

'We delayed our departure from Owlerton on account of the hostile attitude of the crowd which gathered round the dressing-tents.

'Immediately we left in a char-a-abanc we were pelted with showers of clinkers, cinders and stones from crowds of excited people who congregated in the streets.

'Nearly every player was struck. Lyon was hit behind the head with a heavy stone, and sustained a heavy scalp wound. Among the missiles which struck the players were two large clinkers, raw potatoes, a lump of billiard chalk, a jagged piece of earthenware, a penny, and a pearly-handled penknife.

'The outside passengers of every tramcar we passed deliberately leaned over and spat in our face.'

On the field also there was sometimes a graceless lack of sportsman-ship too reminiscent of the present.

A photograph appearing in February 1913 showed two Norwich and Bristol players involved in fisticuffs. The referee apparently did not see the incident for, according to the report of the match, no one was sent off. Nor did players content themselves with the odd punch-up. On Saturday, 10 January, 1914, Warrington went on strike and refused to play at Hull because they had not been given a bonus of a £1 per man for defeating Huddersfield the week before.

There were other examples of skulduggery. Mr H. A. Norris, a director of Fulham, accused Liverpool of deliberately losing a match against Chelsea :

'My own view is that, had the Liverpool team, as a whole, desired to win the match, they could have done so quite readily. It is not for me to suggest reasons for this display on the part of a section of the Liverpool team. One is, however, tempted to ask why they acted in the way they did, and echo answers Why?'

Nothing was proved against Liverpool and the whole business may well have been a figment of Mr Norris's overheated imagination. Yet the theme of money in professional soccer was exercising many. A reader wrote to the *Express* in January 1911 :

'It is about time for an outcry to be made against the disgraceful "deals" that are going on. What was once a good, healthy sport is now converted into a business. As to the leagues, they are a farce, for the final leaders are decided before a football season begins. It is only a question of which team has the most money. Just imagine Bristol City, Gainsborough Trinity, and Southend winning their respective Leagues'. Teams are styled "Everton", "Liverpool", "Blackburn Rovers", and "Sunderland" but they do not deserve their names for they do not represent the talent of their own town, but merely an alien crew of men purchased from all over the country.'

To which a football club director replied :

'The player is only entitled to £10 when transferred. Entitled yes, but as one who has had considerable experience in conducting these negotiations with clubs and their players, included the actual signing-on papers of players, I can vouch for the fact that the rule was ignored in nine cases out of ten for the simple reason that any particularly prominent player refused point-blank to sign unless he received at least £100. Not infrequently £300, £400, and even £500 was demanded and paid.

'None of the more wealthy clubs would have dared to take the extreme step of reporting one of these blackmailing demands. To do so would cause that club to be blacklisted with all professional players, and render any attempt to secure further players worse than useless for all time.

'Again, the law has now been altered, and allows a player on being transferred – or "sold" – to share in the amount realised by the sale up to 75 per cent according to the number of years' service with the club he is leaving. And the player may be safely left to see that he receives at least his full share.

'The whole system of transfer and transfer fees is admittedly an evil, but it is a necessary evil.'

However, some players could lose heavily if they were tempted beyond discretion. As controversy about the ethics of the transfer market grew more ill-natured, the Army felt constrained to warn its star players in April 1911 :

Lieut General Sir H. Smith-Dorrien has issued important orders warning Army footballers against being bought out to become professional players, as according to the established rules of the Football Association, they cannot be eligible for twelve months.

'The General notifies officially that several cases have been brought to his notice where men so purchased from the Army have, instead of earning a living, found themselves stranded for twelve months.'

Despite lapses, however, soccer remained, as the *Express* observed, the greatest spectator sport in the land and the paper invited the distinguished cricketer Prince Ranjitsinjhi to write on the English Football Cup Final of 1903 :

I had never seen a Cup Final until Saturday, although I played both Soccer and Rugby game up at Cambridge. I was asked by 'Speedex' to give some of my impressions of the game, and for once wander out of my path as a cricket writer, and tread on the ground of criticism of a game at which I have never posed – or been posed – as an expert.

I journeyed down to Sydenham [Crystal Palace] in company with my friend, C. B. Fry, who last year was present at the final in the capacity of a player and not that of a mere spectator. We discussed Mr Bentley's, [a football writer] forecast of the match, and Fry asked me which of the rival teams Mr Bentley had given as winner.

'Derby County,' said I.

'Then I shouldn't be at all surprised to see Bury win,' was his reply, 'for last year when Mr Bentley selected Southampton as his favourite we suffered a defeat.'

Mr Bentley is an excellent judge, but one whose prophecies have been unfortunate. Mr Bentley is a fine sportsman, however, and it occurs to me as being quite possible and he may have chosen Derby as the winning side in order to bring luck to the Lancastrians, with whom his sympathies undoubtedly lay.

Bury's surprising superiority lay in their 'rushes' in the fine combination of their backs. On the other hand, the Derby County forwards lacked combination, and were not nearly as quick on to the ball as their opponents. It was nothing less than a great disaster for them and to the spectators when after the second goal had been scored their goalkeeper was disabled and had to leave the field. It quite marred any chance of a 'finish', as the unexpected may happen in any game.

The first two points scored were fluky, and, in a degree, the result of luck but in the remainder of the second moiety it was a procession. Indeed it is not too much to say that but for the determination of the Bury representatives to keep unbroken their fine record of having no point scored against them in Cup contests, the ultimate margin of goals would have been far larger.

When all was over, the Cup and medals were presented by that grand sportsman Lord Kinnaird, an ornament to the game of football who disarms that jeering criticism which I am afraid some of our friends – yours and mine – throw at the game where professionalism rules. Lord Kinnaird said the right thing at the right time in congratulating Bury, and his thought that the victors would sympathise with the losers found many a responsive echo round the pavilion. The speaker also drew attention to the extraordinary fact that Bury had gone all through the competition without having a single goal scored against them.

Mr H. W. Lawson, the Parliamentary candidate for Bury, proposed, and Sir Thomas Poe seconded, a vote of thanks to Lord Kinnaird. The seconder said Derby County would go on pluckily trying, despite disappointments, until they won the Cup.

Ranji unfortunately forgot to mention the score, but at least everyone knew who had won and no one would have been surprised that it was two Northern teams in the final : the south of England rarely had a look-in at the start of the century. In 1900 there was not a single team south of the Wash in the First Division.

It is hard to conceive of the Member of Parliament for, say, Tottenham, giving a vote of thanks to the President of the Football Association at the conclusion of the Wembley Cup Final nowadays. He would not be listened to for one thing. Then deference to men of standing was accepted as proper and right and certain standards were supposed to be observed in all sports. Although the definition of amateurism differed slightly from sport to sport the *Express* was horrified to learn in 1900 that the Islay Golf Club of Machrie, Galloway, was offering a first prize of £100 to professionals and amateurs alike in open competition :

> For the amateurs the extent of the award is out of all reason. Even for the professionals the giving of such a sum cannot be described as good policy. It will not tend to make them satisfied with winning £15 at another time in, perhaps, quite as hard a contest. One does not suppose that amateurs would compete on account of the magnitude of the award : probably they would be just as pleased at winning an ordinary medal : and for that reason the offer is all the more regrettable.

Professionals may have been expected to know their place and rest content with £15, but golf in Edwardian days was no douce, stolid sport; it was alive with gimmickry :

> Alfred Toogood, the 'blindfold' golfer, met Mr A. Tindal Atkinson, the champion of the 'keep-your-eye-on the ball' theorists, in the *Express* match at Sunningdale yesterday. The professional was soundly beaten, but there can rarely have been a pluckier fight for a forlorn hope.
>
> The *Express* match which had for a week been the sole topic of conversation among golfers, was arranged in order that Toogood might demonstrate his startling theory that it is not necessary to keep the eye on the ball. He was blindfolded before taking every stroke.
>
> Three or four hundred formed a great 'V' behind the teeing ground when Toogood stepped forward to make his first shot. He took his stance, and then Mr Guy Livingstone, his co-heretic, blindfolded him with a large violet silk-handkerchief.
>
> The operation was performed with the solemnity of a sacred rite, and the hush that fell over the crowd was only broken by the clicking of the cinematograph machine and the snapping of cameras.
>
> Toogood was suffering from a recent injury in a bicycle accident but his clean shots were a surprise to the crowd who followed the game from tee to tee. Mr Tindal Atkinson, who is in the first rank

among amateurs, played a fine game. He won every hole save three, when he halved with his blindfold opponent.

'I do not admit that my defeat has upset my theory that it is not necessary to keep my eye on the ball,' said Toogood.

'At any rate I think I have shown that I have no difficulty in keeping my head still without keeping my eye on the ball. And keeping the head still, is the main thing in a correct swing.

'I almost think that if a good many learners were blindfolded they would not be so tempted to lift their heads in making a stroke. As for other players who cannot rid themselves of this fault, it is possible they would play far better blindfold than with their eyes open.'

What was exercising golfers on British links was the cost of caddies :

The circular issued from the offices of the National Health Insurance Commission with reference to the position of golf caddies under the Insurance Act of 1912 has aroused indignation among golfers in all parts of the country.

The circular calls the attention of golf clubs to the fact that under Part I of the Insurance Act all golf caddies of the age of sixteen and upwards, if engaged or paid through the club, must be insured even though they are casually employed, and the club is to be deemed to be the employer.

This means that golf clubs will have to pay threepence a week for every caddie employed, and that the caddie will have fourpence a week deducted from his wages.

Already many golf clubs have decided to dispense with caddies altogether.

A reader, John Banks of Wimbledon, retorted that with simple prudence golf need not be an expensive game :

'There is an initial outlay, before one starts the game, and I estimate it, having regard to a particular club to which I belong, as follows :

Entrance fee .... £2   2s   od
Clubs (five) .... £1 13s   od
One dozen balls .... £1   4s   od

'I have not included clothes and boots, because, in my opinion, expenditure on these is not necessary. Clothes that are old enough to be comfortable serve my purpose quite well.

'I live a penny tram ride from my course. I carry my own clubs.

I estimate the average life of a golf ball to be five rounds. (My handi-cap is ten.)

'My round costs me, therefore, about sevenpence. The yearly sub-scription at my club is two guineas. I play about two rounds a week only, all the year round, which works out, for each round, at about fivepence for the green fee.

'That means my golf costs me about a shilling a round in all.'

At least golfers were not harassed with the restrictions laid upon swimmers. The guide to resorts in 1912 reported that Margate and Hastings permitted mixed bathing while Folkestone allowed it 'between the Harbour Pier and Victoria Pier'. Southend, on the other hand, was more censorious, even banning people from going to the beach wearing mackintoshs over their bathing costumes. They were obliged to use cabins or bathing machines.

Swimmers, however, were free as air compared with poor whist players. The game of whist in the early years of the century (and, indeed, till bridge dislodged it in the thirties and forties) was uncom-monly popular. Whist drives ranged from village halls, with a modest sweep, to very grand affairs where prizes included (for men) an oak roll-top writing desk, a walnut cigar and cigarette cabinet and for women a silver rose bowl, pairs of silver candlesticks.

Then the law stepped in. The High Court ruled that public whist drives were unlawful gambling. The *Daily Express* organised a petition to the House of Commons and ridiculed the lengths to which the police went to get a conviction.

Police Sergeant Payner gave evidence to Greenwich magistrates that he had shared a prize of half-a-crown with another man at a whist drive at Amersham Social Club. The promoter, Mr Mendoza, was fined 2s. The 'crime' was that whist was adjudged a game of chance, and this remained the case until February 1913, when to the jubilation of the *Express,* the 250,000 who had signed the Save Our Whist petition and the members of the Whist Drives Protection League, an Old Bailey jury returned a verdict of not guilty on one Sydney Burnett who had pro-moted partnership whist whereby the same two people played together all evening instead of each individual 'progressing' from table to table, changing partners with every game. Apparently the permanent partner-ship rendered skill predominant over chance. What clinched the defence case was the number of respectable people who declared on oath that whist drives kept men away from the pubs and encouraged husbands and wives to go out together.

Another widely popular pastime that came in for harassment and criticism was ping-pong. Members of the National Sporting Club, in whose premises a championship ping-pong table had been installed, complained that manly sports (notably boxing) would suffer and that the craze for table tennis was symbolic of national decay.

Fear of sport rotting moral fibre had been expressed by no less a person than Rudyard Kipling a month earlier, in January 1902. Kipling had written of 'flanelled fools at the wicket and muddied oafs at the goals'.

But men and women clamoured for fresh thrills. Sports writers girded their loins and went to work with a will to make their reporting as colourful and real-life as possible.

The racing correspondent wrote this account of the Derby of 1913:

I have seen many Derbys and always the great race, with its attendant tragedy and farce, supplies something of an adventure; but never, surely, was there a Derby to be compared with this year's.

The horses came into sight at Tattenham Corner, and the customary frantic shouts were heard all round us, 'The favourite wins!' 'Louvois wins!' 'Day Comet wins!' and with undisguised exultation from a large layer 'Aboyeur wins'. Then followed the finish, the obvious bumping and the general feeling that something was wrong.

'The Stewards took half-an-hour before their decision was announced, and it was an intensely dramatic half-hour. All round me were men, more or less racecourse experts, and practically all of them had backed the favourite. On the verdict of Lord Wolverton and Major Eustace Loder depended hundreds of thousands of pounds. One man whom I knew had backed Craganour to win two hundred pounds. He was white to the lips and was biting hard on an unlighted cigar. He laughed and gossiped, but there was all the time a queer nervous twitching in his eyes.

There were a further 1200 words on the race including potted biographies of the three judges who decided the disputed winner – and one extraordinary omission.

There was not a single mention of the woman suffragette who had thrown herself in front of the King's horse and died in her endeavour to publicise the cause.

Such insensitivity to women was certainly not in evidence the following year when the boxing correspondent wrote his account of

Bombardier Billy Wells' triumph in the British Empire contest at Olympia :

A left on his jaw and a sharp follower with the right on the point sent the Australian, Colin Bell, crashing to the boards. Less than six minutes boxing between the men was all the spectators saw for an outlay of as many guineas.

There never was so strange a sight in Olympia. It was not the boxing that was so remarkable but the audience that watched it. There were probably more than ten thousand persons looking on, and hundreds of them were women.

They drove up in evening dress* in their motor-cars – nearly everyone in Olympia seemed to arrive by motor-car or taxicab. They walked across the sanded floor of the great arena as calmly as if they were walking to the Opera. They just held their skirts and evening cloaks up so as not to sweep the sand.

A few of them sat in the circle of seats immediately around the ring, where they could see every blow to the best advantage, and during nearly a couple of hours boxing they looked on as unconcernedly as if they were listening to a sermon. Just once or twice a woman gave a little squeaking 'oh !' of surprise.

Women's influence was non-existent in sport; it was decisive in the theatre. Actresses could command vast salaries, even by the standards of contemporary pop artists. In the USA Miss Maude Adams had a guaranteed salary of £200 a week for a minimum of 40 weeks – whether she played or not – plus a share in the profits of any play in which she appeared. In 1909 this agreement netted her £40,298 – half a million pounds at present values – for her part in J. M. Barrie's *What Every Woman Knows*.

Miss Rose Stahl earned £100,000 (one million plus) from salary and profit in the hit *The Chorus Lady*. There were others – Billie Burke, Ethel Barrymore, Miss Marlowe who earned very large sums, and in England Ellen Terry and Mrs Patrick Campbell could gross £200-£500 a week on occasion. Yet the brightest star of all in cash terms as well as artistic ability was the Frenchwoman, the divine Sarah, Sarah Bernhardt. In 1910, she was contracted to play at the Coliseum, London, for £1,000 a week.

*So were their escorts dressed, though boxing did not measure up to the London theatres which made full evening dress *compulsory* for all gentlemen in the stalls.

Madame Bernhardt not only entranced her audiences, she instructed them. Commenting on the falling marriage rate she remarked:

'When I was young girls had not a tenth part of the liberty they are allowed nowadays. Young girls mixed with the opposite sex in the house of their parents only, and were rarely left alone without a chaperon. The result was that marriage was popular.

'If the youth of today would abandon their butterfly habits' and were not allowed to intermingle so much, without hindrance, the marriage returns would rapidly increase.'

Madame Bernhardt's moral views were echoed by most women and as they determined the play-going habits of husbands and boy friends managements, critics and authorities were obliged to heed them. Plays had to be licensed by the Lord Chamberlain, an officer of the Royal Household, who was protector of public morals and good order.

Mr Alfred Butt had arranged to mount Max Reinhardt's mime *A Venetian Night* set to the music of Friedrich Bermann.

An official of the Lord Chamberlain's office attended the dress rehearsal and this letter arrived on Mr Butt's desk shortly before the first performance.

> Lord Chamberlain's Office,
> St James's Palace, S.W.
> 4 November, 1912

Dear Sir – I am desired by the Lord Chamberlain to inform you that after receiving a report of the dress rehearsal of **A Venetian Night**, he regrets he is unable to license the performance.
Yours faithfully,

> G. H. Crichton (Major)
> Assistant Comptroller.

The *Express* thoroughly approved this action:

We regard the reek of the divorce court as unwholesome and nasty. We do not believe that it is desirable for young girls to be made familiar with sex vagaries. As it is true that the home and the family are essential to the nation's existence, so is it absolutely necesary that we should cling firmly to the conviction that incontinence is an evil not to be condoned, or even discussed, that it is something ill bred and to be ignored.

Strong-minded puritanism had long been expressed by distinguished critics. Mr W. T. Stead, the crusading journalist who exposed baby-farming, observed of Arthur Pinero's play *Wife without a Smile* in 1904:

> I was surprised at the fact that there were four co-respondents in a divorce case being regarded as a joke.
>
> I confess I cannot see anything amusing in misconduct. Divorce court stories may be pitiable; they can hardly be humorous.
>
> The whole tone of the play is bad. If Mr Pinero gives a true picture of the class of people who live on houseboats, then the sooner the houseboats are scuttled the better for society as a whole.

Mr George Bernard Shaw, ever ready to give the public the benefit of his wit and wisdom, while leaving them unsure whether or not he was being serious, commented:

> Why should Tolstoy and I be considered more immoral than Mr Pinero?
>
> The fact is that the serious moral treatment of the facts of life is not tolerated on the English Stage. My play *Mrs Warren's Profession* was refused a licence not because it was immoral, but because it was too moral.
>
> But does the British public want impropriety in the theatre?
>
> The British public does not go to the theatre. The playgoing public is a class by itself. *The Worst Woman in London* was a huge success. How many people do you think go to see a play called *The Best Woman in London*?
>
> I agree with Mr Stead that sex intrigues are not amusing. Nor are they interesting. It would be a good thing for English dramatic art if a return were made to the policy of producing plays in every way fit for a girl of fifteen to see.

Books did not escape either. The Libraries Association, for example, banned from their members' shelves books by W. D. Maxwell, Compton Mackenzie, and Hall Caine in 1913 because of their treatment of sex. Subscribers could only obtain their works by asking for them and inviting the scorn of respectable people. The *Express* endorsed this action too. A leading article stated:

> Life is not all made of divorce court material, and we are certain that

the vast majority of the people prefer to read things that are whole-some, clean-minded, and uplifting. Those who wish to read of certain phases of life – those phases which are not disclosed to the young and the innocent – may appease their appetite for these things by ask-ing for them.

That, however, was mild compared with what Sir William Robertson Nicoll, the eminent literary critic, had to say on the whole field of pure and impure fiction :

> It depends largely on the author's treatment of his theme and the spirit in which a book is written, and sex, deny it as much as we will must, after all, be considered a part of life.
>
> There are authors, however, who deliberately put coarse passages into their novels with a view to attract certain readers and you know it. I know it, and the average man and woman in the street outside knows it too!
>
> Such authors are, not to put too fine a point on it, vermin, and they should be caught, cracked and exterminated!
>
> Let one of the societies which exist for the suppression of this sort of thing obtain that which it considers after taking proper advice, a clear case against an author and prosecute.
>
> I would trust a British jury, guided perhaps a little by a broad-minded judge, to decide definitely the question whether a book is offensive or not.
>
> The effect of a conviction in such a case it would be difficult to over-estimate.
>
> It would be felt among offending authors everywhere.
>
> I venture to believe that there is not much subtlety required to discover whether a book is impure or not, and that the jurymen would be fully equal to their task.

Films were becoming increasingly popular, with some 7,000 cinemas throughout the British Isles and the *Express* reported in January 1914 that 'as there is talk about criminal instinct being excited by the exhibi-tion of certain cinema pictures, it may be as well to remind detractors of the number of good lessons that are being taught through its medium.' There followed the film criticisms for the week :

> *The Road to Ruin* which was shown privately at the Electric Theatre, Shaftesbury-avenue, is a striking production.

The plot is a strong one. A young man named Wyndham goes up to Oxford and encounters many pitfalls. One day, just after a dinner, he dreams, and in his dream he sees very vividly *The Road to Ruin* on which he has started. The misery he is bringing on himself and his family is exceedingly well portrayed, and when he awakes he sees how foolish he has been, and from that day he reforms.

It is altogether a splendid picture.

At the Picture House *From Manger to Cross* is being produced with great success. The music is very fine indeed with selections from *The Messiah, Elijah, Judas Macabias, Olivet to Calvary* and *The Crucifixion.*

The Polytechnic was known at the time when animated pictures were first introduced into England as 'The Home of the Cinematograph'. Now, with the aid of Messrs Pathe's wonderful films, it presents an entertainment full of interest and amusing and instructive to people of all ages. Above all, there is no fear of seeing on the screen pictures that might be distasteful even to the most fastidious.

The policy of running a continuous programme is proving popular at the Scala Theatre in Charlotte-street, Fitzroy-square, and the entertainment is very interesting. Next week, in addition to *The Messiah,* there will be a film of the life of Napoleon (Pathe Freres) exclusive to this theatre.

To impress history on the minds of children nothing finer could be found.

Give Us This Day at the West End cinema is an impressive study of the cruelty of a pauper's life. Mr Davey Pain of the British and Colonial Film Company assured us that when the film was first thrown on the screen the operator had to stop for a time because tears were coursing down his face.

Among films to be produced at an early date are elaborate adaptations of three famous stories – Helene Gingold's *Abelard and Heloise,* Maurice Maeterlinck's *Mary Magadalene* and Mrs Hodgson Burnett's *Little Lord Fauntleroy.*

A number of proprietors of cinema theatres appeared at a meeting of the licensing committee of the Middlesex County Council yesterday to ask for permission to open their houses of entertainment on Sundays.

All were refused.

Audiences were in no doubt what they would, or would not accept, as this report of April 1914 demonstrates:

One forgives the Stage Society much for the sake of the good work it has done, but one does not forgive such a scene as that in the second half of the third act of Mr Frank Harris' *The Bucket Shop* at the Aldwych Theatre yesterday afternoon.

It was bestial – and it was degrading alike to the players who played it and to the audience who in the main shielded their eyes from the offensive sight.

It was the more a pity since the incident had no dramatic or moral bearing on the rest of the play, and appeared to be dragged in gratuitously to offend, or to show the author's daring disregard of generally accepted standards of propriety.

Blanket condemnation of young women ever appearing on the stage was voiced by delegates to the International Congress for the Suppression of the White Slave Traffic organised by the National Vigilance Association :

M Pouresy, one of the French delegates, said it was difficult to separate the profession of actresses from immorality, and declared that the stage was often the entry into a life of shame. He urged that the age at which young women should be allowed to be employed in theatres in their native land should be raised to eighteen, and in the case of foreign countries to twenty-one.

Herr Emie Gaertner of Austria said that so long as the public asked for performances that imperilled the morality of young people, so long would all legislation be of no avail.

A mile from Caxton Hall, where the conference was being held, Mr Justice Darling was dealing at the Old Bailey with one of those accused of corrupting young women by selling their bodies :

Thomas Jones, who was convicted under the White Slave Act in the Old Bailey yesterday wept loudly in the dock.

'Of course, I know why you have been crying and snivelling in the dock perfectly well,' said Mr Justice Darling. 'You think I am going to order you to be flogged.

'Well, I'll tell you why I don't. It is because I have got a certificate from the doctor to say you are unfit for corporal punishment. Otherwise, I should order you to be flogged.'

Jones was sentenced to nine months' imprisonment. And Mr Justice

Darling was regarded as one of the most temperate, lenient judges on the Bench.

The ferocity of feeling against 'corrupting' plays, books, and people, grew as the century advanced for it marched in step with fear that the country was rotting and would form no match for redoubtable, cold-eyed Germany.

Dancing imported from the US was a prime target for moralists. First to qualify for a stern rebuke was the Cake-Walk. As far back as July 1904 the *Express* noted the case of a girl in Bootle who was accused of stealing millinery. She had, said her mother in expiation, 'gone mad about the Cake-Walk' and a representative of the firm employing her said she had been dismissed as 'her thoughts were on the cake-walk to the exclusion of everything else.'

A well-known brain specialist, interviewed by an *Express* representative, thought the matter one which was growing serious.

'When the Cake-Walk was introduced first,' he said, 'I thought it a mere temporary obsession of the brain, like the small boy's desire to whistle "Hiawatha", or the moodiness of a jilted lover.

'Now it has become a matter of grave import. Indeed, it is almost a disease. Not long ago I had a girl brought to me for treatment. Her parents were quiet, old-fashioned people. One morning the girl, who had been to a dance the previous night, entered the breakfast room on her toes, her body bent and her shoulders thrown back. Her brother's bowler hat was tilted to one side of her head, while she cast amorous eyes on the door-jamb.

'The good people were horrified. The girl continued in this state for some time. Then she was hurried off to my house. I diagnosed the case at once, and prescribed a six months' stay in a country village.'

Then came the tango :

The Duchess of Norfolk, the Countess of Dundonald, Lady De Ramsey, Lady Helmsley, and a number of other well-known ladies have vigorously condemned the tango, and declared that they would not allow it to be danced in their houses.

The *Gentlewoman* magazine includes opinion on the tango from a number of prominent hostesses in an article entitled 'The Dance of Moral Death'. Here were some of the comments :

'THE DUCHESS OF NORFOLK : In her opinion such dances are not desirable, for the tango in itself and in the comments that it leads to is surely foreign to our English nature and ideals, of which I hope we are still proud.

'VISCOUNTESS TEMPLETON : I am happy to say I have never seen the tango danced, and, having regard to the many photographs, etc., which are supposed to set forth its attractions, I am in great hope that I may never see it !

'LADY HELMSLEY : I think it is a great pity that the old Spanish dance, the tango – quite graceful in its original form – should in the course of its indirect introduction to our country have acquired so many of the nigger-dance characteristics now associated with it. I am sure it will never be taken up seriously as a ballroom dance.

'LADY LAYLAND-BARRATT : I consider it an immodest and suggestive dance, altogether impossible for any girl of refinement or modesty.

In common with many leaders of society in Paris and Berlin, certain English hostesses unthinkingly accepted the tango as de rigueur for the season.

Then came Queen Mary's emphatically expressed disapproval, followed by the Kaiser's decree to the officers of both services to avoid families where the tango is danced.

Moreover it has also been clearly intimated to those who are likely to be the Queen's hostesses in the near future that she could not consent to visit any house where such performances were allowed to take place.

Miss Gertie Millar disagreed. The musical comedy actress who danced the tango at Daly's Theatre countered that :

'I honestly cannot understand how the most prudish person can accuse the tango of being suggestive when properly danced, for it is not in the very least.

'It cannot be, for the man holds his partner far away from him, and there is none of the hugging which can be made so objectionable in other ballroom dances.

'It is by far the most graceful, stately dance that has been introduced into a modern ballroom, and the people who call it immoral or suggestive cannot have seen it properly danced.'

The management of the Queen's Theatre invited the critical ladies to a demonstration – followed by a yes or no vote on the question 'Is the tango immodest?' The Bishops of London and Kensington were also asked along.

The invitations were ignored.

Staunchly supporting the peeresses (and presumably the bishops) the *Express* fired off a leading article :

Hooliganism in dancing has established itself in the ballrooms of today, and the whole charm and delight of dancing are threatened.

The modern regrettable tendency to introduce any and every kind of eccentric dance into a programme where once the waltz held sway has now reached a point when it calls for protest from all those who do not desire to see any longer the antics of negro minstrels in the ballroom.

These new dances are now seriously taught in London. Certain people of New York indulge in the freak caperings that are known by strange names, and an attempt is being made by certain English hostesses to foist these dances on young people here.

The most outrageous of the latest dances to be imported from New York is the 'Turkey Trot'. It is both ungraceful and disgraceful in the ballroom. There is not one redeeming feature about it.

Its technical description may not sound very dreadful, but the real manner of its dancing can only be judged at sight. The couple wriggle a few steps together, and then take steps sideways, hopping first on one leg and then on the other, after the manner of a lame bird.

The next contortion is a bending of the body downwards with widespread legs so as to look as nearly like a turkey as possible. After that the couples go prowling about in circles round each other. They may make gobbling noises if they like.

Then there is the 'Huggie Bear' dance. The 'Huggie Bear' is capable – as indeed all these dances are – of degenerating into something more than vulgarity.

The gestures and the body movements are indecent in themselves, and this is not surprising when the British public understand that these dances are taken direct from the negro dancing rooms and the night clubs of Vienna, Berlin and Budapest.

The 'Huggie Bear' consists of the two dancers hugging each other and performing a slow, irregular dance with the clumsy movements of bears. It is considered good form to growl during the 'Huggie Bear', and in America they make uncouth noises and sing at intervals :

Babe! Come along!
O kid! O kid!
Hug'em Hug'em!
Put your arms around me, Babe.

In the passion to model its ballrooms after the pattern of the
'coloured gentlemen's' places of amusement, society is learning the
'Huggie Bear', the 'Argentine tango', and the 'Dandy Dance'.

The 'Dandy Dance' begins with the woman dancing along until
she is caught up by the man, who draws her along with the familiar
cake-walk steps, side by side. Occasionally the woman falls sideways
or backwards, as in the 'Apache' dance. Then they gyrate face to
face, and presently they change to a species of a waltz, kicking their
legs backwards like hens scratching for grain. So it goes on.

As an antidote to the ultra-virtuous was the rumbustiousness of actor-
manager Seymour Hicks and the earthiness of flower girl, Eliza Keefe.

Seymour Hicks – 'I adore women, but I get too much of them,' –
believed the stage, far from being the path to moral perdition was the
highway to legitimate fame and fortune. This was reported by the press
and he was inundated with enquiries for jobs. He wrote to the *Express*
in November 1908 :

'So many of the ladies who have been with us are now peeresses and
millionaires' wives (I have lost five this season alone) that there seems
no class of society that is not anxious to be taken into my matrimonial
agency, an agency where the women enter poor and leave rich.

'If every lady in England who wants to become an actress will write
and send her picture to the office of the *Express,* I will select with
the aid of a committee of experts, twenty-four of the loveliest faces
among the million photographs that are likely to arrive. You will
publish these twenty-four pictures and let the readers of the *Express*
tell me which they think are the twelve prettiest aspirants for
histrionic and matrimonial honours, and then to each of these twelve
I will give engagements.'

He was as good as his word.

Eliza Keefe, a Charing Cross flower girl, was also entranced by
the theatre and by one play in particular, George Bernard Shaw's
Pygmalion, with its Cockney flower girl Eliza Doolittle, reformed and
refined by Professor Higgins. So the *Express* published Eliza Keefe's
criticism of Mrs Patrick Campbell's Eliza Doolittle. The paper did

not arrange for her to get a special seat. Miss Keefe, who lived in Drury Lane, did what all true modestly-endowed theatre-goers did on those days. She sat for eight hours on a camp stool with her crochet work waiting for the box office to open.

But Miss Keefe did not wait for the end of the performance to express her opinions. When Professor Higgins remarked to the stage Eliza 'The woman who can utter such disgusting depressing sounds does not deserve to be anywhere,' the real life Eliza shouted 'Rats!' from her front seat in the pit. She went on, in her published comments:

I didn't like the part neither where the professor makes his 'ouse-keeper take away the flower girl's clothes and burn 'em.

It was as much as ter say that flower gurls are lowsy.

And I didn't like Mrs Patrick Campbell's astonishment at 'aving a bath. Wy, we allus 'ave a bath once a week. Some o' 'em may go for a fortnight, but they're only a few.

I thought Mrs Patrick Campbell talked a bit rough at times. I asked people in the pit if I talked as rough as 'er, and they said, 'No, not 'alf as rough.' And another thing – we shouldn't throw our basket o' flowers at a man just because 'e wouldn't buy any.

An now just a bit about the langwidge. There was one word in particular which Mrs Patrick Campbell sed wen she was supposed to be a lidy. The editur ses I mustn't repete it, but it begins wiv 'b' and ends wiv 'y', like this – b x x x x y'.

Well, no self-respecting flower girl would say such a word wen she was on 'er best behaviour, 'specially if she was supposed ter be eddicated and speakin' in a drorin' room.

Still, on the 'ole, I liked the play. It was funny – wot I understood of it.

Some of the things I didn't understand, but I 'spose that's becos Mr Shaw is so clever – he's beyond the likes ov us wen he reely gets going.

One thing – I wish e'd fahnd a better title. Who's ter know that *Pygmalion* 'as anyfink to do with a flower girl.

It would 'ave bin better if e'd given it a good rousing nime like they 'ave for the Lyceum dramas. 'E mite, 'ave called it *From Flower Girl to Duchess*.

We should 'ave known wot it was abaht then.

Eliza Keefe probably summed up the mood of most people in her romantic view of the stage: for the pleasures of the people and against those who would too rigidly circumscribe them.

CHAPTER XV

Advertising

The pleasures of the people were much in the mind of advertisers without whom newspapers could certainly not have been sold as low as one-half-penny.

Advertising in pre-World War I days was very different from the present. It was jaunty, strident, or extremely self-righteous, or, on occasion, it was down-right distortionate. There was no code of advertising ethics. American patent medicine firms were driven out of the States by restrictive legislation, and came to Britain to establish their fortunes. Consequently a great deal of display advertising was aimed at health and particularly at the bowels and bladder : two seats of common disorder as eighteenth century physicians had it.

Copywriters had the difficult task of harmonising the natural prudery of the times with the business necessity of selling laxatives. The methods they adopted showed an ingenuity and flair worthy of a nobler cause.

First there was a cheeky approach tied in with the news of the day and indeed almost indistinguishable from it. Consider this example from the *Express* of 18 June, 1902, just prior to King Edward VII's planned coronation when genuine official decrees were regularly published :

CORONATION

POLICE NOTICE

Soldiers notice it. Sailors notice it. In fact all sorts and conditions of men and women are observant of the fact that ABBEY'S Effervescent SALT keeps YOU IN GOOD HEALTH, for it *moves on* the sluggish Liver, is always quick in *Action* and is a *safe harbour* of refuge from Impaired Digestion, Sick-Headache, Constipation, Biliousness, and all kindred ills. ABBEY'S SALT taken every morning will crown your daily efforts with success.

When the coronation had to be postponed for two months due to the

King's operation for appendicitis, Abbey Salts' advertising agents were not confounded :

> Appendicitis
> Would be out
> of Fashion
> *If Abbey's Salt*
> *were used regularly*

Philosophy was substituted for current affairs in a full page advertisement in April 1907 which contained the following lofty quotations in the boldest possible type :

"Peace hath Higher Tests of Manhood than Battle ever knew.' – (Whittier).

'His Life was Gentle, and the Elements so mix'd in him, that Nature might stand up and say to all the World THIS IS A MAN !' SHAKESPEARE.

'There is no Death ! What seems so is transition : this life of mortal breath is but a suburb of the life elysian whose ports we call death.' – Longfellow.

'Into Man's hands is placed the rudder of his frail barque that we may not allow the waves to work their will.' – Goethe.

And what did this bombardment of literary quotations aim to do? Persuade the public to buy Eno's Fruit Salts 'which rectifies the stomach and makes the liver laugh with joy'.

A lyrical approach was favoured by Beechams in 1908 :

AGAIN it is the Youth of Nature ! The scented earths answer to the joyous impulse, and laughs forth in buds, in flowers, in foliage. Sunshine and gentle shower smile on the tender star-sprinkled grass. The birds are seeking their mates with chirp and warble. And we, too, feel that 'old things have passed away' with dreary winter, and that youth once more is on the wing – coming alike to all of us. Yes, none need despair of a share of Nature's lavish bounty. Old and young look forward with rising hope and delight to the glorious promise of spring. But there is one condition, and one only, that Nature's demands shall be fulfilled, in order that we may enter into the completeness of her Spring Joy. Not riches, nor fame, nor learning, but HEALTH is the essential qualification. Nature wants the blood to throw off its impurities and flow fresh and bright through our veins,

like the new sap in her plants and trees. And so she urges our intelligence to seek out those natural medicaments which will best aid her benign intention. The bowels are made to act with quiet regularity, and the functions of the kidneys are vastly improved. So that, on the whole, BEECHAM'S PILLS may justly claim to be the most efficacious and reliable SPRING MEDICINE obtainable.

Kutnow's Powder concentrated on simple name dropping or, more precisely, title dropping :

The Royal Family, Clergy, Dukes, Marquesses, Earls, Viscounts, His Majesty's Household, Army, Navy, Statesmen, Judges, Barristers, Solicitors, Professors of Medicine, Use Kutnow's Powder :
But
do you know
The Evils of Substitution?
The well-known efficacy and great popularity of Kutnow's Powder has caused many counterfeit productions to spring up. Such substitutes have been analysed and found to be absolutely worthless, and in most cases injurious to health. It is, therefore, most important that you see the Deer on the Rock, which is the registered trade-mark of Kutnow's Powder.

Cereal firms naturally concentrated on the health aspect. A 1903 advertisement for Quaker Oats had the conventional line drawing of a firm-jawed, clear eyed young man thrusting forward a strong right arm with the caption :

Men who Achieve – with hands or brain –
Who Rise, who Lead, who Win, who Act –
They fight on simple grain –
On Quaker Oats – to be exact.
The Will and Brain that conquer Fate,
The Rugged Health, the Bone and Thew –
There's every trait that makes men Great
In QUAKER OATS – the food for You.

Some years later a more off-beat approach was adopted by the company. A drawing showed a father beating his small son across the bare bottom with the back of a hairbrush accompanying the text :

THE MORE PAINS-TAKING THE PROCESS the more certain the results. Quaker quality oats are sorted and cleaned by machinery through forty painstaking processes before they are ready for milling into Quaker Oats.

But the most effective piece of cereal promoting was produced in 1904 by Shredded Wheat who secured W. T. Stead to write up an interview with General William Booth, head of the Salvation Army, and present it as a straight news story. This opened with a description of the General preaching and lecturing to a host of followers for nigh on two hours. (Part of his subject was the possibility of turning Rhodesia into a 'new-start' colony for the down-and-outs of Glasgow, Leeds, London, and other big cities.)

'How do you do it, General?' I said. 'How do you preserve this inexhaustible and nervous energy? Most men after such a meeting would be quite pumped out, and you are as fresh as paint. Have you got any secret food, or drink, or what?'

The General turned to me full of animation at once. 'Yes,' said he, 'I have found an ideal food.'

'What is that?' said I.

'Listen,' he said, 'and I will tell you.' And he at once began to tell me the system under which he dieted himself. 'I eat very little meat,' said he; 'often none at all; but I eat Shredded Wheat. Have you never seen Shredded Wheat?' he asked me. 'Get some and try it.' I find it splendid. I have it with milk and perhaps a roasted apple at breakfast, and again at supper. It is made of the whole wheat grain, so that none of the ingredients of the wheat are lost. I find it most digestible and very palatable.'

Phosferine, the patent tonic manufacturers launched a series of portraits from the lives of different categories of workers, extolling the advantages of the product. A typical one, from June 1903, was:

LIFE STORIES ILLUSTRATED
A Busy Housemaid

THE COMFORTS OF HOME are, as everyone will admit, greatly increased and intensified by the diligent service of that much criticised person, the Domestic Servant.

AN IDEAL MISTRESS is possessed of the womanly appreciation which recognises that there are occasions when the numerous details of

Household Duties accumulate beyond the capacity of the most industrious maidservant, and such a mistress has a sympathetic consideration for the Vexatious Hindrances which prolong the labours of the day many weary hours beyond nightfall.

THE BUSY HOUSEMAID, whose numberless duties always seem to require attention at one and the same moment, sometimes, not unnaturally, becomes harassed and careworn under the responsibility and unvarying monotony of her work, and develops what the Great Specialists In Nervous Disorders describe as 'House Nerves'. To one in such enfeebled health the daily repetition of the same tasks is a very trying ordeal, and if persisted in will end in complete nervous collapse. It is, however, possible to avert such a breakdown and permanently restore the Nerve Force by the use of Phosferine.

That was a mild, reasoned request compared with the efforts of an earlier, American, advertiser to sell his remedy for unhappy scalps. In July 1902 this little item appeared:

AS OTHERS SEE US

Ladies! when you go to service on Sundays pray remember that your headgear and toilet, especially the latter, are subjects of very keen criticism on the part of your friends of both sexes sitting in the pews behind. The noble lord of your bosom friend – she who is never absent from your 'At Home' – sits making comparison between your appearance and that of his wife, and on the way home inquires, 'What on earth is the matter with Tom's wife's hair? It looks unhealthy and clammy and dirty, and she seems to be half-bald.' Such and similar remarks pass Sunday after Sunday between husband and wife, young lady and fiancé, brother and sister, the young 'get about' and his chum, concerning the hair of nine out of every ten lady worshippers. It is anything but a pleasant reflection surely. Ladies! *Un petit mot.* Mrs Brown Potter, the beautiful American actress writes: 'I use only "Tatcho".'

Princess Eugenie Christoforos Palmlogue says: 'I would not be without "Tatcho" on any account.'

Mr Geo. R. Sims, to whose inventive bent the world is indebted for 'Tatcho' in an interview with the editor of the *Daily Mail* said: 'In "Tatcho" I have discovered a remedy capable of working wonders.'

Even that was modesty exemplified compared with a still earlier Ameri-

can effort that breathed of credulous pioneers bamboozled by covered
wagon quacks in the wild and woolly West:

SICK MADE WELL
WEAK MADE STRONG
Marvellous Elixir of Life Discovered
by Famous Doctor Scientist that
Cures Every Known Ailment.

Wonderful Cures are Effected That
Seem like Miracles Performed –
The Secret of Long Life of
Olden Times Revived

The Remedy is Free to All Who
Send Name and Address

After years of patient study and delving into the dusty records of the
past, as well as following modern experiments in the realms of
medical science, Dr James W. Kidd, 402 First National Bank-build-
ing, Fort Wayne, Ind., USA, makes the startling announcement that
he has surely discovered the elixir of life. That he is able with the
aid of a mysterious compound, known only to himself, produced as a
result of the years he has spent in searching for this precious life-
giving boon, to cure any and every disease that is known to the
human body.

There may have been a case – just – for Hennessy Brandy to claim in
1908: 'On many occasions when life and death have been in the
balance Hennessy's turned the scale.' But there was none at all for this
one (again American) from the paper of January 1911:

Consumption has been Cured. Marvellous as it may seem after
centuries of failure, a remedy for Consumption has at last been
found. After many years of almost ceaseless research and experiment
in his laboratory, the now renowned Derk. P. Youkerman has discovered a specific which has cured the deadly Consumption even in
fairly advanced stages.

Nor for the equally specific – and as cruelly deceptive – statement from
a Mr Elmer Shirley: 'I Cure the Deaf in 30 Days.' He took a full page

Consumption has been Cured.

DERK P. YONKERMAN, WHOSE DIS-
COVERY OF A REMEDY FOR CON-
SUMPTION HAS STARTLED THE
WORLD.

Marvellous as it may seem after the centuries of failure, a remedy for Consumption
has at last been found. After many years
of almost ceaseless research and experiment in his laboratory, the now renowned
Derk P. Yonkerman has discovered a
specific which has cured the deadly Consumption even in fairly advanced stages.

ad to say that in September 1912 and backed his boast with 38 testimonials from satisfied customers, all of whom provided name, addresses and photographs. Although he offered £500 to anyone who could prove the testimonials were not genuine, it was significant that the cures had all been effected within the previous five months : there was no way of checking long-term recoveries.

A wistful story-book approach was favoured by a regular advertiser of Edwardian times, Dr Williams' Pink Pills for Pale People :

Saddest and most pitiful of sights is a young girl gradually drifting to the grave through the dire influence of Anaemia. Weak for want of blood – starved, because without blood she cannot digest and use her food – she has nothing but Consumption to look forward to. And all sorts of added discomforts beset her. She cannot walk upstairs without waiting to rest, for she is out of breath when she begins to climb. Her eyes are dull, her lips pale, and on her face is the bony hand of death. The sight of her brings tears to parents' eyes.

There is no need for all this. These Anaemic Girls can be cured. All they need is Blood – new Blood put into their veins by Dr Williams' Pink Pills for Pale People.

There was nothing demure or winsome about another form of advertising which would, again, be considered unthinkable today. With a bold wanton flourish, the advertisement of August 1911 proclaimed :

LET US MAKE YOU EAT

We will prove at our own expense that it is No Longer Necessary to be Thin, Scraggy, and Undeveloped.

We particularly wish to hear from the excessively thin, those who know the humiliation and embarrassment which only skinny people have to suffer in silence. We want to send a free 2s 6d package of our new discovery to the people who are called 'scrags' and 'laths', to bony women whose clothes never look well, no matter how expensively dressed, and skinny men who fail to gain social or business recognition on account of their starved appearance.

The company manufacturing this remedy, Sargol, repeated their admonitions at frequent intervals, ending up in 1914 with :

HOW TO GET FAT
AND BE STRONG

although neither of these advertisements could match the pithiness of
Stuart's Dyspepsia Tablets in 1901 :

GET FLESH

Fashion in the first decade of the twentieth century was much in favour
of the well-endowed women. Shape was all. Bosoms were prominently
presented and waists were pinched by corsets. The corset makers were
as alive as anyone else to the old business adage, 'Never let a good
chance slip by!' so when war began in August 1914, British manufacturers rushed into patriotic print against the hated German rivals :

TO EVERY WOMAN OF
THE BRITISH EMPIRE

We ask for your support of the British Corset Industry; not only for
patriotism's sake – but also because it will pay you.

Some corsets are obviously German, with German names, although
purporting to be British. Refuse them.

Some corset firms hid their alien identity behind high-sounding
fancy titles. Other concerns are American with German-American
Directors. Some even call themselves British, though their Principals
are German.

Refuse to buy any but entirely British Corsets. Not merely for
patriotism's sake, but also because no other corset in the whole world,
be it German, American or French can compare in quality, dura-
bility, and price, with the best British-made numbers.

The strongest guarantee of British make behind a corset is the
'J.B.' trade mark. Ask your dealer distinctly for 'J.B.' See the initials
'J.B.' on the pair you buy!

The good durable Coutil covering is mostly made in Lancashire.
The Busks are made in London. The steels come from Sheffield.

War, real or threatened, provided colourful copy. Bovril was the first to
spot this and early in the Boer War pointed out – with pardonable
pride and a little sleight of hand – that Lord Roberts' convoluted movements in South Africa spelt Bovril. Later it was able to record recom-
mendations from Baden-Powell and Rudyard Kipling and took pride in
a commercially-minded soldier :

An Army Corps man, attached to Buller's victorious legions, has
made a lot of money by the sale of hot BOVRIL. During the very cold
nights which characterise the Transvaal Summer this sustaining

beverage has been greatly appreciated by the men of his company, who have readily paid 6d for a cupful, which remuneration proved eminently profitable to the salesman.

But the most remarkable blend of advertising art with current affairs occurred in October 1910 :

TO THE DAY

The Anticipated German Invasion of 1913 Has Furnished the text for this advertisement :–

'To the day' is the toast that is drunk nightly at every mess on every battleship, cruiser, destroyer and torpedo boat of the German Navy.

'To the day' is the toast swallowed in silence by every officer in the German Army.

'To the day' means the time when the Fatherland finds itself strong enough to strike out for the World Empire which we possess, and which she considers we are not strong enough to hold.

Early in this year a gentleman residing at Newmarket wrote to the papers saying that he had just sold a horse, and that a German had bought it for the German Army. On the seller remarking that he was sorry to lose sight of the animal, the German said, 'You will see him back in less than three years.' This expresses the opinion of nine-tenths of the German nation.

However, it is by no means certain that nine-tenths of the German people want war, but they believe it is inevitable.

Our citizens, our men and women, young and old – are they ready for the hardships and the horrors of 'The Day?'

The strongest evidence suggests that Holland and Belgium will be the beginning of Britain's fight for existence. Methods and weapons have changed, but the spirit and stamina of the race is the same if we will only exert ourselves by keeping our bodies fit and insisting on our rulers, whoever they may be, doing their part.

What can we do, then, to fit ourselves, not alone for any trials that may be war, but the daily battles of our struggle for existence in the office, the factory, the field, the home?

The medical and nursing world tell us – tell us decisively, conclusively, 'Hall's Wine' – get the new, extra large size bottle, 3/6d, and be fit for whatever any day brings!

Hall's Wine was not wide of the mark. The war began in 1914 and the cause of Britain's entry was the German invasion of Belgium.

CHAPTER XVI

The Unready Land

War for Victorian civilians was something that happened to other people in other places. In 1899 it still happened in another place, but large numbers of civilians found themselves joining up with the regulars to fight the Boers in South Africa.

The Boers, or Afrikaaners, a dour, brave people of Dutch, French Huguenot and German stock, had established two independent republics, the Orange Free State and the Transvaal in the mid-nineteenth century. They had trekked north to these territories to get away from the British who governed the Cape and Natal. But the Afrikaaners, especially of the Transvaal, yearned to link up again with their countrymen who had remained under British rule. They dreamed of re-unification – of a Great Transvaal. Similarly the British itched to get their hands on the 'anachronistic' Boer republics, especially after gold was discovered at Johannesburg. When in the summer of 1899 the British perceived a Boer threat to Natal they sent out reinforcements from home. President Kruger of Transvaal demanded that they be sent back. Britain refused. The Transvaal and the Orange Free State declared war.

'The last of the gentleman's wars' is what the Boer War came to be known as.

At its height, in January 1901, the *Express* recorded that the Boer leader, President Kruger, was ill in bed and had 'received a cart load of New Year cards'.

On 9 May, 1900, Colonel Baden-Powell, British commander of beleagured Mafeking, telegraphed to London accepting the honour of a complimentary dinner which members of the Powell family were desirous of giving him upon his return to London. The message, sent off by runner to Ootsi, a small place about sixty miles north of Mafeking, was as follows : 'Delighted accept kind invitation directly fortune permits. BADEN-POWELL.'

Another telegram, sent from Mafeking on the same day, was received at Dewsbury by Mrs Whiteley, from her husband who was mayor of the town.

Though these messages were reassuring, yet they did not tell everything. It was left to Lady Sarah Wilson to give a few details of Mafeking's sadly depleted commissariat.

Telegraphing to her sister, Lady Georgina Curzon, on 3 May, Lady Sarah gave the daily menu thus : 'Breakfast consisted of horse sausages : lunch minced mule and curried locusts. Well.'

It was a great time to be a hero and the greatest of all was Colonel Baden-Powell, defender of Mafeking and founder of the Boy Scouts :

What made him beloved of all who know him is his never-failing fund of humour. 'He is the funniest beggar on earth,' remarked one who is proud to be included among his circle of admirers.

As a boy he was full of the joy of life. 'A grin always covered his face,' says Mr Harold Bogbie in his *Glory of Baden-Powell,* issued yesterday. The spirit of fun looked out of his sharp, brown eyes. 'He was forever making the other chaps roar; keeping a football field on the giggles; sending a concert audience into fits.'

It was the age of noisy, unashamed patriotism. The rector of a church in Belgravia remarked that the fall off in weddings, early in the war, was due to the fact that 'young men in a fervour of patriotism have vowed that their weddings will not take place till the British flag is flying over Pretoria.'

With the news on 19 May that Mafeking had been relieved the whole of Britain went mad. The *Express* reported :

At the Alhambra Theatre the orchestra struck up 'Rule Britannia', and a darkened house read on the lantern screen the fateful message.

There was a pause of one second, and then the audience rose to its feet at a common impulse and started shouting, screaming, singing. It was a very chaos of exultation.

In the OP box, among a party of ladies and gentlemen, was Lieutenant the Hon Arthur Hill, invalided home with a wound in the leg received at Spionkop.

He was on his feet in a moment, despite his lameness, and, standing forward, led the National Anthem. The house and the band took up the familiar strains in a wave of electric impulse. The volume was wonderful to hear : the sight of the vast audience singing earnestly was even more wonderful.

Piccadilly Circus got the news from an enthusiast on top of a bus, waving a flag. The Circus stopped its business of moving slowly to

'A lot of the dialogue (of *The Importance of being Earnest*) is really mine,' said Lord Alfred Douglas. He is pictured at the time of his libel suit over Arthur Ransome's critique of Oscar Wilde; the print shows the editorial marks made at the time.

Songs and ballads were sung about them. Dr Crippen was as well known as Dr Frankenstein and better known than Dr Livingstone.

It was the age of noisy, unashamed patriotism. Jubilation at the relief of Ladysmith was surpassed when the Boer siege of Mafeking was broken. The whole of Britain went mad.

LORD ROBERTS TRACES THE NAME ON THE SAND.

Careful examination of this Map will show that the route followed by Lord Roberts in his historical march to Kimberley and Bloemfontein has made an indelible imprint of the word Bovril on the face of the Orange Free State.

This extraordinary coincidence is one more proof of the universality of Bovril, which has already figured so conspicuously throughout the South African campaign.

Firing on the Red Cross Flag.

The "Daily Graphic" of March 3, 1900, contains an interesting narrative by a surgeon of the Royal Army Medical Corps, describing the capture of Spion Kop. The writer says:—" Cases now began to pour down from the hill on stretchers, and I soon ran short of my little supply of bandages ; but Major —— sent up what I sent back for, with a supply of BOVRIL and other comforts for the sick. Suddenly the Boers opened fire on us, and their bullets went into the fire, knocking the sticks about."

How One of Buller's Men Made Money.

An Army Corps man, attached to Buller's victorious legions, has made a lot of money by the sale of hot BOVRIL. During the very cold nights which characterise the Transvaal Summer this sustaining beverage has been greatly appreciated by the men of his company, who have readily paid 6d. for a cupful, which remuneration proved eminently profitable to the salesman.—Vide " Tit-Bits."

Always First Aid to the Wounded.

Extract from the " Lancet " of March 17, 1900.

After describing the conveyance of wounded from Spearman's Camp to Chieveley, a distance of twenty-four miles, the writer of the article says:

" The end of the train of stretchers and waggons came into view. Hot BOVRIL and stimulants had already been prepared by the men of the Royal Army Medical Corps, great pots of the former resting in the kitchen."

think out what this meant. Then a newsboy came along with a placard and the secret was out.

There is no doubt that the Circus was extremely sceptical to start with. And it is not essentially English. It swarms with foreigners, some of whom love their brother-Boers, or, at least, do not love the British.

First place on this score were the Irish nationalists. One of them, Hugh Corberry of Armagh, was reported killed fighting on the Boer side. His fellow patriots erected a statue to him in Ireland. But Corberry was alive – and when he heard of the statue he asked that it should be sold and the proceeds sent to him in South Africa !

But the newsvendor and the news-carts came up hot from the trade – the circulation of the evening papers dissipated scepticism, and the scene quickly changed. Vendors of flags sprang up from the ground as if by magic. They were sold out in a few minutes, and capitalism allied to faith and patience found its reward of 100 per cent of the outlay.

There is a suspected pro-Boer at Finchley Park. His windows were broken.

A shopkeeper in Holloway-road opened at eight a.m. on Saturday morning and sold over 400 flags in an hour.

Every visitor to the Hippodrome received a picture of Colonel Baden-Powell. Ten thousand were distributed.

In Kentish Town tramcars were stopped and not allowed to proceed until 'God Save the Queen' had been sung.

An old soldier and ex-police inspector went into a shop at Brixton to buy some patriotic ribbon, but when he spotted on the box 'Made in Germany' he left the shop in indignation.

Patriotic labourers at work in a French steamer in the Victoria and Albert Docks on Saturday threatened to strike work if the ship was not decorated. The captain cried *'Peccavi'* and promptly hoisted half-a-dozen flags.

British generalship was so dreadful at the start of the South African War – and later, when it became a guerilla struggle – that the Archbishop of York proposed a Day of Humiliation to recognise 'God's chastening of our national and personal sins'. The men responsible for these failures were Sir Redvers Buller, Sir George White, Lord Methuen, Sir Charles Warren : duffers all. Yet the worst that was said about them was 'that there is nothing much to be said for Warren'. The *Express* was prepared for White to be given a baronetcy, adding only the proviso that as he lacked private means his son might find it difficult to sustain the dignity of the title!

By a strange and sinister quirk of fate a war conducted with extraordinary chivalry, gave birth to the term 'concentration camp'. These were camps for concentrating the civilian population out of harm's way. Many Boers did died in them due to disease and neglect (many British soldiers died from the same causes in their own camps) but there were no atrocities practised there. Boer prisoners were far more frighened of the sea which they'd never seen – and believed they were being marched into the water when ordered down to the hold.

The war ended in May 1902 with unconditional Boer surrender and the absorption of their republics in the Union of South Africa. The struggle cost 22,000 British and Empire lives : the Afrikanners lost 4,500.

*

The British Army that emerged from the Boer War was changed, but not essentially so. Khaki – to blend with the sun-scorched veldt – had taken over from the familiar red tunics. The fire power of the infantry – to match the accuracy of the Boer farmers – had reached an astonishing rapidity (which was to take the Germans by surprise in the Great War) but, basically, the Army was still a force for winning colonial wars. Only massive reinforcement by hundreds of thousands of volunteers from the UK, Canada, Australia and New Zealand had enabled us to win. Writing in the *Express*, Conan Doyle, the creator of Sherlock Holmes, agreed : 'We beat the Boers because we had a great preponderance of numbers which enabled us to outflank them and much better artillery. Otherwise we could never have conquered their country.'

In certain respects the Services were still eighteenth century in their outlook. The *Express* reported on 4 January, 1901, that the crew of H.M.S. *Barfleur* stationed at Hongkong have mutinied in consequence of over-severity of discipline *and alleged unfair treatment in regard to loot taken in China,* (after the crushing of the Boxer Rebellion in China). Naval punishment included IOA which compelled a defaulter to stand on deck at all times and take his meals there under the eye of the sentry.

Regimental orders of the 3rd Battalion Grenadier Guards, stationed at the Tower of London, stated :

'In future any man caught coughing in church will be ordered to remain in quarters during Sunday and reported to his company commander for punishment.'

This was still the day of a shilling-a-day Tommy Atkins and out of that shilling he had to pay 3½d for messing and washing plus another fourpence for recreation, shooting practice, haircutting, boot blacking and insurance against damaging his barracks. There was small incentive to recruitment and the Army remained a miniscule force compared with the conscript legions of the Continent.

Its policing role was summed up in two dramatic despatches to the *Express,* one in May 1903 describing a battle against the Mad Mullah of Somaliland, the other in July of the following year recounting the victory over the Tibetans – who appear to have roused the ire of our Viceroy in India by being secretive about their way of life. Just in case their secretiveness concealed a deep-laid Russian plot (it didn't) we sent a military expedition to make sure.

But first the Somaliland clash. Headlined :

PLUNKETT'S STAND

A STORY OF DESPERATE

HEROISM

the Reuter message read :

Colonel Plunkett was about to conclude his reconnaissance when the enemy was sighted. He moved into the open, the column manoeuvring with the utmost precision, and formed square.

The scene of the last stand was an open space, with only patches of shrub and bush. Just as this open spot had been reached, a large body of the Mullah's hordes were seen advancing. All further retreat was cut off, and the force was completely hemmed in.

The enemy's horsemen swept down upon three sides of the square. Spearmen and dismounted riflemen attacked the rear, while the flanks and front were completely engulfed in a surge of charging horsemen who, with cries of 'Allah, Allah', rushed upon the devoted soldiers.

Every man was soon engaged in a fierce struggle. The horsemen fired from the backs of their ponies, while the front ranks of the square lunged and stabbed with their bayonets, after emptying their rifles into the dense press.

Every dervish of the attacking parties seemed to be armed with a rifle, and to carry in addition a sheaf of spears. The horsemen whirled round and round the square until the impact with the British force itself stopped their furious rush. Time and again the heads of their horses were dashed upon the very muzzles of the British rifles : time and again the Mullah's cavalry precipitated themselves into the square itself.

In the background were hundreds of women inciting the spearmen to fresh efforts with their shrill outcries.

Just as the enemy delivered a charge under a telling fire the remnant of the gallant force, by orders of Colonel Plunkett, broke up the square and hurled themselves into the midst of the besetting foe.

The dervishes fell back here and there, but the attack was pressed at fresh points with unabated vigour. More men fell, and some who had been wounded were wounded again, but still a firm front and magnificent courage were maintained, and finally the brave little band succeeded in cutting its way through.

The Tibetan adventure was headed :

BRILLIANT FEAT OF BRITISH ARMS

and Reuters' special correspondent wrote :

There is no more stirring story in the annals of Indian frontier warfare than that of the capture of Gyangtse Fort, held by 7,000 Tibetans, by a mere handful of British and Indian soldiers today.

The excitement of a long day culminated in the scaling of a breach in the walls of the jong by Lieutenant Grant, of the 8th Gurkhas, followed by a mixed company of Gurkhas and Fusiliers.

We watched with bated breath these heroic men climb a cleft in the rock in face of a hail of fire and torrents of stones which were hurled on their heads by the frantic Tibetans.

A stone struck Lieutenant Grant and swept him off his feet, as it seemed, to certain death below, but he recovered in a wonderful manner, and was the first man through the breach.

As I write at dusk the battle is not quite over. One still hears fitful bursts of musketry, but the jong is ours. It dominates the town below and the monastery beyond.

Our ten-pounders, hitherto employed generally in firing at the jong and the town turned their attention to making a breach in the wall between the two towers on the face of the cliff, beneath which was a small ravine or cleft.

It was all very well taking on the Mad Mullah and the Dalai Lama but compared with Continental Armies the British did not rate. Nor did they compare with the Japanese, about whose prowess the *Express* correspondent in the Far East had written, with remarkable prescience, in October 1900 :

> I am inclined to think that the Japanese have probably the best army in the world to-day, because, in addition to assimilating ideas that could be usefully learnt in Europe, they have really improved upon them by the neat and practical way they have carried them out.
>
> They would be ideal soldiers composing an army such as the world has never perhaps seen but for one great blot. The baser metal of their cruelty is perpetually showing through the electro-plating of their civilisation.

*

Very different was the position of the Fleet, unchallenged and un-challengeable since Nelson's time. The *Express* bewailed the defence cuts of 1900 :

> The result of the reductions in a word, is as follows :
> The Channel Fleet is reduced from sixteen battleships to twelve. The Atlantic Fleet is to be reduced from eight battleships to six. The Mediterranean Fleet is to be reduced from seven (as it stands at this moment, or eight, its normal constitution) to six ships. If that is not a clear loss to the sea-going battle fleet of seven (or eight) ships, what is it?
>
> In addition, the two cruiser squadrons attached to the Channel Fleet and the Atlantic Fleet respectively, are to be reduced from six ships each to four ships each.

After the cuts the Royal Navy remained stronger than the next two fleets put together. But the shadow of Imperial Germany, now launched on her war ship building drive, was already falling across the Cabinet table in London.

From 1907 fear of invasion grew. When the Army carried out an exercise to test the efficacy of our East coast defence, the Treasury demurred at the cost : £100,000 and Essex landowners objected to the soldiers interfering with game. Significantly, the point on the Essex coast chosen for the landing was that nearest to Germany.

There now began the great spy scare. Colonel Lockwood, MP, for Epping, told the *Express* in July 1908 :

> 'A case has been brought to my notice of three Germans who are now

living in my division. The entire district has been sketched, photographed, and mapped.

'The men, I am told, visit inns, and obtain from coachmen, grooms, hunt servants and others, particulars of horses kept in the district, the quantity of forage, and any general information that may be useful.'

Immediately a flood of 'I spy' stories descended on the Press. W.M.A. of London wrote :

I caught three Germans, evidently naval and military officers, on the sand hillocks at Weybourne Hoope, near Sheringham-by-the-Sea, a little time ago.

They were taking sounding, bearings, and photos of Weybourne Hoope, which since the time of the Romans has always been considered the very weakest spot on our North Sea Coast.

Owing to a natural series of three bays and other natural surroundings the tides are always full in and the water is deep at all times of the day and night. A hostile army could easily land there.

Another correspondent wrote :

For years past I have had among my pupils numbers of German officers who made no secret to me that they did not come to England to learn the language, but to get thoroughly acquainted with the country from a military aspect. These gentlemen travelled about into all parts, some taking one direction and some another. I had no idea such a system was unsuspected.

By 1909 the handful of German agents had reached the proportion of an epidemic, according to Major A. J. Reed of the Perthshire Tories :

'In the industrial centres of Scotland alone there are at the moment no fewer than 1,500 persons, male and female, in the employ of the German General Staff. It is now known that the whole of the defence of Scotland has been secretly investigated during the past two years and reported on to Berlin.

'The number of Germans regularly collecting information in England, more especially on the east and south coasts, is computed to be over 5,000.'

Apathy in Government circles and amid the broad mass of the

middle classes at the alleged plot against British security prompted a
satirical verse :

> I was playing golf the day that the Germans landed
> All our men had run away
> All our ships were stranded
> And the thought of England's shame nearly put me off my game.

Considerable furore was caused by the production in London's West
End of a play *An Englishman's Home*. This portrayed a raid by Germans – or at any rate foreigners looking remarkably like Germans – on
a middle-class house in Essex owned by a pacific gentleman named
Brown. Mr Brown was against armaments until he was the victim of
other people's armaments. He then grabbed a gun himself and was
promptly shot.

The play was frankly propagandist and the moral was crystal clear.
If you want peace, prepare for war. *An Englishman's Home* was an
immense success and stimulated recruitment and the campaign, headed
by the veteran Field Marshal Lord Roberts, for national service. It was
written by Daphne du Maurier's uncle who was with the Colonial
Service in Africa when, unbeknown to him, the play was launched on
the West End stage by his actor-impresario brother, Gerald. The play
attended, naturally, by Mr Winston Churchill 'applauding as heartily
as any galleryite' spawned another on the same lines, *Invasion* which
prophesied the foreign occupation of London if the torpor continued.

The *Express* urged, on 8 January, 1909 :

> The duty of taking a share in national defence should be as much an
> obligation on every citizen as is the duty of contributing to the
> national exchequer. It is unfair to ask a few men to do what all
> should do. It has been shown over and over again that unless Great
> Britain possesses a sufficient army to make a surprise invasion a
> certain failure the safety of the country remains in constant peril. It
> is now evident that such an army cannot be provided unless every
> citizen undergoes the military training necessary to enable him to be
> an efficient soldier if the time of danger should occur.

As Germany speeded up her naval and military preparedness the British
Government decided to do something about the growing menace. It
launched an advertising campaign.

Full page announcements appeared in the press from 1912 onwards extolling 'good wages, good food and unique opportunities for sports and games – the surest way of keeping a man fit for service in the field.' In retaliation, the Kaiser made football compulsory in the German Army.

Appeals to the volunteer spirit met, however, with a poor response and so deep-rooted was pacifism and distaste of the military values in Liberal England that some nonconformist churches issued leaflets calling for the Boy Scout movement 'with its military overtones' to be crushed. That was the extreme attitude – for most people the belief that it could never happen, that a European war was impossible overlaid mounting fear and distrust of Germany. But only just. By the time of Edward VII's death in 1910 'the German menace' in trade, colonial expansion, diplomacy and above all in the open challenge to Britain's naval supremacy was a real part of every thinking person's life. The newspapers reflected prejudices, but they also reported facts. And the facts were chilling enough for all but those totally dedicated to seeing only the good in human nature to be convinced that Germany was resolved to be first among nations and to impose its Prussian spirit on Europe.

The changing attitude to Germany, from approval to outright hostility, was charted clearly in the columns of the popular press.

CHAPTER XVII

German Menace

The first message welcoming the *Daily Express* into the world of print came from Kaiser Wilhelm II of Germany. No man, in the years to come, would so dominate the news as this stiff unbending disciple of Prussianism, whose waxed moustache and messianic eyes would personify for millions the destroyer of the world. Of course Wilhelm was a far more complex being than the cardboard figure of hate he was made out to be. He never exercised anything like the dictatorial powers possessed by Adolf Hitler and in his day Germany enjoyed independent courts, newspapers and freedom of speech. Yet the Kaiser did become the demon figure of World War I and long before that he was the most talked about, the most respected, the most feared figure in Europe.

To start with he was a favourite with the quality British press as with the popular, with Liberal-inclined newspapers as with Tory ones. Wilhelm was the much-loved grandson of the great Queen Victoria. He led the most scientifically advanced and culturally-conscious nation on the continent. The Germans were 'like' the British in a way the French never could be.

England had been almost perpetually at war with France for two centuries. Prussia had often been Britain's ally. And yet . . . as the *Express* went into production German commercial competition, along with American, was posing a severe threat to British supremacy even among her own colonies, and Germany's jealousy of British hegemony was daily displayed in German press attacks on British 'barbarites' in South Africa. (Thirty-five years later, Hermann Goering was to rebuke a Briton protesting about concentration camps by consulting his dictionary. 'Ah, yes, concentration camps. First established by the British in the Boer War.')

Mindful of its debt to the Kaiser for his telegram of good wishes, the *Express* reported on Mafeking Night, 1900 :

In pursuance of the policy of the *Express* which is to select the good news from the bad news, a representative writes that the German population in London heartily joined in the jubilations of Saturday, toasting the health of Baden-Powell in copious libations of Munich beer, crying '*Hoch, hoch, hoch*!'

The event appealed to their inbred military instincts and the pros and cons of the war were unanimously waived. '"Baden-Powell is a fellow, a clever fellow, a good soldier, who has fought with his head," said one of a beaming group in a Soho restaurant, tapping his brow to accentuate the value of brains in warfare.'

Undoubtedly the Kaiser's diplomatic send-off telegram to the *Daily Express* had something to do with these international fraternisings.

A benevolent attitude towards the All-Highest continued intermittently. He gave an interview to a British diplomat which was published in all the principal newspapers. Among his observations :

'You English,' he said, 'are mad, mad, mad as March hares. What has come over you that you are so completely given over to suspicions quite unworthy of a great nation? What more can I do than I have done?

'I declared with all the emphasis at my command, in my speech at Guildhall, that my heart is set upon peace, and that it is one of my dearest wishes to live on the best of terms with England. Have I ever been false to my word? Falsehood and prevarication are alien to my nature.

'When the struggle [the Boer War] was at its height the German Government was invited by the Governments of France and Russia to join with them in calling upon England to put an end to the war. The moment had come, they said, not only to save the Boer Republics but also to humiliate England to the dust.

'What was my reply? I said that so far from Germany joining in any concerted European action to put pressure upon England and bring about her downfall Germany would always keep aloof from politics that could bring her into complications with a sea power like England.'

Most sensational was the Kaiser's claim to have invented the plan that won the South African war for Britain (just possibly it did have German origins : with its farm burning and barbed wire entanglements, it was ruthless enough). Declared the aggrieved Kaiser :

'I bade one of my officers procure for me as exact an account as he could obtain of the number of combatants in South Africa on both sides, and of the actual position of the opposing forces. With the figures before me, I worked out what I considered to be the best plan of campaign under the circumstances, and submitted it to my General Staff for their criticism.

'Then I despatched it to England and that document, likewise, is among the State papers at Windsor Castle, awaiting the serenely impartial verdict of history. And, as a matter of curious coincidence let me add that the plan which I formulated ran very much on the same lines as that which was actually adopted by Lord Roberts, and carried by him into successful operation. Was that, I repeat, the act of one who wished England ill? Let Englishmen be just and say!'

Shortly after this interview, the German press attacked the Kaiser for his pro-British sentiments and Prince Buelow, the German Chancellor, offered to resign because, although he had not seen the interview he had, by implication, endorsed it. His offer was refused. But it is likely that the Kaiser realized how antagonistic to Britain were large segments of the German people. As with the Hitler peace offers later (Hitler had some very kind things to say of Britain in *Mein Kampf*) it is impossible to decide whether his published pro-British sentiments were genuine, transitory or merely designed to lull the British into a false sense of security.

However much the Kaiser might try to make tactful remarks about the British – such as advising German lady cyclists to dress becomingly like their English sisters – bad feeling between England and Germany grew as the century advanced.

Again and again the militarism, authoritarianism and the heartlessness of Young Germany was pointed up by British newspaper correspondents in Berlin:

Friday, 4 July, 1902:
As is well known, no officer in Germany is allowed to marry without being able to prove that either himself or his intended possesses a certain amount of private income with which to eke out the miserable stipends provided by the Government.

Now, in addition thereto, the Kaiser commands that full details shall be given to the superior officer by any officer tired of single life respecting not only his private means and those of his fiancée, but also the latter's parentage, reputation, and education, and whether she was previously married, and if so, to whom : if divorced, why and when : if a widow, how long. In fact every possible step is taken to ensure that the army will be pure and above reproach. The reason for this regulation is that many marriages have been contracted wherein the sole question determining them was the amount of the fiancée's dowry.

Tuesday, 14 April, 1903:

A naval officer named Huessner and a lifelong friend, Hartman, who was performing compulsory military service by serving as a private in an artillery regiment, have been spending the Easter holidays at Essen, where their respective fathers are prominent residents.

Last night Huessner, who was in uniform, met Hartman. The latter, being in plain clothes, did not salute the officer, but greeted him as a friend.

Huessner peremptorily commanded Hartman to salute him, and when he refused drew his sword and plunged it into Hartman's breast with terrific force.

The weapon pierced one of Hartman's lungs and passed right through his body coming out at the back. Death ensued in a few minutes.

Wednesday, 20 January, 1904:

More details concerning the latest military scandal in Pirna (Saxony) have come to light, and furnish singularly realistic illustrations of the descriptions of military life.

Lieutenant Krohn, of the 64th Field Artillery, is a painstaking officer and affectionate husband and father. His wife, though young, is by no means prepossessing in appearance. She seems to have been a sort of provincial Messalina who gave her love and also cash to quite a number of officers, preference being given to those of her husband's own regiment.

Lieutenant Krohn, who was prepared for the General Staff, was aware of nothing until the scandal became so great that his superior officers felt it was their duty to inform him of what was going on in his house.

According to German ideas of honour, Lieutenant Krohn is obliged to challenge all those who have carried on 'intrigues' with his wife. So far three pistol-duels have been fought, in all of which Krohn remained victorious, disabling his adversaries for life. Several more duels are to follow.

Thursday, 17 October, 1906:

The editor of the *Hamburger Echo,* M. Wabersky, has been sentenced to ten months' imprisonment for lèse majesté.

The municipal authorities had declared that it was a criminal offence to pick leaves and flowers from the public gardens. Recently, however, the Kaiser sent the Mayor of Hamburg a flower which he had picked from a soldier's grave at Metz.

M. Walbersky drew a parallel between these two incidents in a recent issue of his newspaper, and criminal proceedings followed.

12 May, 1911:

Baron von Richthofen, when little more than a youth, needed money, and borrowed £1,250 from Baron von Gaffron, who stipulated that £2,000 be returned to him within a year.

Baron von Richthofen's elder brothers, one of whom is a judge and another is an official in the German Foreign Office, intervened as his guardians, and when they learned the particulars of the transaction they refused to pay the exorbitant rate of interest demanded. They settled the debt for the amount borrowed with interest at 6 per cent.

In addition, the brothers caused Baron von Gaffron to be socially boycotted as a usurer. The Baron, resenting the discredit in which he became involved, assaulted Baron von Richthofen in a Berlin restaurant.

Baron von Richthofen submitted the affair to a military court of honour, which decided that a duel must take place under severe conditions, owing to the grave nature of the insult which Baron von Gaffron had offered Baron von Richthofen.

Baron von Richthofen, having killed his opponent, reported himself to the military authorities. He will be tried by court-martial and will certainly be sentenced to detention in a fortress – probably for a short period, owing to the fact that a military court of honour expressly ordered the duel to take place.

Exactly one year and a number of duels later, General von Heeringen, the War Minister, explained to the German Parliament why duelling was necessary to the spirit and honour of the German Army :

'It is a fundamental principle of the officers' corps that an officer must stand up for his honour with his whole body.

'The same views prevail in the armies of all the great European countries where there is universal service and an officer is the severest judge of himself in the matter of the defence of his honour.

'It was its highly strung sense of honour which enables the officers' corps in the great wars of the past century to carry the German arms to victory, and if the sense were shaken more would be lost than would be good for the Fatherland.'

19 January, 1914:

Captain Hansmann of the artillery at Cracow was entertaining a number of other officers to dinner in his rooms last night when he considered himself insulted by Lieutenant Ziegler.

He summoned his orderly, and, placing a revolver in his hand, ordered him to fire on the lieutenant.

The soldier obeyed, and Lieutenant Ziegler fell mortally wounded. The captain and his orderly were arrested.

In fact the German-sounding officers were Austrian, for Cracow was part of the Austrian Empire but that would not have been common knowledge in Britain. Readers would naturally assume that Germans were involved as the despatch was datelined Berlin.

Perhaps the most sensational story illustrating the hard face of the Prussian military caste concerned the Lions of Zabern. The 'lions' were three German officers, Colonel von Reuter, Lieutenant Schad and Lieutenant von Foerstner. Zabern, in Alsace, was then part of the German Empire having been annexed following France's defeat in the war of 1870-71. The Alsatian population of Zabern did not like the German garrison. They made fun of the goose-step, they spread stories – which originated from the soldiers – that Lieutenant von Foerstner had promised recruits five marks for every traitorous Alsatian beaten. The Lieutenant gave an example of what he meant by using his sabre and badly injuring a crippled shoemaker. For this he was sentenced to forty-three days close confinement by court martial.

Meanwhile the natives had, not unnaturally, become restive. The officers claimed that the townspeople were unfriendly and that the local police did nothing to protect the dignity of the German uniform. Colonel von Reuter then decided to teach the locals a lesson. He told a civilian official, 'You ask, will I allow bloodshed? My answer is blood can be shed and under certain conditions it is quite good that blood should flow, for we are defending the prestige of the Army.' The result was a minor affray in which a number of citizens were arrested (one of them 'for being about to laugh') and several were hurt.

This occurred at the end of 1913 when Europe was tense as never before. France yearning for revenge and the recovery of the lost province of Alsace and Lorraine was responding to the appeals of university students, among others, to increase compulsory military service from two years to three. The sight of crippled shoemakers being slashed by brutal Prussian officers was too much for French emotions.

Worse was to follow. Colonel von Reuter and Lieutenant Schad were court-martialled – and acquitted, and a superior court-martial overturned the sentence of forty-three days imposed on Lieutenant von Foerstner. The three officers went scot free. It was, said the *Express*, 'Victory of Government by the sword over the constitution. Militarism is the strongest force in Germany.'

That was nothing new. German militarism's mesmeric power had been shown to an extraordinary extent in the uproarious case of the Captain of Koepenick.

A cobbler named Voight perpetrated a hoax, a highly successful robbery, in 1906, by playing on German officialdom's unquestioning obedience of anyone wearing an Army uniform. He walked off with £8,000 in cash from the Town Hall of Koepenick, a small town near Berlin. The *Express* of 18 October recounted the amazing tale :

The supposed captain, who wore the uniform of the first Regiment of Infantry Guards (borrowed from a theatrical costumier) accosted a detachment of soldiers when marching back from drill to barracks and directed them to follow him, saying he carried an imperial decree ordering him to effect important arrests.

The military detachment occupied the town hall. When the robber heard that the police superintendent was before the door, he summoned him, and told him he required assistance. The superintendent like all the others was completely duped, stood at attention, and after receiving the captain's orders proceeded to execute them.

He summoned eight policemen, and directed them to keep order among the crowd which had collected around the town hall in order that the captain might carry out his imperial orders without being disturbed.

Mayor Langerhans of Koepenick, in giving his account of the affair, says he was sitting in his office at a quarter to five in the afternoon when the door opened suddenly, and an officer, followed by two grenadiers with fixed bayonets, entered.

'The officer, who was wearing the full uniform of a captain of the 1st Regiment of Infantry Guards, came close to me,' said the Mayor, 'and asked, "Are you the Mayor of Koepenick?" When I answered

The fall-off in weddings, early in the Boer War, was due to the fact that 'young men in a fervour of patriotism have vowed that their weddings will not take place until the British flag is flying over Pretoria.'

For Kaiser and Fatherland . . . German reservists going to their homes to take leave of their families, August 1914.

For King and Country . . . Scots Guards called to the colours in August 1914. They were to become part of the immortal 'contemptible little Army', the Old Contemptibles.

in the affirmative, he continued, "You are my prisoner by the Kaiser's orders. You will be immediately conveyed to Berlin." I began – I beg you – but scarcely had I uttered these words when the captain interrupted me roughly saying, "You have nothing to beg, I have already said you are my prisoner." '

Langerhans then proceeded to explain how he arrived at the military guard-house in Berlin, where the soldiers escorting him handed him over to the officer on duty, whose astonishment was unbounded. Meanwhile the detachment of soldiers whom the sham captain had pressed into his service had been missed from their own barracks, and a patrol had been sent out in all directions to search for them.

An extraordinary feature of the affair is that the 'Captain' before occupying the town hall called at the post office and ordered the officials there to cut off the town from all telephonic connection with the outside world during the ensuing two hours, adding that he was about to effect arrests there by the Kaiser's orders. The post office officials blindly obeyed the brigand's commands and consequently when the imprisoned municipal officials endeavoured to telephone their plight they found it impossible to obtain replies.

As soon as the troops withdrew at the time arranged by the 'Captain' the municipal officials sent the following piteous telegram to the prefect of the district : 'Town hall occupied by troops. We earnestly beg an explanation of the reasons in order to pacify the agitated population.' When this extraordinary communication arrived the prefecture thought it was a joke, but telephone inquiries soon revealed what had happened.

The official description circulated throughout the country to facilitate his arrest give a good idea of this remarkable criminal. It is as follows :

Age 45 to 50, height 5 feet 9 inches: long grey moustache, sunken pale cheeks; one cheekbone protrudes prominently so that the face appears almost deformed. Nose presents the appearance of being crushed. One shoulder is higher than the other, so that his figure presents an imperfect appearance; bow legs.

It is a measure of the bureaucrats' credulity and suspension of reason that they could mistake someone who bore a passing resemblance to the hunchback of Notre Dame for a Prussian officer. Voight was captured, but released before he had served his full sentence, thanks to the intervention of the Kaiser.

Year in, year out from 1908 on British readers were regaled with stories of the rising might of Germany, on land, at sea and in the air.

In a speech to his generals in January 1909, the Kaiser proclaimed his full agreement with the military assessment that Britain, France, Russia and Italy were intent on suffocating Germany and her ally Austro-Hungary. He gave his blessing to the naval race with Britain, to outbuilding the allies in the air and having no equal on the land.

The whole pre-1914 scene was summed up in a tragically prophetic front page headline in the *Daily Express* on 3 March, 1913:

STAMPEDE

FOR

VAST ARMIES

France and Germany

rushing to a

climax.

CHAPTER XVIII

The Great Change

'Never have the prospects for world peace been so bright. Never has the sky been more perfectly blue.' So spoke David Lloyd George, Chancellor of the Exchequer on 1 January, 1914. He was not the only British Minister to take a sunny view of the international situation. Sir Edward Grey, the Foreign Secretary, announced the formation of an Anglo-American committee to organise 1914 as 'The year of rejoicing for peace'.

Politicians have a habit of making sweeping – and usually inaccurate – statements, but there was some reason for the euphoria of 1914. Europe had, in the previous year, passed through the Balkan War without the Great Powers becoming involved. This was a very significant achievement for the Balkans were the place where, if anywhere, a European war was likely to break out. Russia sought access to the Mediterranean at the expense of Turkey whose Empire was visibly crumbling. Austria was desperate to prevent Russian expansion because the Slavs within the Hapsburg Empire would turn to their fellow Slavs and natural champions, the Russians, to break free from Vienna's rule. Germany supported her Teutonic partner as the best way of keeping the Slavs in their place and blocking Russia's path into central-southern Europe.

So when in 1912-1913 the little countries of the Balkans, Serbia, Greece, Bulgaria, fell to fighting the Turks – who still ruled part of the Balkan penninsula – and then, joined by Rumania, fell to fighting among themselves there seemed every prospect that the giants, Russia, Germany and Austria, would be drawn in: Germany and Austria to defend Turkey, Russia to succour the small Slav states. Russian involvement would suck in her ally, France, and the long foretold Armageddon would begin. But it hadn't happened. For the second time (in 1908 the Austrians had 'acquired' the provinces of Bosnia and Herzegovina from the Turks) the Balkans had threatened to drag all Europe into war and for the second time calm statesmanship had averted calamity. Suppose

that were to be the pattern? Suppose the nightmares were only nightmares?

At the back of their minds, Lloyd George, Grey, Asquith and all the
others probably knew that a show-down with Germany was inevitable.
The nation was bursting with pride, demanding its place in the sun,
sweeping all before it in world markets. The German menace was, by
1914, part of British folklore : in books, in advertising, on the stage, in
countless speeches. The German fleet was believed to be just waiting to
sail across the North Sea and settle the issue, once and for all, in an
afternoon. And yet . . . and yet. . . .

The longer war could be postponed the greater the chance that
national economies would be so entwined that no one would want to
tear them apart. Capitalism, international finance, would make war
impossible.

So hope and fear jousted with one another at the start of 1914 with
hope edging ahead.

During the early summer press and politicians were obsessed with the
Irish problem : the Liberal Government's resolve to give the whole
island Home Rule and Northern Ireland's rock-like insistence that she
would fight rather than submit to Dublin (and Roman Catholic) rule.
Civil War seemed imminent. Then, on Monday, 29 June, 1914, the
lead story in the newspaper changed :

HEIR TO
AUSTRIAN THRONE
MURDERED

———

ARCHDUKE AND HIS
WIFE SHOT DEAD
IN THE STREET

The *Express* correspondent in Vienna told the story that was ultimately
to send millions to their death and change the world more fundament-
ally than any other event in history :

Vienna, the gayest of European capitals, is a city of the dead tonight,
for the murdered Archduke, in spite of his aloofness and his somewhat autocratic disposition, was very popular among the Austrophile
section of the heterogeneous subjects of the Empire.

That the assassinations were carefully planned beforehand there
can be no possible doubt. Two separate attempts were made on the
lives of the Archduke and his wife in Sarajevo.

A bomb was thrown at them as they were driving from the Arch-duke's headquarters with the army – he had been acting as Com-mander-in-Chief during the manoeuvres of the last few days – to the Town Hall, where a civic reception had been arranged.

The bomb struck the car, but was thrown off by the Archduke, and rebounded on the road behind, where it exploded in front of another car containing four members of the suite.

Colonel Merizzi, one of the Archduke's aides-de-camp, was struck in the neck by a splinter, and badly injured. The other persons in the car were also hurt, as were several people in the crowd.

The Archduke behaved with magnificent courage. He ordered his chauffeur to stop the car and, alighting, walked back among the crowd to see what had happened.

After ascertaining the extent of the injuries of his aide-de-camp, and giving peremptory orders to have him removed to hospital, he went back to his car, and in spite of the entreaties of the members of his suite, declared his intention of proceeding to the town hall.

At the entrance he was received by the burgomaster and the mem-bers of the town council, and it was clear to all that he was then in a furious temper, and bitterly resentful of what had happened.

The burgomaster stepped forward to read the address of welcome, but the Archduke could contain himself no longer. He waved the burgomaster aside, and in fierce, passionate tones, cried :

'Herr Burgermeister – We have come to Sarajevo on a friendly visit. We have been met with a bomb. It is outrageous.'

A terrible silence followed the Archduke's fierce indictment – fiercer in its tone and temper than its actual wording.

The burgomaster fell back, but the Archduke imperiously waved him forward, with the command 'You may now speak.'

As soon as the burgomaster recovered himself he proceeded to stumble through the address in frightened tones and amid a dead, ominous silence.

The Archduke, in stern tones, made a brief reply, and the crowd broke into cheers.

After half an hour he and the Duchess, who had also behaved with great coolness, left the town hall, the Archduke announcing his intention of driving to the Garrison Hospital to see Colonel Merizzi.

He was told that the military had been ordered to clear the streets, but he promptly countermanded this, and declared that all the festivi-ties and arrangements must go on as if nothing had happened.

The car was passing through the open space at the corner of the

Appel Quay when a young man stepped out of the crowd and fired two shots from a Browning pistol, point-blank at the Archduke and the Duchess.

The first shot lodged in the Archduke's face.

The Duchess made a wild attempt to save him. She rose in the car and threw herself in front of him with arms outstretched.

She received the assassin's shot in the breast, and fell forward across her husband's knees.

The Archduke made a feeble effort to clasp her in his arms and they fell together on the floor of the car in a last embrace.

The assassin was a young Serbian student named Gavrilo Prinzip.

It is believed here that the assassination was carefully prepared by Serbian conspirators, and a fresh outburst of indignation against Serbia has already taken place.

(Sarajevo was the capital of the province of Bosnia annexed by Austria and claimed by Serbia.)

The next day, the *Express* correspondent reported widespread anti-Serbian riots in Austria as it became clear that Gavrilo Prinzip and his fellow conspirators (members of the Black Hand Organisation, as it was later disclosed) had the active sympathy of Serbia. At last the Austrians had a legitimate excuse to deal with Serbia and, at the very least, by humiliating her to scotch Serbian claims to Austrian territory and Slav aspirations to freedom. Before the reckoning, however, there was the funeral. The correspondent observed :

The bodies of the Archduke and his wife are being taken to Vienna. After they have lain in state they will be interred at midnight, on Friday, at the Castle of Artstetten, where the Archduke erected a mausoleum during his lifetime.

This will render it possible for the bodies to rest in the same grave. Had the Archduke been interred in the imperial vault, according to custom, his wife could not have shared his last resting-place, for she was not of royal blood.

The aged Emperor (Franz Joseph, aged 84), on whom all thoughts are centred, returned to Vienna yesterday, and he was loudly cheered by the crowds which awaited his arrival.

Three weeks went by as Austria prepared and delivered an ultimatum that would be both a punishment and an example. When it was issued it barely made the front page of the *Express*, which was devoted to the collapse of inter-party talks on Ireland and the dramatic trial for murder of Mme Caillaux, wife of the French Finance Minister. Yet the *Express* did not hide from its readers the gravity of the European situation; it simply thought of it as a matter concerning Austria and Serbia.

Austria made the most far-reaching demands. Serbia was required to dissolve anti-Austrian nationalist societies; modify her Press law to stop criticism of Austria; dismiss Army officers and officials considered by Vienna to be enemies of Austria, and to submit to investigation by *Austrian police* of all aspects of the murder conspiracy in Serbia. The Serbs agreed to all the conditions save the last although they were willing to accept this too were the International Court at the Hague so to decide. The Austrians rejected the Serb reply. Vienna wanted unconditional surrender, and promptly declared war.

Now the *Express,* and other newspapers in the UK, and France, began to see a sinister design in all this. The timing, the issue, were too pat.

Russia, an autocracy, might find it hard to support Serbia which had plotted the murder of a Royal heir.

France, bound by her alliance to support Russia, was ill-tuned for war. The President was abroad. The Government was shaken by the Caillaux scandal.

Britain, which had an 'understanding' with France was wholly concerned with Ireland where open fighting had begun between troops and populace. What better time than now for Austria to settle accounts with Serbia?

Thus in a couple of days the whole complexion of the European crisis in the popular British Press altered from wary neutrality to downright hostility to Austria.

At this point, 28 July, 1914, feelings towards Germany were still muted. The *Express* correspondent in Berlin reported:

Demonstrators passed before the British Embassy in the Wilhelmstrasse, and shouts of 'Long Live England!' were heard. Such a demonstration has not been heard in Berlin for years.

Immediately on his return to the capital today the Kaiser had a long conference with the Imperial Chancellor. I am informed that he is determined to do all in his power to maintain the peace of Europe if this is possible.

There is optimism in Government circles that he will succeed, especially as Austria has not yet moved into Serbian territory.

But now the machinery of war, based on mobilisation by railway time-table, was taking its frightful course. Each nation was afraid of being caught out by its rivals. Russia mobilised against Austria, so Germany countered by mobilising against Russia and that led to France calling her troops to the colours.

In the event of war the French target was the provinces of Alsace Lorraine, lost to Germany in 1871. The German objective was to out-flank the French by marching through Belgium and Luxembourg. When they did this at the beginning of August they swept away the Liberal Government's last lingering doubts (the Tories had always been hot for war, regarding Germany as the enemy Britain had to fight) and, apart from a handful of Radicals, Britain went unitedly to war in defence of little Belgium, the sanctity of treaties and the protection of civilised life in face of Prussian aggression.

Appendix

Appendix

The Ownership of the *Daily Express*

Arthur Pearson, an enterprising go-ahead man of the new century already owned *Pearson's Weekly* when he founded the *Daily Express* in 1900. He edited it himself for the first two years, then briefly handed over to Mr Fletcher-Robinson. Shortly after the end of the Boer War a young American, Ralph Blumenfeld, who had represented US newspapers in the UK for some years, became editor. He headed a syndicate that took over from Pearson when the latter began to go blind in 1908.

But Blumenfeld and his associates were short of money. They were advised by Andrew Bonar Law, the leader of the Tory Party, to contact a young Canadian who had just become a British MP – a Mr Max Aitken. Mr (later Sir) Max Aitken offered the paper a loan of £25,000 in return for which he expected, and got, a fair amount of publicity for his activities. The *Express,* however, still suffered from severe financial difficulties and in December 1916 Sir Max Aitken bought the paper outright for £17,500 (he had already become the *Express's* first mortgagor at a cost of £40,000). Two years later, Lord Beaverbrook, as he had become, began to exercise a decisive influence on the newspaper's editorial columns.

On 24 April, 1900, the first leader to appear in the *Express* set a tone that has been consistently followed ever since :

This paper will not be the organ of any political party, nor the instrument of any social clique. It will not provide a parade ground for marshalling the fads of any individual. It will advertise all men, but no men in particular – outside its advertisement columns. Its editorial policy will be that of an honest Cabinet Minister – inspired by a sincere desire to do and say what may best serve our country, a resolute determination to combat influences making for the national detriment.

315

We do not carry any political trade mark. Our policy is patriotism. We have no axes to grind, no personal end to serve.

It is our business to give you news. We will try to make sure that it is true news. So far as we may honestly exercise the right of selection, it will be good news. Life is like English weather, various. The daily chronicle of the world's doings must include accident and disaster, the crime that is expiated at the scaffold, the paltry misdoing that is dealt with at the police court. But we have no scent for blood, no appetite for horrible detail. For choice, we will tell you of the comedy of life, putting its minor tragedies in the background. We will try to bring a smile to your breakfast table for every morning in the year.

An editorial in October of the same year calling for strong military forces remarked:

So long as England, the pioneer of freedom, is prepared to guarantee peace by being ready for war, so long will the hope of peaceful years be cherished and the onward progress of our race to the quiet dominion of the world be assured.

Pearson adopted many of the propaganda methods later to be associated exclusively with Beaverbrook. There were front page boxes containing slogans extolling the benefits of Tariff Reform – later, under Beaverbrook, to be known as Empire Free Trade. The Crusader trademark in the very early years was the slogan:

One People
One Empire
One Destiny

Ralph Blumenfeld brought a lighter tone to the paper when he started editing it and his diary provides some of the snippets that he passed on to reporters or gossip columnists, or obituary writers. One such concerned Billington, the hangman, who departed this life – happily through natural causes – on 18 December, 1901. Blumenfeld, not yet editor but hopeful, noted: 'Billington the hangman is dead. He was mightily overcome recently by having to hang Patrick McKenna, a bosom friend and townsman of his at Bolton. Billington had complained recently that the authorities did not appreciate his importance. He ceased to get oysters and champagne for breakfast before executions and this had been reduced to bacon, eggs and tea, while the fee remained at £10.'

As soon as he took over as editor Blumenfeld had Dr Starr Jameson (leader of the Jameson Raid on the Transvaal in 1897 which attempted to overthrow the Boer Government) complaining that 'the long Christmas break in England will be the undoing of this country. If this goes on England will be off the map in twenty years.' That was in 1902. Blumenfeld himself felt that things were rather going to the dogs. In 1908 he noted : 'We are becoming negligent in dress. Down in the City today, where I talked with the Hon Claude Hay, MP, I noticed that he wore a soft collar, such as golfing men wear, and brown boots. Also he had no gloves. Many men in the City go about in bowler hats nowadays instead of top hats, which shows the trend of the times.'

Blumenfeld, who was more English than the English, nearly went down himself in 1914 when his name lent apparent substance to the allegation that he was a German. The *Express* published this front page explanation :

It has come to our knowledge that certain rivals, evidently smarting under the phenomenally successful competition of the *Daily Express* are sedulously spreading false reports calculated to damage the prestige of this journal.

For the benefit of the many of our readers who have written to us on this subject we beg to state that

The Chairman and Editor of the 'Daily Express is not and never has been a German.

The paper on which the 'Daily Express' is printed is not and to our certain knowledge has never been made in Germany.

There is not one German on the staff of the 'Daily Express'.

We shall be greatly obliged if any reader to whom these false and malicious statements are made will kindly communicate to us details of such conversations, including the name or names of those making the statements, so that we may take steps to bring the spreaders of falsehood to book in the Courts.

Spurred on by the *Express* example firms like General Electric Company took space to explain to their customers that contrary to hostile rumour, 961 of the shareholders in Osram Lamps were British while a mere 41 were continental or American (who might or might not have German connections).

Blumenfeld gave added emphasis to his Englishness by running stories on 'The War and Cricket'; 'The War and Football'.

He continued to edit the *Daily Express* for twelve years after Lord Beaverbrook took full control, relinquishing the post to another North

American, the Canadian ex-serviceman, Beverley Baxter in 1930. He was followed, in turn, by Arthur Christiansen and, after twenty odd years, by Edward (later Sir Edward) Pickering and a number of notable journalists.

Lord Beaverbrook died in 1964 and was succeeded by his son, Sir Max, who, along with the members of the Beaverbrook Foundation, transferred control in 1977 to the Trafalgar Group for £14 million. Mr Victor Matthews of Trafalgar then became Chairman and Chief Executive of Beaverbrook Newspapers.

Index

Index